In Loving Memory of Lori Ann

I dedicate this book to Terry, Jesse and Myah who carried me through the darkness and whose presence brought me into the light.

I would also like to dedicate this book to my big brother Gord, who stood by me so many times and whose strength and unconditional love made me want to go on.

Praise for

Butterfly Woman

With *Butterfly Woman*, Lutze leads us through the horrific true story of Hannah and her metamorphosis from innocent child victim to an empowered role model we could all learn from. The story is full of events that cause heartache and pain, but Hannah's spirit stays vibrant throughout.

Emily Lutze is an excellent observer of life, well beyond its physical boundaries, and is truly a gifted woman and writer.

-Rick Rose *Film Maker, Screen Writer, Toronto, Ontario, Canada*

With *Butterfly Woman*, Emily Lutze offers the reader a gift of love. Butterflies emerge from cocoons after a mysterious process of metamorphosis. They are beautiful, delicate, seemingly fragile creatures, a symbol of the lightness of being, of hope and love. The butterfly represents the healing message of the book, but the journey of girl to woman is fraught with pain. Hannah's courage is inspiring. Finding inner strength in the company of loving others, butterfly woman — the character and the book — honors the human spirit.

-Daphne Read, *Associate Dean, University of Alberta, Faculty of Arts, Canada*

A memoir I have had the pleasure of reading and a person I am proud to call a friend. This story is about the continuous journey into womanhood and mental maturity and trying to keep one's sanity in times of such dysfunction and loss.

Emily allows us to see such naked truth about our own transgressions through telling her own story.

A message of hope for women...in knowing part of moving on, is dealing with our past.

-**Ronaele Pound**, *Broadcast Journalist, Calgary, Alberta, Canada*

RAW HONESTY! Most women experience a violation at some point in their lives. This compelling story will give them something tangible to relate to, ultimately opening up a necessary dialogue.

-**Gaylene Boucher** *Librarian, Alberta,Canada*

Butterfly Woman is an intimate peek into one young woman's struggle to come to terms with her haunting past.

A heartbreaking tale that had me laughing, crying and cheering all on the same page.

On one hand the author tells a story that many women will relate to; on the other hand, part of the story will be so utterly unfamiliar that you will want to read the book from start to finish.

The writing style of the author is transformative; and is juxtaposed with the transformation the protagonist also goes through. In the beginning of the story we can sense the protagonist's vulnerability in the tone of the writing; by the end we are aware of how much she has evolved.

-**Kelly Quessy**, *Business Consultant, Alberta, Canada*

The best scenes are almost cinematic. And the chapters move from one to the next with grace. The work is cohesive and interesting.

-**Bethany Lyttle**, *Author, Editor, New York, United States*

INSPIRATIONAL...I was unable to put it down; I read it from start to finish. It made me believe that there is hope no matter what you go through.

-**Morgan Boucher**, *Legal Assistant, Alberta, Canada*

"A poignant first novel that sings to a soul's longing and nostalgia. A song that heals as the reader travels along its pages."

-**Tracey Allen**, *B.Ed, M.Ed, Head Librarian, Beaumont, Alberta, Canada*

BUTTERFLY WOMAN

A NOVEL BASED ON TRUE EVENTS

ISBN: 978-1-4269-2812-3 (soft)
ISBN: 978-1-4269-2813-0 (hard)

Library of Congress Control Number: 2010902581

Our mission is to efficiently provide the world's finest, most comprehensive book publishing service, enabling every author to experience success. To find out how to publish your book, your way, and have it available worldwide, visit us online at www.trafford.com

Trafford rev. 3/3/2010

 www.trafford.com

North America & international
toll-free: 1 888 232 4444 (USA & Canada)
phone: 250 383 6864 ♦ fax: 812 355 4082

We delight in the beauty of the butterfly, but rarely admit the changes it has gone through to achieve that beauty. ~Maya Angelou

TABLE OF CONTENTS

Acknowledgements

Firstly, I would like to thank all of the students in my Write 298 course at the University of Alberta for giving me the strength to tell my story. Also, thank you Professor Daphne Read for believing in my talent and encouraging me to never stop writing my truths.

I would also like to thank my dearest friends; Aileen Mac Isaac, Freda Lannon, Linda Fraser, Sarah Hauck, Andrea Wright, Cheryl Alonso, Laura Haynes, Marcia Rigney, Andrea Dunne, Kelly Quessy, Gaylene Boucher, Lisa Mayes and Paul, Julie and Donald Michaud for lifting me up, loving me unconditionally and having the courage to share your stories with me.

A special thanks to Marybeth Zelent and all the ladies at Marybeth's Coffeehouse for your support and understanding and the free flowing cafe caramels that juiced me up daily in my little corner of the coffee shop. You gave me a beautiful setting that inspired me to write. Marybeth, our friendship means the world to me, thank you for all the times you let me cry on your shoulder, laugh over the counter and in my secret nook.

The Watton Family, when I was lost you took me in and supported me through one of the most difficult times in my life. You asked for nothing in return and shared your home with me as I regained my strength and confidence. I would not have made it without you and for all of your love and kindness I am eternally grateful. Jane, you are my sister, thank you for your unconditional love and support.

To my parents: Though our road was rocky and filled with regrets, I have always felt your love. This is the last stage of my healing and the blanket of darkness has been removed. Now, I am left with all of the positive and incredible gifts you gave to me throughout my life. I am given a second chance when I see you light up in the presence of my magnificent children and in my heart I know you have always had that love for me. I am so glad we have moved on and have left the past behind. You have taught me the most important lesson in my life, to forgive. There is not a single more important lesson. Also, I thank you for allowing me the freedom to write this difficult story and share it for a greater purpose.

In order to find out if this book was worth reading I needed a test audience. Daphne Read, thank you for being the first to read it and provide me with a very valuable critique. Your feedback resulted in a much better product. Also, thank you to Minister Faust for meeting with me and taking the time to share your knowledge on the best approach. Also for my dear friends and avid readers from every walk of life who took the time to read and provide testimonials for the book. Without all of you I would have known whether it served its original intention. Nadine Janus, my first friend to open the pages, thank you for all the heart to hearts and friendship. Andrea Wright, the world's most fabulous neighbor and a down to earth woman who I adore. Also, to Freda Lannon, a fellow mom and dear friend who was there every week to laugh and share with me through all of the ups and downs. Gaylene Boucher, an incredible influence on me, a woman whose nurturing spirit has gotten me through so many challenging times and whose laughter is contagious. Ronaele Pickup, a woman whose strength is inspirational and a woman who I instantly connected with. Rick Rose, an old friend who by chance I reconnected with, thank you for your professional advice and the fabulous final edit. Thanks for your kind words, support and marathon edit. Kelly Quessy, a fellow mom and a woman whose opinion I greatly value, you have made my life so much richer. Also, thank you to Colleen Peterson Copley for your incredible input and assistance with the cover copy and your friendship. Morgan Boucher, an incredibly strong young woman who I have complete respect and faith in, you can do it! Tracey Allen, thank you for taking the time to offer your professional opinion and friendship. Thank you so much to my friend Judith Crystal for passing the novel on to Bethany Lyttle, a publisher and author in New York.

Finally, to the world's best husband, Terry Lutze: you have given me the most incredible gifts in life; your unconditional love, our two remarkable children, and the opportunity to realize my lifelong goal and ten year process of writing this story. You have made so many sacrifices in supporting me and I will always cherish that. You are one of a kind and I feel so blessed to have you as my partner in this life. I will always be thankful that we found one another. You are my best friend and I love you with all of my heart.

Prologue

Butterfly Woman is not intended simply to be a novel that tells a traditional story. When I tell people that I have written a memoir, they look at me quizzically and ponder what a 35 year old could possibly write about her relatively short life.

I wrote this book for every woman and for every man that wants to understand the psyche of women.

As women and children we can be creatures of vulnerability, and we are faced with many challenges and situations that tend to be repressed. In the past society has brushed taboo subjects under the proverbial carpet and this has stifled the necessary dialogue that should be allowed to thrive.

During my short time on this earth I have been faced with many harsh challenges that are universally experienced. In order to heal from them and release them from my subconscious I personally needed to release them in stages. Three specific stages: talk therapy, assisting others going through these situations, and finally writing about them.

I refused to let these horrific experience rape my life of happiness any more than they already had, so these steps were my necessity.

I always assumed I would market this book as a memoir so that my readers would know that these events are true. To me releasing it as a memoir meant that people would put more stock in what was written and discovered through my process, therefore gaining more from the experience of reading it. One thing I didn't realize until the novel had been completed was the legal ramifications of publishing a memoir. An attorney explained to me that any of the 'characters' in the novel could come back and sue me for slander if they didn't approve of what I'd written about them. If I was to publish this novel as a Memoir I would have to get permission from every person that I wrote about. I have no desire to seek out many of the individuals that caused me pain so this seemed like an impossible task. I struggled for many years over what to do about this conundrum.

This novel is my story. The names have all been changed to protect the identities of individual characters in the novel. Keep in mind this is my personal interpretation of the events that occurred throughout my life, many of which were difficult to rehash. As I sat down to write each chapter I was transported back to that time and place and the words would just flow out of me organically. Memories are personal and obtuse so I feel that it is impossible to slot this novel into a category.

My goal in writing this novel is to reach out to individuals that could relate to my story and give them hope. Hope that no matter what you are faced with you can evolve and grow into who you always wanted to be.

Sincerely, Emily Lutze

Lost Child

Present Day

As she sipped her hot coffee she opened her old family photo album and looked at the photo of herself at age three. The yellowed photograph captured an innocence in her own infant eyes that was unfamiliar to her until only recently. The bright navy blue eyes of the toddler reminded her of the last time she felt safe. Overcome with an intense sensation of loss, she longed to rediscover the feeling of complete innocence that she silently mourned for the last thirty years.

She seemed to have the 'perfect' cleaver type family in the beginning, until "it" happened. On the next page she saw the only portrait of her whole family taken before her Dad abandoned her for the first time. In it, the whole family smiled while posing in their cheap polyester pant suits…emanating true happiness…yet there was a hint of falseness to it…She searched aimlessly for one comforting memory from that time but was always unable to find it in the scattered files of her mind. After all these years she finally realized that the polyester family never existed. Her image of her mother was one that she had created in order to survive her nightmare of a childhood. This being the reason that letting go of the woman that gave birth to her was so difficult. She was mourning the loss of the imaginary mother that had been there and nurtured her throughout her life. Through the fog of trauma she was unable to recall any of the positive memories. It was liberating to finally give real credit to those who played that role for her. Childhood memories of her father were scarce and mostly created out of bitmaps from photos that she had seen over and over again. She had survived three decades but her only tangible memories were from the last five years, everything before that was black.

Her older sister Lou Lou swears that their life was great before their Dad left. Only eighteen months older than her baby sister Hannah she had always played the role of mother to both her and their older brother Jory. Hannah admired Lou Lou's strength of character and independence and had always leaned on her for guidance and answers to her tough questions. Lou Lou took no bullshit from anyone. She was tough on Hannah's delicate spirit for a higher purpose. She strived for Hannah to be her own person and not a chameleon adjusting to everyone's whims.

The lack of guidance in Hannah's life had caused her to lack confidence and an ability to be aware of whom she really was. Her journey would be a long and torturous one full of anguish and challenges that would test her to the very core. Along the way there would be times where she was barely clinging on to life but the feeling that there was always a purpose for her that she had yet to reach carried her. She waited patiently for the day that the cards of her life would unfold and present themselves to her.

VULNERABILITY

"The female butterfly deposits her eggs on a chosen plant and then abandons them. A few days later, a tiny creature that looks like a worm will hatch."- Emily Lutze

Missing

September, 2008

The long drive to my sisters' farmhouse was filled with anxiety, unanswered questions and nervous chatter. I kept seeing Lou Lou, in flawless clarity-walking beside the white line on the side of an abandoned road enveloped in darkness; she was walking towards me, staring blankly at the bright lights of our oncoming vehicle, her mahogany curls dripping wildly down her shoulders, her clothes soaked and cold, the wind striking her hard, attempting to effect some reaction. An upturned canoe, drenched lifejacket, and tackle box floating casually in the muggy, black water. The lonely, antique, baby blue Ford perched on top of a bumpy hill overlooking the rugged man-made boat launch. Her faded jean jacket strewn haphazardly across the torn bench seat sits waiting for her warmth to re-envelop it.

The flashes terrified and comforted me as we drove closer to her farm. I searched frantically into the dank, night air needing so badly to see her, never to have her materialize. Was it her lost soul in between dimensions, calling out to me for help?

When we arrived I sobbed for my vanished sister, I sat on her deck and screamed silently into the darkness. Her black lab, Dr. Jones laid his head tenderly on my lap and stared helplessly at me. As torturous sobs escaped my lips his deep brown eyes connected with mine and he placed his damp paw up on my shoulder and crept in close to my body. I wanted to find her, hold her and never let go.

Drenched with wet snow I opened the door that led into her office in the mudroom. Her handwritten notes were still tacked to the walls, to do lists still left unchecked, her Day-Timer opened to yesterday's date. My hot tears warmed my clammy cheeks as I looked painfully at the calendar I made her hanging from a rusty old nail. The pale green construction paper framed a photo of her dressed up like Amy Winehouse, holding a bottle of wine with a hysterical expression on her face wearing a bright neon green sweater and a white crinoline skirt. I stroked the image and willed her to walk in the door behind me. In the kitchen, hung haphazardly on her mahogany cupboards were 81/2 X 11 sheets of paper, with wildflowers, weeds and flora scotch-taped and labeled in her handwriting, a learning tool created for her four children.

I heard sniffles and the faint sound of a woman's voice humming coming from the living room adjacent to me. As I entered the dimly lit room I saw her four year old daughter still awake and she stared at me with tortured sadness in her innocent eyes; those eyes plead violently for me to take the pain away. She whispers sweetly in her tiny voice, "My mommy went away, and she hasn't come back, she doesn't know you're here!" She curls her body into the curves of her daddies mom and opens one eye slightly to look at my confused stare as I hold in the floodgate of tears that is about to flow out of me. I bend down to kiss her exposed cheek and I whisper "I love you" in her ear. I sit silently in the room trying to stifle my tears in front of my niece. When she falls asleep, her grandmother brings her to bed and my tears turn on like a violent faucet. Her husband Eddie's mom shushes me saying "maybe she just ran off, it will be OK." I try to stifle my emotions but reality has hit me hard.

Lou Lou's face and form standing there, lost on the side of the road, lit in the abyss of the night only by a set of headlights. Flickering on and off like an antique motion picture with no sound. The image of her started to fade away as I fought to keep myself awake propped up on the oatmeal sectional, threatening to dissipate into the confines of my mind. When the early morning dawn awoke me with a start, the daylight stole my vision away viciously, leaving me empty and hopeless.

Masked Magician

Summer 1978

Hannah's mother, Magda Rush was newly divorced, with three kids, a mortgage and a full-time job teaching special needs kids. Her hermetically sealed world was crumbling like the Berlin wall and she felt like her life was spinning swiftly out of control. Still madly in love with the children's father, Rex, her mind played tricks on her. She often blanked out in the middle of a lesson and conjured up fantasies of him returning, scooping her up into his arms, whispering hoarsely "Magda, I can't live without you! I need you! I need our three precious children! I must come home with you tonight!"

Her fate had been sealed six months ago when clouded by intimacy she kissed a young man in her drama class at teacher's college that had been carpooling with her each day. On their daily drives they formed an instant connection that consumed Magda's fantasies. Her husband Rex had grown distant of late and was on the road more than he was home, her longing to be held overcame her in the heat of the moment. In the end it was her that could not live with what she had done. Guilt consumed her, and in a matter of weeks she ended up in the town's psychiatric ward. While in the white padded room free of furniture or sharp, predatory objects her visions of "Rex: Her Knight in Shining Armor, The Ying to her Yang, The Jelly to her Powdered Donut" ran fiercely through her mind. The minutes turned into days and he had yet to come swoop her off her feet. Judgment day finally arrived. She saw his ruggedly handsome face staring at her, stoic through the tiny square window at the top of the padded door. Her urine soaked gown transformed into a baby pink satin negligee covered in

5

dainty jewels. As she glided across the room she smeared on her imaginary tube of lipstick and smoothed down her short, erratically untamed mousy brown hair. She had never felt more stunning and knew that this was THE magical moment…

A nurse unlocked the door and motioned for him to enter. He scrunched up his nose and held his breath as the stale, pungent odors washed over him. She swirled over to embrace him and he held his arms solidly in front of him, shoving her back towards the padded wall. The disgust he felt for the woman was palpable. He took her firmly by the arms and pushed her wanton thighs away from his lap and onto the imitation tile floor. "I am indifferent to you Magda and I am leaving you." She was still smiling brightly as he exited the room without even a look back at the mother of his children. The door slammed…the lock clicked…and with that deafening sound reality struck her…her heart felt like it had been pierced by a lead pipe…animalistic sobs escaped her lips and penetrated the muted green hallways of the hospital ward in haunting muffled notes.

Within the year his phone calls became scarce and increasingly distant; divorce papers sat idly in her incoming mail pile; she heard a woman's voice prompting him in the background when she spoke to him on the phone. He had a new, younger lover; someone who could have hot sex at the drop of a dime; someone who had the firm body and tight vagina of a prenatal woman; someone whose vocation and hobby was swimming; someone whose life was unscathed and simple…

Before the shit hit the fan, it is said that she was a great mother. She had been a stay-at-home mom for the past seven years since her first born, Jory arrived. She used her Teacher's Certificate to open a Nursery School to provide her family with extra income so that they could still be together. It was in a one hundred and fifty year old abandoned school that remained fairly intact and had loads of character. She and Rex had transformed the basement of the school into a wonderland with vibrant colours on the walls and giant murals of rainbows, birds, bears and other assorted animals. Magda's pride and joy was the seven foot tall apple tree that was painted on the south wall. On each child's birthday a red or green construction paper apple was placed on the apple tree bearing their name.

After Rex left, she went there and collapsed on the floor beside her prized apple tree. She stared up at the yellowed drop ceiling and begged God for the strength to get over this nightmare. She begged him to turn back time, to steal back that meaningless kiss. Tears rolled down her cheeks as she rolled beige paint, the consistency of yogurt, over top of her child's wonderland. When she was done packing up the Nursery School the only proof that it existed was one sticky handprint of a small child etched on the foggy North window. He had washed his hands of the Nursery School, his unpredictable wife and three small children within weeks. Magda felt too overwhelmed to keep it going and being there reminded her too much of her true love lost.

Due to a fairly large alimony payment from Rex she was able to stay home during the day and go to school at night. In Ontario a new law had recently be issued that all teachers needed an Education Degree to teach in the classroom. Magda's Teaching Certificate was now null and void. It took a few years and several dozen babysitters to get through the next couple of years.

For several months her youngest child, three year old Hannah, would sit curled up, rocking back and forth on the creaky wooden rocker that she had purchased from the Mennonite Colony on the outskirts of town. Saying nothing Hannah chewed the corners of a frayed, crochet knitted blanket, with its rainbow coloured squares, waiting for her Dad to come home. She would simply rock…back and forth, back and forth…Minutes turned into hours as she stared blankly out the window at each approaching vehicle, stopping only for supper or for a quick pee. As the night drew dark she would see headlights brightening the suburban road reflecting off the electrical box across the street and her excitement would well up inside, she would pop up sure that these were the headlights that would turn into her driveway. At first she had the company of Jory and Lou Lou who took turns keeping vigil but they soon grew weary and went back to playing "ping pong champion" downstairs. Hannah kept her brown velour slip on sandals within reach so she could quickly slide them on, run out and be scooped up into her Dad's strong, secure arms. She kept visualizing their reunion over and over in her head like rewinding, putting into slow motion and re-watching your favorite part in a movie. Eventually she grew tired of the endless disappointment and started to slowly spend less and less time in the rocking chair by the window. Six months later she refused to sit in the chair anymore, she realized that her life was forever changed and her Dad was never going to return.

For the years after Rex left, Magda scrambled every night to find babysitters for the kids. She had to complete her degree so she could return to work so she used up all her favors first, asking neighbors, her church family and friends for the first little while. After she had exhausted all of her favors she started collecting numbers of teenagers around town who could watch her kids in the evenings. Jory, the oldest of the three kids never stopped smiling and you couldn't help but love him with his thick glasses. He had been born with a lazy eye and had several surgeries to correct it. When he looked directly at you his eye would wander around the room. Lou Lou was confident and sure in front of strangers, but with her brother and sister she definitely took the role of organizer, caretaker and advisor. Hannah was cowardly and would cry at the drop of a hat. She was the baby and her main goal was to draw as little attention to herself as possible.

The run of babysitters took its toll on Magda and the kids. Most of the babysitters would talk on the phone the whole time they were there and ignore the three kids completely. The kids would try and get the girls attention by throwing darts at the bulk bags of flour in the crawlspace, letting the loose powder expel into the air. Jumping on the furniture or screaming at the top of their lungs was also a revered pastime. Each babysitter incited a full blown preschooler rebellion. They went through a new babysitter pretty much every night; it was very rare for the sitters to return for round two. One night Jory's anger suddenly erupted. A fifteen year old girl named Tammy was babysitting and she was very bossy with the three kids, Jory lost it and grabbed a child sized chalkboard and smashed it over Tammy's head. She passed out cold and the kids were afraid to rouse her so they hid in their makeshift cardboard box fort in the crawlspace under the stairs, whispering hoarsely about what they were going to say when their mom returned. No one over three feet could squeeze in there so they could hide from the horde of teen and preteen babysitters that were frequenting their crumbling home. When Magda returned she nursed the babysitter's goose egg with an ice pack, slipped her an extra $20 bill and drove her home. While she was gone the kids quickly got themselves ready for bed and by the time Magda returned they were all pretending to be asleep. She peeked into their rooms, and then walked to the dining room, its table covered with papers that she still had to attend to. She pounded the circular dimmer hard with the side of her hand and held her breath as she slid down onto the old rickety wooden chair. When Jory woke up the next morning he found his mom laying on the papers, black streaks under her eyes. He put his arms around her and whispered, "Wake up Mom." She looked at him, pulled him onto her lap and squeezed him hard.

After the chalk board incident, word spread like wildfire around the neighborhood about the "unmanageable Rush kids and their crazy mother." Magda knew she had to find a regular babysitter that would be firm yet good with her children. It broke her heart that she had to spend so much time away from home when she knew right now they really needed someone on a consistent basis. In the past few months she had come home to a babysitter with a bleeding nose; a house full of inebriated, stoned teenagers blaring music while her kids cowered in her walk in closet; two teenagers screwing in her marriage bed…Her exhaustion and aspiration had hit its limit and she decided she would get her pastor to announce her dilemma at church on Sunday.

The following Sunday she asked the kids to dress in their Sunday best and to be on their best behavior. She stated her case to them and told them if she didn't find someone to watch them soon they would be in the poor house. They all had to work together as a team in order to accomplish their goal.

After the sermon, Pastor Doug announced the families position to the congregation. A Caribbean woman named Rose raised her hand and spoke out, "Well Amen, my son is looking for work right now, and he's very good with kids and would be the perfect fit for your family. Deary, we can talk after the service."

After church Rose invited Magda and the three kids back to the house for a Caribbean feast of jerk chicken, corn fritters, homemade macaroni and cheese and collard greens. The kids devoured the food as though it had been their only meal in weeks. Hannah secretly wished she could go and live with Rose and eat her food every day all day. After they ate she took them downstairs to meet Derrick, her twenty year old son. He was watching TV in the dimly lit basement. As we they began their descent down the plush basement stairs Derrick looked over at them and greeted them with dark sparkling eyes. He stood up and smoothed down his plaid button down shirt and introduced himself; first to the kids and then to Magda. His mother relayed Magda's plea and he was quick to respond. The adults agreed that this would be the perfect arrangement for him to work for the family every weekday afternoon until 9pm.

His hand is so cold and smooth…I wonder why his skin is so dark, but the inside of his hands are pink like mine…hmmmm…weird…he is soooo tall like a giant and his arms are really big…he and his mom have neat accents…I like the way they talk…he has a nice smile…I hope he's nice to us, I think he'll be nice…his mommy is nice so he is too…

The following day was Monday and it was Derrick's first time babysitting the kids. Instantly, the three kids fell in love with Derrick. He was by far the most attentive and friendly babysitter they had had over the past months. He knew all sorts of magic tricks and he brought over large

Tupperware containers of his Mom's home cooked Caribbean food. Unlike all the other babysitters he actually played with them the whole time he was there, so the kids listened to him and showed him every respect. The first week was exciting and fun for the kids, especially Jory; he especially had been missing the male companionship his father had provided. He taught the kids lots of finger plays like "Two Little Blackbirds" and "Little Bunny Foo Foo". Derrick had a kind, kind face and a smile that could melt your heart. The kids and Magda had grown to love him as one of the family after just one week. Magda was happy that her kids were finally in good hands and she didn't have to worry anymore. Her kids had been through enough and she really began to depend on Derrick.

Halfway into the second week;

When Derrick looks at me I feel weird inside, like he is looking right through me...he looks at me like Daddy looks at his new girlfriend sometimes...I feel icky...Tonight when he was showing us a magic trick he made me put my hand in his pocket...He said "inside it there is a surprise, especially for you!"...Lou Lou and Jory were sitting on the rug in front of us...Inside his pocket there was something hard but soft too...it was poking through a hole, I felt all yucky and gross so I tried to pull my hand away...He grabbed my hand through the fabric on his jeans and wouldn't let it go...I wanted to scream real loud and run away but he was so strong...my tears were so hot on my face, they felt like they were going to burn holes right through my ivory skin...his grip tightened...my delicate bones were burning from the pressure...

I heard a loud 'CRACK' and saw Jory's large, yellow, metal Tonka truck bounce off the arm of the sofa and onto the floor...As his hand released mine I stared at the thick, blood running in slow motion down the side of his cheek...Before my shriek became audible I felt Jory tugging on the arm of my pastel, fairy pajamas...Lou Lou was screaming "RUN, RUN, HANNAH!" Frantically the three of us ran out the front door into the chilly September night...the sun was innocently setting and I stalled for a moment to capture its beauty...My feet were burning from the roughness of the cement as Jory and Lou Lou called for me to hurry up...We just kept running until we reached the forest behind our crescent...We stayed there huddled together, shivering in the night air, surrounded by the distant rush of the creek water and other nocturnal noises...

We tiptoed back to our house when we saw Derrick's mothers' car drive up the road and turn into her driveway just up the street. When we came in the door my Mom held us and cried real hard, harder than I had ever heard her cry... I washed and washed and washed my hands until the water started burning me…I didn't like that magic trick…I didn't like Derrick anymore…I went in my room and pretended to be asleep for the rest of the night, I kept seeing what happened over and over and I could hardly breathe. The next day Mom cried a lot more and yelled on the phone a lot to Rose. She kept saying loudly while she cried "If I ever see your son near my kids again, I'll go to the police!" Derrick never came back and neither did my 'Mom'.

A few nights later I fell asleep in my pale green room with red and white checkered curtains and matching bedspread. I awoke to the pungent, chemically scent of fresh paint. My Mom was looking into my sleepy eyes as she dangled a silky, pink 'bed-in-a-bag' and sang her good morning song brightly….."Good Morning, Good Morning, Good Morning it's time to rise and shine, Good Morning, Good Morning, Good Morning, I hope you're feeling fine! The sun is up above the hill, another day for us to fill…!" I squinted in disbelief as I sat up in bed and soaked in my walls that were now painted pale pink, the colour that was splattered all over my mother, and realized that my bed was in the middle of the room, all the other furniture vanished…"Get up so I can make your bed! Don't you just looovvee this colour sweetheart? I sanded down your dressers so I can repaint those; they're ready for the first coat. Would you like to help?"

That night Mom was rushed to the hospital with her first 'nervous breakdown'. A neighbor had called the ambulance when they saw my Mom outside in the garden weeding naked and preaching to the heavens. An old couple came to live with us for a while, Mom called them the "Who bodies", I never really understood why, maybe that was their last name, I don't know. They were nice to us. The lady smelt really flowery…when I stood too close to her I felt like sneezing. They let us stay home from school sometimes because they said they felt sad for us and that we needed time to heal. I liked Mrs.Whobody, but I stayed away from the man…

Jamaican Momma

Fall 1981

Love is in the Air
&
Love is in the Heart

With Love Karol Hodgkin

That was the note that Karol left for us when Mom finished telling her she was about to get married to the troll Ross Hodge. Her last message to us was accompanied by a blank almost horrified look. My Mom told her that her services would no longer be needed because Ross was going to be a stay-at-home dad. Karol had been our 'during the week Mom' for the last five years. All three of us kids quietly held vigil in front of her door while we listened to her compressed sobs and the discreet squeak of the imitation leather suitcase as she rammed her modest belongings into it. Karol abruptly closed the door of Lou Lou's frilly, pale yellow room leaving only a bed with hospital corners and the trace scent of Vick's vapor rub behind. My tears stung me as I thought about how much I would miss her Jamaican dialect and nightly braiding sessions. She had a firm way of dealing with us and it comforted me to know she cared enough to scold me and hold me accountable.

September 2008

As I brush my sister's six year old daughter, Chastity's long, silky, chestnut hair I suffocate my tears. As I hold the three, thick strands in my hands I recall those long, muggy evenings in Lou Lou's banana yellow childhood bedroom. Her holding my thin, strawberry blonde strands in her fragile hands; pursing her lips together while attempting to add the loose hair hanging at the sides of my face into each singular strand just like Karol used to do; flushed with tenderness. Her thin legs clenched around my petite hips. Stealing glances at her determined expression, exposed to me in the oval, wood trimmed vanity mirror. Our treacherous path exposed, yet I was comforted knowing I would not have to walk down it alone.

As the French braid took shape and I began running out of hair to add to the strands I choked on my despair, knowing that Lou Lou would not be there to nurture this child. I wrapped the shimmering, orange elastic around the thick end of the braid, gave Chastity a hug and excused myself. I stole my woolen sweater coat from the barn board coat hook in the mud room and snuck out the door. With no trees to shield my sorrow, I hid in the field behind a stark, spindly bush. I could feel the thirsty, yellow grass poking into my blue jeans as I sat cross legged. I closed my eyes and begged Lou Lou to give me a sign that she could hear me. After a few puffs I felt magnificent warmth escalate from my hips and radiate upwards, sitting in my belly for an extended moment in time. On my last visit to this farm Lou Lou and I sat in her shed out in the yard, talking and laughing. At one point in the evening she had turned to me; her face transforming; her features became gentle and serene. Asking me to close my eyes, we sat in silence. After a few moments I felt this familiar intense warmth radiating in my body, she said she was hugging me. While I felt her presence there behind that bush I promised her that I could be strong for her and that I would love her four kids forever. As soon as the whispered words escaped my lips the warmth slipped secretly from me and I was left cold and alone assaulted by the autumn prairie wind.

1978-1981

Karol was a tall, husky Jamaican woman with a great sense of humor and a kind hearted soul. Her vibrantly patterned jewel toned house dresses made her warm and approachable. The Rush kids instantly trusted and respected her. She was the first person to truly care for the children since the babysitter incident after Magda's divorce to Rex. Her thick accent made her friendlier in some way, the deep, comforting tones felt like home. Even when she raised her voice they would all end up in fits of laughter because she was all talk no action. Her favorite line was, "GO LIE ON YOUR STOMAK FOR TEN MINEWTS, I WILL COMB OP THA' AN' WACK YO' ASS!" When she yelled out the phrase the guilty child would go straight up to bed and lay as still as a corpse and the other two would grab something to threaten Karol with and hide behind the accused kids' door. When Karol charged up the stairs ready to whack some prepubescent honky ass the other kids would start swinging their makeshift utensil weapons at her until they all rolled around on the floor in hysterics.

September 2008

As I lay next to my sister's teenage daughter Brooke on the makeshift mattress on the living room floor, her breaths lull me into an unsettled stupor. Suddenly, I am aware that I may never sleep beside my sister again. When Karol was our caregiver Lou Lou and I sacrificed our childhood rooms and were moved into the barren master suite. Though we seemed miniscule on the king sized bed, we spent many hours bickering over who got what blankets and how much of the bed we were each allocated. At one point Lou Lou brought in a roll of thick, transparent packing tape; she then proceeded to make a line in which I was not to cross for any reason. Though many of the nights were spent nit picking, more numerous were the nights spent whispering silly stories or revealing deep secrets. Our bond adhered during those five years; we became closer through our mutual struggle. I want so badly to call someone, ask for a life line, but I have no clue who to call. I want to scream and cry in someone's arms, but her arms are the ones I crave.

Magda had a habit of staying out until all hours with strange men and asking Karol to do more than they had agreed on in the beginning yet not paying her more for services rendered. Karol became resentful and inwardly annoyed and angry at Magda, but she refused to abandon those children. Magda would fade in and out and her moods were so unpredictable, though Karol was not the type to judge, she didn't believe that Magda was fit to care for these three children. She was meant to have her weekends off to go home to her family in Scarborough. This was time for herself. Being a full-time live in nanny and housekeeper to the Rush family gave her no rest. She coveted her weekends off spent in the company of her people, her family. Being stuck in a white suburb all week could be challenging. When she took the Rush kids out, people in the hermetically sealed suburban community just gave her the forced smile, and the "Oh! It's so apparent that you're the hired help" kind of look.

One weekend Karol took us home on the Greyhound bus to meet her family. When we walked in the door of the third floor condo, we were assaulted by the smell of deep fried food and cigarettes. I was instantly drawn to the deep, autumn paint that covered the walls and the collection of cherub sculptures that surrounded us. My favorite was a ceramic angel with delicate silver wings, etched with tiny flowers and swirls.

Her family came to the door with warm smiles and an offering of hugs. There was Momma Gemma who was about Grandma's age and she was short and very round. Auntie Necie who held out her left hand to shake while she held her smoke in her right; slender and beautiful, her smooth golden brown skin shimmered against her vibrant red wrap around dress. I studied her delicate, sophisticated movements and when I was in the tiny, cluttered condo bathroom I practiced holding my invisible cigarette taking pseudo puffs while I moved my tiny six year old hips in a gyrating motion and sprayed her perfume on my wrists. Uncle Odell had a very muscular frame and he was a very loud talker. He liked to wave his hands around a lot when he talked. I tried to stay as far away from him as I could. I hid in the folds of the crisp, fresh smelling fabric of Karol's billowy, vibrant batik dress. She never complained or tried to push me off of her. As soon as an older man was near my body would tense and I would feel hot, like I had a really bad fever. I would feel like running as fast as I could and hiding forever where no one would ever find me. I felt like a wound that is being doused in alcohol, the sting festering for an extended period of time…

That night Karol and her family planned on taking us to their church. I had overheard her and Momma Gemma arguing about whether we should attend or not. Karol said she didn't think it was the place for three white children. Momma Gemma argued that we were all God's children and there was more than enough room at Bathurst Baptist Church. We dressed in our Sunday best and sat on the dingy bus stop bench outside their apartment saying nothing. Finally the bus arrived to take us to our holy destination. I wondered why everyone on the bus kept staring at us. It really made me uncomfortable because we were so quiet on the bus you could have heard a pin drop. Momma Gemma, Auntie Necie and Uncle Odell had smuggled some squares of warm corn bread onto the bus and were bent over jamming pieces into their mouths and giggling. Momma G offered me some; it smelt so good drool was forming inside my mouth, but Karol shook her head no. I felt like you do when you're hungry, but it's not cause you're hungry it's cause you have the butterfly barfs.

Three transfers later we were standing outside the door of a small, simple, white, very traditional looking church. It looked just like one of the mini plastic ones that people use on their wedding cakes. It had a big, black, iron cross just over the door and was nestled in amongst a few run down strip malls; one housed a Chinese Restaurant called "Smiley's Good Food Place"; and on the other side there was a pawn shop called "Hawk and Haul"; open twenty four

15

hours and a coffee shop called "The Good 'Ole Coffee Hole". Karol spent about five minutes straightening us up, making us presentable for her congregation. Momma Gemma started to hop up and down, her fat jiggling around her belly. "I have to use the facilities are you gonna bring those kids in 'ere or what?" Karol told us to hold hands and in we went. As I walked through the double doors I heard the sound of Calypso music and the hundreds of voices screaming "HALLELLLLUUUUIIIIAAAA!!!!", "PRAAAIIIIIISSSSE JEUSUS!!!" Everyone in the church was standing, dancing or waving their arms around, most were clapping vigorously and they all looked so joyful. An intense energy filled the room, injecting me with the most warm, nurturing, feeling. The three churches I had been to were so bland and boring like a diabetic shortbread cookie. This church was vibrant, colourful, and intense like a slice of rich, triple berry cheesecake with hot chocolate sauce, mountains of whip cream and a ripe, juicy red cherry on top. No one stared, no one tisk tisked…they all were wrapped up in the glory of the Lord. They welcomed us into their sacred world and it was so special I felt like I was in the right place at the right time. These people left an indelible imprint on my heart…

In the morning I awoke to the sounds of Karol's nasally yet delicate snores. She slept on a cot next to the double bed Lou Lou, Jory and I shared. The two beds crowded the tiny room leaving only a foot between the cot and the bed. I looked at the clock, on its face I read five o'clock am. I still had a few hours left to sleep but I decided I would rather spend my time memorizing Karol's kind, face that showed more lines for its twenty-eight years than a woman's should. There I sat wondering what her life had been like. Had she worked for other families for long? Cooking and cleaning for other people? As I stared at her chest, watching it heave up and down tenderly I clenched my eyes shut and slid off the edge of the double bed. The space between the beds was just big enough for me to kneel in. As I sat I held my hands together and prayed on my terms. I asked God to please give Karol a family of her own to look after. I wanted her to have a family that wouldn't abandon her after years of caretaking and loving. She always made me feel loved. She gave me a slice of normalcy that would remain in my fractured heart…

The Albino, the Lemonade and the Subway Station

Spring 1982

I thought all Grandfathers looked like my Mom's Dad. I also thought that I was born at the "H" Hospital and every time we passed those green signs displaying the white, block letter "H" my childlike voice rang out excitedly, "That's the hospital I was borned at!" For some reason no one ever corrected me. During the most troubling years of my childhood I spent many weekends at Grandma and Grandpa's. Mom's birth mom had passed away during the delivery and my present Grandma had actually been Mom's childhood housekeeper. Grandma (Adele) was French Canadian and had the rawest sense of humor. Grandpa was devoid of pigment in his hair and body due to the fact that he was Albino. He also only had 5% sight. When he was a young man he had ridden a motorbike and driven a car, blind and all. When he told those stories I always pictured him with his friend navigating on the back of the bike with a face also devoid of colour due to all the blood rushing out of it; yelling from the back of the bike, "There's a 90 degree turn coming up in .5 seconds!"

"There is a red light coming up rigggggggghtttt about now...Oh... PEDESTRIAN!!!"

Grandpa had too much pride to admit he had any "disability". It kind of made me sad that he never knew what I looked like. His personality was pretty icy 95% of the time unless you asked him to take you down to his workshop in the basement. He had the full range of the most rare vintage model train sets;

Markin, "HO", Lincoln and American Flyer. He also had the most intricate village set up downstairs with miniature buildings, tiny trees of all shapes and varieties, lights that illuminated when you passed over certain parts of the sophisticated train system running around the perimeter of his imaginative world. When you stepped foot in his dimly lit world his eyes would light up like a little child receiving a puppy on Christmas morning. Transformed, he would talk at length about each train and all of its features and intricacies. We would go on a pre-scripted tour of his workshop: small sets of drawers methodically labeled with one of those label-makers that spits out the sticky plastic strips with popped out white printing. I felt closest to Grandpa then, even though I didn't understand much of his train talk I valued my time with him so I listened attentively.

He was one of the only people in Canada that knew how to fix the old fashioned Braille machines. Though he was blind he worked with the utmost precision and was a highly valued member of the CNIB. People from all over Canada would ship their antique Braille machines to him for servicing and knew they would always be satisfied with the workmanship. On our last visit he was close to tears when he mentioned that he had not found an apprentice to carry on his work, it became a lost art and soon the antique Braille machine would face extinction.

When I went to Grandma and Grandpa's it was a refuge of calm predictability. A break from the chaotic life I had with Mom. Routines were set in place, announced by the chime of the old Grandfather Clock that sat on the shiny, white marble fireplace mantel. The old television; one of those ones that is embedded in an ornate mahogany wooden box; was always on when we were in the house and Grandpa was a permanent fixture sitting less than a foot from the screen in his plastic covered floral armchair. He would squint with his face right up against the screen to make out the fuzzy images that coordinated with the dialogue. As I sat across from him I would watch him with fascination, wondering if he could really tell what Angela Lansbury looked like. Or if he knew that Andy Rooney had hair almost as white as his. News, Soaps and Mystery's became such a part of my viewing that I had the formulas memorized at a very young age. I fell in love with the "stories". The exaggerated storylines of the soaps; trying to solve the mystery during "Murder She Wrote." I enjoyed those shows so much that I began to get bored with shows targeted at kids my age; they were too immature…

If it was particularly sunny we would all go outside during the lull in programming between 2 and 3pm. Grandpa would putz around in his garden and Grandma and I would sit on the squeaky vinyl couch swing…the awning *carefully protecting us from the harsh rays of the Eastern sun...We would sip lemonade as we were lulled into relaxation listening to the gentle squeaks of the old swing, the melodic songs of the birds and the dull muffled sound of city traffic...*

On a particularly humid and stifling hot day...you know the days where your legs stick to the chair and when you get up you have to peel yourself off... Grandma and I went into the house to make some lemonade...Grandma passed me the lemons and my job was to squeeze them into the tall glass jug... As I turned to look at Grandma I lost my coordination and the lemon knocked against the side of the jug knocking it off the edge of the kitchen table...The floor was drowning in the sticky, bitter liquid...ice cubes sailed all over the black and white porcelain tiled floor...rapidly spreading to cover the expanse of the kitchen...Grandma and I hopped onto our chairs to avoid soaking our feet...Grandpa hollered from the living room "WHAT IN THE HELL WAS THAT?...Fear rose up my spine and plunged into my heart making it throb...I could hear his heavy footsteps and the sound of his hand sliding along the wall to find his way towards the kitchen...I stifled my cries hoping if I was quiet he wouldn't find his way to the kitchen...He reached the dining room entrance of the kitchen "WHAT DID YOU DO?"Grandma clammed up as she always did when Grandpa lost his temper, she didn't move a muscle...it was as though she was playing a game of "frozen tag" and she was trying not to be made 'it'...Tears streamed down my face...unseen by Grandpa, "It was an acccidddenttt" I squeaked..."CLEAN IT UP YOU CLUMSY CHILD!!! YOU'RE JUST LIKE YOUR MOTHER!!!" he spat violently... I knew how much my Mom annoyed my Grandpa so I took that as the biggest insult...That was the first time I saw my Grandpa lose his temper...He usually maintained a stern yet monotone mood...After that I felt more cautious in his presence, scared to make one wrong step, afraid that Grandma and Grandpa would stop taking me for our weekends...

When I was about six years old, Grandma and I chose a particularly rainy day to go downtown Toronto for a girls only shopping trip...We planned on hitting all the discount stores and a craft store and having lunch at "Mr. Green Jeans"...Grandma loved having the company...we were a great duo always making one another laugh...We held hands as we exited her old historic home... The first street we needed to cross had become a very busy thoroughfare over the years so Grandma reminded me to hold tight and keep up...As she squeezed my petite hand I could feel the transparent smoothness of her aging skin...We walked two blocks to the Sheppard Avenue subway station...We descended the concrete stairs and the familiar scent of stale urine and musty concrete filled my nostrils…I took a deep breath in and tried only to breathe through my mouth hoping that by doing that I would escape having to endure another whiff, also worried that I wouldn't breathe so hard that I would taste it…We reached the small glass cubicles housing the ticket master, Grandma passed me a shiny, dime-sized subway token and she placed hers in the metal and glass container, I placed mine in after and watched it spiral down the metal slide into the shiny pool at the bottom of the container…Grandma waved to the weathered old Asian man sitting in the box…we heard the click of the turnstile-an invitation to enter… we walked swiftly towards the rushing sound of the in and out coming trains… Grandma's grasp tightened as we rushed to catch the next outgoing train… Anxious not to miss it…the sound of our rubber-soled shoes padding quickly upon the snot green commercial tiled floor…I snuck glances at the illuminated adds for Coca-Cola and Doritos…Feeling overwhelmed with all the stimulation…people bumping into me…subway rails screeching…babies squawking…I felt the walls closing in on me…Once we got to the top of the escalator my small heart skipped a beat and perspiration moistened my brow as I stepped onto the escalator hoping this wouldn't be the time when I would lose my footing on the moving steel stair and tumble to my death…A cold wind blasted us as the Southbound train exited on its way towards its destination…We were carried along down the stairs as our subway pulled into the station, we reached the level platform and noticed the subway was jammed packed…There was a sea of bodies of all shapes and sizes animalistic…shoving each other into the metal tube, covered with grime and graffiti. Grandma quickened her pace, me trailing behind her, my legs doing double time because they were half the length. She followed behind an Asian couple who pushed their way in through the narrow double doors of the subway car. Grandma squeezed in just after the "ding, ding…" warning sounded, with no notice the doors closed rapidly right onto mine and Grandma's clasped hands. We had to let go of one another so we wouldn't get our hands crushed. Grandma was trapped inside, her already pale face turning completely white. I was standing alone on the platform, fear and anxiety rising up in my body like sour bile. Grandma frantically motioned for me to go to the next station. I anxiously awaited the next train, feeling severely alone and vulnerable. Five years old-ALONE-stifling my sobs…trying to blend in and be unnoticeable…

It took forever for the next train to come, but when it did I pushed myself on with some hesitation. I took the short, wobbly ride to the next station and got off the train. I searched every corner of the station for Grandma, but she was not there. I waited for a while and then, took the southbound train back to Sheppard Station. She had vanished into thin air; she was nowhere to be found. I didn't know what to do next. I couldn't find her. Too scared to stay at Sheppard

Station and too scared to go back to the next station, I stayed put for a while. I thought it was a long time, but for all I knew it could have been only three minutes. I made the decision to go back to Grandma's house. I had been down there so many times; I figured I should be able to find my way back. Fearful that I was going to be in deep trouble no matter what I did I felt I needed to get out of there, away from the prying eyes of onlookers. Tears flowed down my face as I walked with my head down towards Grandma's house. When I reached the back door I turned the handle slowly, trying to be discreet in case Grandma hadn't returned. I was terrified to face Grandpa alone. The handle turned easily and I heard the door click as I opened it quietly. I heard the muffled sound of the TV and noticed that Grandma's shoes were not on the mat. Frantic and miserable I descended the narrow wooden stairway to Grandpa's workshop. I hid in one of Grandma's square plastic clothing holders. I snuggled in amongst the numerous fur coats and floral polyester dresses. There was a faint smell of mothballs that made me want to sneeze. I felt a good one rising up, tickling my nostrils. I held it with as much power as I could muster in my five year old senses.

It felt like I was crunched up in that cheap clothing closet for hours, the weight of my curled up body denting the thick cardboard bottom. Finally I heard the back door open, Grandma yelled "ANNAH! JOHN IS 'ANNAH 'ERE???" I heard my Grandfather's slow but steady shuffle down the hall and him bellowing "What, why the hell would she be here, she was with you!" Grandma replied, "We got separated at de station and I cannot find 'er!" I figured this was probably the moment when I should show myself. Grandma was there to protect me now from Grandpa's vile temper. I slowly ascended the stairs, trying not to make them squeak with the heaviness of my feet. Grandma turned around and saw me, she squealed, "'annah! What har you doing 'ere?" I said sheepishly, "I tried to go to the next station and I waited for you for a long, long time, but I couldn't find you and I got scared!" She said, "Why were you 'iding?" The tears just started to flow and I said nothing, not wanting to reveal the fact that I was scared of facing Grandpa alone. Grandpa spat, "That was a stupid thing to do, you silly girl!" Grandma put her arms around me, sheltering me from his cruel words, knowing why I had hid. She brought me into her bedroom, sat me on her white chenille bedspread and held me in her arms, rocking me, saying nothing but "I'm so sorry!!"

I loved my Grandma more than anyone in the whole wide world and she knew it. I wanted to leave Mom and come live here forever. Grandma was silently protecting me from all the mistakes and horrors my Mom had exposed me to. She was unable to take me away permanently but she let me escape to the safety of her home whenever I could.

Bahamian Friends
We Love You!!!

Winter 1981

Life was really good when Magda was not involved with one of her many male callers. She had a large chart on the back of the kitchen door in the kitchen with a list of each child's daily chores. Her household started to mimic the milieu of her Special Needs Class. Although the ironic thing was she refused to open her eyes to her own children's special needs. Hannah, Lou Lou and Jory would come home from school and complete their chores obediently; they wanted to prove to Mom that they could function, just the four of them. They didn't want a new Daddy and they made every effort to make their Mom's life as pleasant as possible.

One night when we got home from school we planned out this whole idea that we'd pretend that we were running a fancy restaurant...We started out by cleaning the house from head to toe...then we made up a really detailed menu written in fancy calligraphy on white stationary backed with purple construction paper...We spent almost an hour planning out the dinner fare for the night...For an appetizer we would have a veggie plate made up of carrot and celery sticks, followed by vegetable soup (Campbell's of course), the main course being maple flavored beans with chopped up beef wieners, and the dessert, Flamingo butter tarts a la mode...We thought that our meal was close to perfection and that Mom would love it...Each of us had a role to play: Jory was the Maitre De, I was the Chef and Lou Lou was the Waitress... We scrambled to go find clean, crisp outfits to match our prestigious titles

22

before Mom arrived home after school...While I was searching for my long sleeved button down white shirt I heard Lou Lou scream from the kitchen... "HANNAH, GET IN HERE! You burnt the beans and the wiener pot is boiling over!" I felt so stupid, I ruined everything...I felt the tears welling up inside ready to come flooding out, Lou Lou had a sixth sense when it came to my emotional outbursts and she held me by both arms, turned me so that I was forced to look directly in her eyes and said calmly, "Hannah, we'll fix it, Don't Cry! Please Don't Cry! It is going to be OK!" I ran into the bathroom and breathed in and out hard trying to focus myself...Lou Lou was right, me crying would ruin the whole night...I had to pull it together...

Dinner had been ready for about an hour by the time Mom's brown Chevy Nova pulled into the driveway...We had all been waiting patiently by the window in our crisp white shirts, black shirts and pants...Jory ran down the stairs with a blue and white checked dishtowel folded neatly over his forearm and stood patiently by the door with his brightest smile...When Mom opened the door she was welcomed by her eldest son...He took her bag and coat off for her and said "Welcome to Chez Rush Madam." She looked exhausted when she first came in, but when she saw the three of us all dressed up, presenting her with a menu for the night her face lit up and a genuine smile spread across her lips...She noticed every detail of what we had done and thanked us over and over for a special night...Even though the wieners looked like your fingers when you've been in the swimming pool too long, and the beans were blackened, with every bite she took she reacted as though this was the best meal she had ever eaten...a meal made from love...

Mom had a secret plan that she had been keeping from us, something she had been saving for a very long time...All we knew was that it had to do with the church and the fact that a family from the Bahamas had come and lived with us for a month at Christmastime the previous year...For months the church had been collecting money by doing Garage Sales and Bake Sales to raise money for some special event that was all hush hush...On Sunday the pastor at our church said something about reaching their goal and Mom's face lit up...When we got home she said she had something to tell us...We were so excited and wondered what we had to do with the churches goals and stuff...

Mom sat us down in the living room looking like a happiness bubble about to explode..."We're going on a Church Exchange for a month to the Bahamas!!!"...Oh My God, did I just hear right, I pinched myself hard until I flinched and then noticed Lou Lou and Jory were already running around the living room screaming and shouting "YES! AWESOME!" We all swarmed Mom and soon she was up jumping and screaming too…All this time, everyone from church was raising money for us to go to the Bahamas for a church exchange…We would be staying in a condominium right in Nassau, and we would be spending all our time with the family that came here at Christmas…

We didn't have much, we all knew that, so the fact that Mom had pulled the money together for such a huge trip touched us deeply and we worked extra hard to help Mom as much as possible…Life was really good, everyone was happy…

When we stepped off the plane we were greeted by three Bahamian locals in bright, floral sundresses, they placed strings of fresh fuchsia orchids around our necks…I felt like a Princess and I almost melted as the fresh, warm summer air caressed me…The air was fragrant and as I looked to my left I just about fell to my knees when I saw the most beautiful pink, orange and fiery red sunset…I had just entered heaven on earth…

Mom glowed the whole time we were there…the pressure of raising three kids and running a classroom full-time, alone seemed to slip off her back the minute she stepped off the plane…It was the beginning of our adventure…"The Rush's take Bahamas!!!" Apparently the family that was sponsoring us were definitely Upper Class, because they had set us up in a beautiful furnished condo that was nicer than our house…we had unlimited access to a pool and hot tub and we each had our own bedroom…We spent almost every moment at the condo splashing around in the pool…there was no one else in it, ever! We had the place to ourselves except for this one leathery old lady, who never left her lounge chair on the side of the pool and always held this aluminum foiled looking cardboard in front of her face…she never spoke to us, but she also never complained about the noise…

One day while we were swimming, we hardly noticed her anymore as she had become like a permanent ornament of the pool area…She had mumbled hello as we jumped into the pool that afternoon and we went about our splashing and frolicking…As we were playing a game of Marco Polo, I was It so my eyes were closed, but I heard Lou Lou and Jory climb out of the pool, I said "Hey you guys are cheating!" They screamed for me to go and get someone…The leathery old lady had started convulsing, her tongue was hanging out of her frothing mouth, her breathing had become labored and shallow and her eyes had rolled back!! It was like a scene out of The Exorcist…After the Ambulance left Mom told us that it was a good thing we were there because the lady had sun stroke and could have died if we hadn't been there…We didn't see her anymore after that, but her empty plastic lounger haunted us for the rest of the trip…

We had the most amazing time while we were there; we went on a glass bottom boat and as we sailed around we watched the floor come alive with schools of vibrantly coloured fish, eels, sea lions and starfish greeted us as we skimmed along the crystal, turquoise Caribbean water...It was like Mom was healed, she focused all her energy on us, she wasn't scattered or weird, she was vibrant and beautiful, strong and lucid, I was proud she was my Mom...I knew that leaving this island would mean leaving utopia so I tried to cherish every single moment and burn it into the cells of my memory...One thing about having a great imagination, I know I can always count on it to transport me back to the places where I felt safe, and loved...

We also had a brush with fame while we were there, apparently we were quite special because somehow we received an invitation to spend the day with the Governor of Nassau and his family...We drove up to a large white mansion in the centre of town, surrounded by iron gates and fences, a security guard had to buzz us in...We had lunch with a room full of delegates and people in fancy dresses and suits...I wore my grey dress with the large square collar with my patent leather shoes, with my boyish haircut I felt quite ugly compared to all the Bahamian girls with their long braids and frilly pale yellow dresses... Mom did not put much value in clothing, so we didn't have much to wear...I didn't care though...They took a picture of us with all the important political people in Barbados and here we were, the three little Rush kids in the very front row...The picture was featured the very next day on the cover of Nassau's most esteemed daily newspaper...though I was excited that we were almost famous now I was horrified that I looked like a boy in a frock!

The remainder of our days were spent frolicking with our great Bahamian friends in the ocean, having bonfires on the beach, collecting conch shells and preparing a tuna salad type dish with the conch snails meat...I felt at home there, these were the most friendly people I had come across in this lifetime... they didn't judge me in any way, and they never criticized me for the way I was...They just played with me and helped me feel joy in the everyday life on the Island...This was my paradise amidst the tornados...my oasis before the dark side opened and swallowed me whole...

Her World is Falling

During the summer of 1986 Hannah's Dad and stepmother had taken the three kids on a whirlwind trip to Expo '86 in Vancouver, then San Diego, and Disneyland. Though Disneyland was a magical place that many kids dream of, Hannah had an underlying heaviness that remained in her chest, a sense of urgency. That night in the hotel room, she was unable to keep the violations of the last four years to herself. There needed to be a way to escape from this hell on earth that they were all living in back in Newmarket. The thought of having to return home to her mentally ill mother and pedophiliac stepfather was more than her twelve year old soul could fathom. Lou Lou and Jory watched Jaws One, Two and Three and then began to watch Piranha to the chagrin of Hannah. The violence and negativity only intensified her anxiety making it unbearable. Her only desire was to feel safe; it was not simply a desire though it was a MUST! She attempted to communicate to her brother and sister the only way she knew how, a floodgate of tears. At first her brother was crass and poked fun about her situation with Ross "you let Rossy touch you, eewwwwww!" The tears continued to flow and Lou Lou and Jory's frustration with what was Hannah's typical behavior pattern transformed into empathy. They too were caught in this web of horror and were searching for a way out. They then began to encourage Hannah to go down to their Dad and step mom's hotel room to tell on Ross, coaching her about the best way to approach it.

The silence of her footsteps on the plush carpet of the hotel hallway released questions and thoughts that raced through her mind at a rapid pace:

What if Dad doesn't believe me? He has never trusted me or had faith in me. He always says "That's silly!" What if he says I'm just telling another one of my stories? What is he gonna do about it? What if he just sends us back without doing anything? He's not very emotional. What if he doesn't feel sorry? What if he doesn't hug me? If I just walk back to the room I can be with Lou Lou and Jory and we can keep on pretending. I can't live like this anymore; I have to go to him.

She reached the high gloss; cream coloured door marked 321 and stood with her hands clenched by her sides. Barely able to breathe she tried to muster the courage to knock on that door. It was her chance: *They're gonna think I ruined the trip! Oh God! O.K. Who cares I have to do this NOW!*

Knock on that damn door Hannah! Her knock was so gentle that it could not be heard by her Dad and his wife. She tried again, just a little harder this time, then she heard the squeak of someone getting out of the leather chair and footsteps coming towards the door. The tears started to flow again as her stepmom Karen opened the door saying "Well, Hello Hannah! Rex its Hannah!" with an overtly perky, yet forced tone of voice. Two sets of eyes stared at her with a sense of urgency. "Well what's the matter?" At first all that came out of her was a squeak. Following the squeak came a single tear and then Karen put her arm around Hannah in a genuine, nurturing way. The floodgate was opened and out poured the dirty secrets that had been rotting her soul for the past four years...

*Ross has been doing things... Hurting me...*Hannah you need to calm down, just try and calm down, your safe with us now, tell us what is going on..."Rex I knew that man was no good!"...

He comes into my room at night and sits beside my bed...he breathes on me... the stench of his breath is disgusting...he comes when everyone is asleep...I'm trapped and no one knows he's there...What carries me in the darkness is the vision of the man without a face and the two small ones...who materialize each night in the corner of my room...comforting me with the knowledge that they are my future...They take me away from this place...He said if I told anyone he would kill my Mom and Lou Lou and Jory too...He scares me...

"What does he do when he sits in your room Hannah? You have to tell us so we can help." you...*He licks me and the smell of his saliva makes me want to vomit...He is such a pig...So dirty...He touches me down there...and he puts my hand on his...I try to pull away and he hurts me...I can't do this... please don't make me tell you anymore...*

Directly after Hannah's tearful confession her father called her Mother. She loved her mother and fantasized about her father heroically rescuing her from this nightmare. She was willing to give up being with her mother to get away from the hell that was her home life. Her Stepmom held onto her hand and wept silently as her father spoke to her mother in hushed tones.

She heard bits and pieces of the conversation "take them away," (*Oh My God! I am going to escape that prison!*) "How could you have been so stupid?" (*Mom knows what is going on, what did she think was going to happen. She lost me after she left me with him in her marriage bed on Christmas morning...I'll never forget when she opened the door and saw him laying with me...just looking with a blank fucking stare and saying "breakfast is in ten minutes"...Mother's are supposed to protect their young...Why didn't she save me...I thought she was finally going to save me...But he held me hostage as I stared at his silver dime holder and mini square wind up clock on the night table...That was two years ago...She let it go on for two more years...Well, now she can't turn a blind eye can she...I will just have to deal with whatever consequences there are to telling my dirty little secret...Lately I have been fighting off my stepfather...I tell him to go fuck himself and that if he comes near me I'll scream my head off and cut his balls off...I told my best friend Candy what he was doing and she said to do that...At first I was scared too because I thought he might actually kill me...but I would have rather been dead than have him go near me again so I tried it one night...The first night there was a struggle but I got him off of me...I kept myself awake and ready to fight, so after a few nights he stopped coming...He started to physically abuse me after that, it really sucks but I can handle it...Like the day I went downstairs to get a cushion for my friend from Sunday School...He had been raising chicks in the basement of our bungalow...our friggin' house smelt like a barn...so much chicken shit just festering on the ping pong table that he set up to be a coup...We weren't allowed to go in his makeshift farm room, but that was where the cushions were...We were no longer on speaking terms so there was no way I was going to ask...I tiptoed down the stairs...aware that I wasn't sure where he was...I reached the back room (or farm) and started to relax as I reached around the corner and snatched a cushion...I got one...now I just needed one mo...CRACK! CRACK! I felt an intense pain shoot up my back and on the top of my head...I had been struck...I whipped around and as I did I came face to face with Ross...there was so much evil behind those crystal blue eyes, it was like standing face to face with Satan himself...In his hands he was holding a 2 by 4...I screamed at the top of my lungs and bolted up the stairs...I told my Mom what he did...They had a screaming match and I ran away for the fiftieth time...Life would go on like that for at least another year...Him waiting around corners and sheepishly abusing us physically while my Mom was away from the house...The scariest times were the times when Mom had her "nervous breakdowns"...If we didn't have a place to go we would have to stay with him ALONE! We all scrambled to find friends to stay with as often as we could...Many of these four years are black...In order to survive our memories seem to strategically lock things out that are too dark to reveal...I still have so much anger at my mother for not leaving him...when she met him he was 40 years old and still living with his mother and father...their old rickety house gave me the creeps...it was full of miscellaneous dollar store crap covered in layers of dust...We all had the creeps as soon as we met Ross...kids know who they can trust and who they cannot...The three of us had begged and pleaded with our Mom up to and on the Wedding night Especially Jory... When we were decorating the hall Jory had screamed at Mom to "CANCEL THIS STUPID FUCKING WEDDING", after his outburst, Ross struck him upside the head in front of everyone in the hall...Jory took off...Lou Lou and I took off after him...after a few hours of searching all his hideaways Lou Lou and I headed home with great hesitation without him...He was there in the morning with a fresh bruise welling up on the surface of his pimply preteen skin and a defeated look in his eyes...*

Hannah and Lou Lou ended up returning home after the trip to California that summer of 1986, while Jory stayed on in Edmonton. Rex and Karen had convinced the girls that Ross would be gone from the house when they returned as per a condition they discussed with Magda (actually a threat, but that is simply semantics). If he was still there the girls were to contact Rex and Karen and let them know, whereupon they would be sent right back out to Edmonton permanently.

My heart felt like it was going to break in two when Dad walked me and Lou Lou onto the plane that summer...He came right on and held me as he placed me in my seat...tears ran down both of our faces...Jory had a blank stare...he would be safe now...our secret alliance would be broken... who would I go to in the night when I needed to talk?...could Lou Lou and I handle looking after Mom on our own?...I wanted so badly run right off that plane, but loyalty kept me from my desires to be free...Mom was not capable of functioning without us...she was too far gone and had no control over her bipolar disorder...She would need someone to survive this with her...Our loyalties and a fear of the unknown outweighed our desires to live in a safe, nurturing environment...

Magda had promised that he would be gone when the girls returned. She had 'technically' removed him, but he refused to go without a fight...

As I walked into my room upon returning from Dad's safe haven I noticed that my bed was not made...I was always particular about the way my bed was made...it was almost an obsession...the sheets had to be straight and taught...the pillows had to be perfect rectangles with no indentations or signs that they had been slept on...my heart fell down into my kneecaps as I walked hesitantly over to my bed...As I slowly pulled back the covers I noticed that the pillow had a large indent which was filled with a dirty, grimy round patch...his sweaty bald head had been on my pillow...I threw back my pink floral comforter and noticed a crunchy, substance smeared into the sheets with more grayish brown grime...I vomited in my mouth and ran to the bathroom to release it into the toilet...He had slept in MY BED while I was away...the tears flowed quickly down my face as I went into the room...the tears turned to rage as I tore the sheets and pillowcase violently off the bed... If he couldn't invade me, he had to invade my sacred space...FUCKER...I stormed over to my next door neighbors'...Maureen was like a true mother figure to me...though we never spoke about it I always knew she was aware of what was going on behind our closed doors and shut up windows...Even in the scorching, humid, summer heat Ross would never allow us to open the windows or blinds...Hiding his evil he was...When I stumbled through the door of Maureen's kitchen she jumped..."You're back honey, we mis...What is wrong sweetie?... all the secrets rushed out of me pouring in liquid form all over Maureen's green veneer kitchen table...

Ross would stalk and torture Magda and the girls for almost a year. Neighbors' that were on the lookout would call and let the girls know that he was watching them. The stalking got so bad that they had to escape to their mom's friends place. Magda's friends, Mary and Kathy were away for an extended trip so Magda and the girls stayed at their place for a while. He would come at late hours in the night and bang on the doors, wiggling the handles, trying to get in. The three of them would hide under the mahogany kitchen table and grasp hands as he would try and break down the door. Why wouldn't he leave them alone? Did he have no conscience? Did he have no remorse? All of a sudden he stopped coming around. This was the time when Lou Lou felt it was finally safe for her to move to Edmonton with Rex and Karen as well. She and Hannah agreed that their Mom still needed someone to live there, so Hannah volunteered with trepidation.

By Grade Eight he had been long absent from Hannah's life. The healing was slow, but she was finally starting to feel happy. Things were going well. It was just her and her Mom now and things were actually really great. Her Mom pretty much let her do whatever she wanted. Like let her have friends over after school and have parties on the weekends. As much lenience as her Mom gave her, she felt a deep sense of longing for the kinship of her siblings, and a secret desire for her mom to care enough to set some boundaries.

Every Sunday after church Hannah and her Mom would go on long drives: her Mom would let her drive on the back roads. It was during this time in the week that they would update each other on everything that was going on in their lives. Hannah always appreciated the fact that her Mom would never judge her or get mad, no matter what she had to say. Her Mom showed outwardly the fact that she loved Hannah unconditionally no matter what.

Hannah's Grade Eight Graduation was soon arriving so they were planning out all the details on their Sunday drive one week. Grandma Adele would make her dress; white satin, with puffy three quarter length sleeves and a red sash and trim. The night of Grad was filled with hope for the future and the security that her Mom now lived for her and her siblings. They had let the past disintegrate into the deepest part of their conscience for several months now. Her Grandma and Grandpa sat proudly on the outermost edge of the third bleacher in the gymnasium. Her Mom had just joined them and upon seeing them waiting there Hannah waved to them excitedly. She was going to be in High School next year...She couldn't believe she had made it here in one piece...

I wonder what Huron Heights will be like? That's so cool that I'm gonna be in High school...What? Where did Mom go?...Why is Grandma staring at me like that?... What is going on?...Is that Mom yelling in the hallway?...

Magda was being pushed backwards into the gymnasium. Her flat soled Tender Tootsie shoes squeaked as she tried to grip the gleaming linoleum floor with her feet. Hannah could barely see what was going on because her friend Sheila turned her by the shoulders and held on trying to force her not to see. Ross was forcing himself into the gym, in front of all those people. He was shoving Magda towards the stage where Hannah was standing dumbfounded, waving a pink envelope in his hands, yelling, "I JUST WANT TO GIVE THIS CARD TO MY DAUGHTER!"... Hannah's face turned white with disgust, embarrassment and rage. *"Why the hell would he come here? Hasn't he done enough?"* Mrs. Lake, Hannah's Grade Six teacher ran over and also started shoving the short, fat bald, pedophile out of the sacred ceremony. A buzz lurched out of the audience full of family members and faculty. Hannah blanked out for a few moments as more people came to help Magda escort Ross forcefully out of the gym. The next time Hannah would see Ross there would be a judge and jury present…

A note from Hannah: *As I wrote this chapter my two month old daughter Ruby slept peacefully on my lap, she offered a veil of protection that surrounded me in a circular fashion as I wrote. From the heavens she protected me as a child while I was there and the beauty of having her here at last in flesh and warmth, her soft sweet breath sending love and keeping me grounded so that my mind kept itself from going to intensely back to that toxic, unsafe place.*

Life with Mom

Before Mom was diagnosed with Bipolar disorder our lives were literally consumed with chaos...Everyone loved the sweet, bubbly special needs teacher who spread her love around like wildfire...Resentment filled me every time someone would say, "I just love your Mom, she's so nice and she lets you do anything you want. You're so lucky to have a Mom like her!"...Yes, my life was such a Hallmark card...wasn't she just the Mary Poppins of mothers?... She could definitely keep up appearances...she was the Mistress of Disguises... Calling Social Services on parents of abused kids in her class while her own three children were being tortured daily by her obtuse husband...Oh yes, life was a vase of colourful Gerber's for the Rush kids wasn't it?

I never criticized her because the first few times I tried my friends would rush to protect her name as though she was Mother Theresa or something...I held my tongue for so long that it felt like a piece of lead pipe weighted down with cinder blocks...

In Thornhill, Ontario, the town we lived before Newmarket, she had summoned up quite the reputation for being a loose cannon at the wheel of a car...The average person probably has one accident a decade...My Mom was lucky to get through the week without an accident, especially during the winter months...Each winter she would run straight into each one of the stop signs on her route to and from school, each time bending the steel with the dented bumper of her rusted, brown Chevy Nova...She did it so many years in a row that the town eventually replaced all the steel posts with long wooden 2X4's... From then on Mom's car was the only blemished party...None of our friends ever took a ride a second time from my Mom, they politely declined by saying, "Oh, that's OK, I'll just call my parents.."

Mom slammed on her brakes so hard all the time in that Nova that after ten years she had worn a hole right through the floor under the brake…you could see the road passing by and when it was slushy her boot and the bottom of her pants would be wet and soiled with the salty ice…Mom had a major accident while Jory was in the car…She actually drove right into the side of a semi truck…Fortunately, neither her or Jory were injured but after that we were all filled with intense anxiety when we stepped into the car…She had three pre-teen backseat drivers to deal with from that day on, shouting directions and warnings at her…After the semi Mom had to take her car into the shop so she rented a car from Rent-A-Wreck…The day came upon us where it was time to return it…At the time we had a Springer Spaniel named 'Sheets' and he was on medication…Apparently Mom had accidently taken the dogs medication so she was feeling 'a little off'…With much hesitation we hopped into the rental car and headed towards the agency…We were driving on a divided highway and mom couldn't remember where the place was…All of a sudden mom spotted the yellow sign across the four lane highway…she made a sudden left turn as though possessed and drove into the ditch like she was Bo Duke from the Dukes of Hazard…Lou Lou and I held onto the dogs ears and screamed as Mom just pinned it down into the ditch and up the other side… Jory held onto the dashboard, his knuckles white, as Mom drove right in front of the oncoming traffic straight into the parking lot of the Rent-A-Wreck…I had noticed a salesman standing outside the shop and he had been watching the whole thing, his mouth gaping open…We all thought we were going to die after that so that was the end of Mom's driving…We got her to take us to the country in the evenings and teach us to drive…We took turns driving and crossed our fingers that the police would not pull us over…

1985-1989

I thought after Lou Lou left to go live with Dad, and Ross was gone out of our lives for good that Mom and I would be happy…finally…I thought that this would be our fresh start and that we would have a good life just the two of us… Though we were desperately poor for the first few years…I was finally fourteen and able to get a real job…I started working regular hours at the "White Rose Crafts and Nursery" I was able to help out financially on my $3.25 per hour wage…When Mom was not dating life was just peachy…we would hang out

in the evenings, her marking her school papers and I doing my homework...
we would listen to music together and go for drives...She was really growing
during those years...She had finally been diagnosed with Bipolar Disorder
and her lithium helped make her more stable...She was focused and present
for me...I still took on the "mother role" but at least I felt like I was the key
person in her life now...for the first time I felt important...we made decisions
together and consulted each other on everything...she was really flexible and
let me do pretty much anything I wanted because she trusted me...

Then she started dating again...

I realized that my Mom's hunger for men would always eclipse me and
my needs...As soon as she started dating I became invisible once again and I
would slip into the cracks and hide and anticipate moments where she was in
between men and would pay attention to me...

Vincent

Was basically a slimmed down version of Ross...Old and desperate...
never married and fifty years old...he tracked Mom down and for months left
a different sentimental card (you know the ones with the watercolour pictures
and two page sappy poems written with a calligraphized font)...I swear he
bought her every one ever created...sliding them in our mailbox at different
times throughout each day hoping to woo her with sappy clichés...She resisted
his pathetic ways for longer than usual.. Vincent would not give up...he would
show up at the door at all hours unannounced...Mom and I would try to figure
out how to get rid of him...It was actually kinda fun because I didn't think
my Mom had it in her to be malicious or dishonest in any way...

Mom's tendency to 'feel sorry' for people and do things to make people
happy even though she didn't want to overrode any sense she must have had...
Eventually she cracked and was caught up once again in another 'sick' web of
unhealthy obsession... Mom gave in and agreed to go on a date with him...
All my red flags went up and I refused to be at all cordial to that man...his
desperate attempt for a relationship at 50 was pathetic and I knew there was
a reason he had never had a wife...I was so angry at my Mom for betraying
me and going out with him...Maybe she was flattered by his attention...
Maybe she felt so sorry for him she was just doing it to be nice...or maybe she
was just undeniably horny and was out to get laid...I really didn't know why
she agreed to not only one date with him, but many...The cards kept coming,
and Mom kept falling for his corny bullshit...at that point I gave up hope of

ever holding onto her for long…as long as there were stupid men, there would be stupid mom…

When Mom was out me and my girlfriends would phone party lines and talk to horny older guys…or we would pin up new posters of hot teen heart throbs like Brian Bloom, Corey Hart, Corey Haim or Corey Feldman…what the hell was it about guys named Corey in the eighties…why did they all have the same friggin' name…

Or we would invite boys over and play truth, dare, double dare, promise to repeat down in my basement…this was when I had my first kiss with tongue, and my first cigarette…my friend Tanya introduced me to them one day and they soon became my comfort…Cigarettes were the only ones I could count on through anything…they never let me down…unless one of them snapped in half or I dropped one in a puddle…They would be the constant in my life for the next decade…My addiction to cigarettes was much like Mom's addiction to men…She just couldn't bear to go without them even though they were slowly choking her…

One night, after she had returned from a date with Vincent I lost it…I told her it was me or him…she had to decide…I was not going to sit around while she fucked up her life for a man again…I told her that I needed her to put me first for once in her fucking life!!! I needed her too…I was still healing from all the years of torture from her last mistake…Her fear of being alone was ruining her life and mine…I begged her to just be happy with us…

This worked for about a month…She got rid of Vincent once and for all… She knew she was just dating him out of pity so it was easy for her to end it… Again we were both well because all we had was one another and our pets…

We both kept finding stray cats and bringing them home…after two months we had five all together…Misty was a shy calico…Pee Wee was an orange one with a white belly…Hailey was grey with really ratty fur…Jimbo was one that we rescued around Halloween, he was all black and escaped every time we opened the front door…and last but not least was Tiny Tim, a malnourished dwarf kitten that was feeble and white with brown stripes…he had a hard time walking and needed lots of love and nurturing…It seemed like Mom's addiction with men was slowly being replaced with an addiction to animals…Did I forget to mention the large white goose that she brought home from the lake…It followed her everywhere, thinking Mom was her mother…it shat wherever it wanted and even went to school with Mom…I was embarrassed because Mom taught at the school in town and of course everyone knew about Mom's baby goose…One day my friends little sister said she saw Mom walk by her grade two classroom and there waddling behind her was the Goose...littering the hallway with shit squirts...sometimes I felt like my life was just a big joke and that I would wake up one day sleeping in a normal house with normal parents making me eggs and bacon and two slices of toast...

Some evenings I would make supper and wait for Mom to come home to eat with me...all proud of myself for the nice meal of beans, wieners and creamed corn I had made and she would not come home...at all...I would wait, and wait, and wait...we had no television so eventually I would call up my best friend Candy and ask if I could go to her house...We would watch slasher movies, spike our blue-berrilicious kool-aid with boos from her parents bar, put whoopee cushions under her senile Grandmothers settee and laugh when fake farts erupted from her bedroom, and eat marshmallow cream right out of the jar...her parents would let me sleep there for a couple days until Mom showed up again...It was like she was oblivious to the fact that she had an eleven year old daughter at home...sometimes I felt like she thought I was an adult or something...like I could look after her but I was mature enough to look after myself...I wasn't though...I really needed her and I really needed therapy for all the years of abuse I had faced at the hands of her pedophiliac second husband...

The next two years was littered with random men that floated in and out of our lives...I only ever liked one of them...he was a cool, handsome man... kind of rugged with wavy long, dirty blonde hair...he wore torn jeans and faded plaid button down shirts...he had a nice body and was actually younger than my mom...He was too cool for my mom, but I guess he liked her wild, free personality...she had no inhibitions...no control over herself at all... Things were actually going really well with him...he had a daughter who was about twenty named Carolyn...she was about six feet tall, around twenty years old, slim with long straight blond hair...she was really pretty...there was no hardness about her, she was really nice to me too...she had this habit of chewing on the inside of her cheek, that was kinda weird...but because she did it, I thought it was cool so I started doing it too...every time I drank orange juice or anything acidic it would sting like a son of a bitch but I thought I was cooler than shit...They dated for about six months on and off...and they were getting really close...Mom had a few other men on the side that I was pissed off about...I couldn't imagine why she would want to sabotage the best relationship she had ever had since Dad...well definitely the most normal... My secret fantasy was that I would hear wedding bells in the near future once again...and it seemed like they were getting close...I would pick out Mom's clothes for her every time she went on a date with him and I would put my make-up on her to mask the rosacea that covered her face...I would do her hair...if left undone it was a huge wavy mess sticking out all which ways... those nights when I did her up she actually looked really stunning...Her eyes would sparkle and she looked happier than I have ever seen her...not just that flaky happiness that she existed in permanently, but "real" happiness...genuine happiness...I was happy for her...I felt like it was my responsibility to make sure that she would not end up with another loser...this was my life too and it had already been fucked up way too many times...my life was on the line here...Her happiness and mine was my focus...One thing about Mom was that she was gullible...I could feed her any line of bullshit and she would believe it...I started to wonder if that was why she fell for so many losers...she was like this pathetic target that sorry ass men just gravitated too...

Back to Tony...we actually thought there may be a commitment within our grasp...but who was I kidding...it eventually fell apart...I had prepped Mom before her date one night...she was looking all hot and wanton and Tony came promptly to pick her up...she looked smitten with him and was a bubbling lunatic as soon as he walked in the door...his smile was slightly forced and looked as though it was a delicate piece of china with a slight crack... My gut cried out...No! I can't go through this...I need him to be my Mom's boyfriend or husband or whatever...I was sugary sweet to him...if he liked me maybe he would stay with Mom, I don't know, it could work...They went out at their usual time that night but something was stirring within me... something called a slice of doubt spiced with a dash of holy fuck... I stayed up all night listening to records on my red, plastic, portable record player..."I wear my sun glasses at night so I can so I can..." and "It was the summer of sixty-nine...Oh ya!" I didn't want to tie the phone up so I closed the blind and did a fashion show...I raided Mom's closet of all her vintage lingerie from the Busy Bee Second Hand Shop and tried on each piece in front of our wall of mirrors in the dining room...Ross had taken the dining table so that room was still empty and perfect for dance shows and the fashion styling's of Hannah Louise Rush...As I danced erotically to Eurasian Eyes by Corey Hart in a mid-length, mint green lace balloon mini-dress I saw the bright lights of Tony's pick-up truck reflect off the wall...Oh, No their home early...I threw a throw over the pile of lingerie and ran into my room...I threw on the pink sweats and tie dyed t-shirt that were laying crumpled up on my floor...I heard the doorbell ring..."why is the doorbell ringing?" I wondered "if Mom is with him?"...I raced down the stairs and opened the side door connected to the driveway...Tony was holding Mom as though he was carrying her over the threshold...his face red and strained...Mom was wrapped up in a plaid wool

*camping blanket...she was somewhere else and was laughing hysterically...
she looked like a lunatic and Tony and I exchanged fearful looks...He placed
her down on the landing and out poufed the stench of fresh urine mixed with
wet wool...he said "I had to bring her home early because she peed in her
pants...I put her in the back of the truck with my dog so she wouldn't get pee
on my upholstery...She's your responsibility now! Sorry!"...I took Mom by
the arm as I said good-bye to Tony...Mom was in hysterics so was too out of
it to say good-bye...Tony looked horrified and left in a hurry...I cleaned the
urine off my mother and shoved her clothes and the blankets into the washing
machine...She was somewhere else and I needed to calm her down before I
could get her to sleep...I put her striped, flannel pajamas on her and sat her at
the kitchen table...she told me the whole sordid story about how her and Tony
were walking through the forest...he told her a really funny joke and she had
lost the contents of her bladder in one fell swoop...*

*Tony never returned any of her calls after that...Shit! What was I going
to do with this woman? She was going to have to start over again and my
future was once again uncertain and being mapped out by my mentally ill
mother...*

*I began collecting things obsessively and cleaning the house with the utmost
amount of precision...I threw all the clutter and second hand junk in the
garbage and Mom was oblivious so I had complete control and no one to answer
to...Mom was so manic that she was flitting about all over the place buying
things...remortgaging our tiny bungalow for the fourth time and we were more
broke than we had ever been...there was never any food in the cupboards and
the fridge was bare accept for the dried up grapes in the crisper and syrupy
substance that crawled along the frosted coating on the bottom shelf...I tried
to get more hours at White Rose to pay for groceries and I got a second job as
the drive-thru girl at McDonald's (I lied about my age to get the job, amazing
what a little make-up can do)...I don't know what Mom ate, but I mostly
survived on the expired burgers and fries that were left over at McDonalds
and what I could buy with my tiny paychecks...*

*Another friend of mine from school was Minnie McNealy, she lived a
block away and her parents were Scottish...they had thick trilled accents...
their home was full of warmth and a sense of family...they welcomed me into
their home with open arms...When Ross had been in my life and Mom was
hospitalized I would sneak into their open garage and sleep in the rafters on
a shelf that housed the families ski collection...Michelle knew I was there but
I asked her to keep it a secret...I didn't want to tell her parents about Ross so
she helped me keep my secret and let me take shelter in her garage...she would*

39

sneak out food and snacks for me and was a true friend...During the day I would hang out with her family and then we would pretend to say good-bye and I would run back a few minutes later and climb the wooden ladder up to the rafters...The nights I spent in the rafters were some of the best sleeps I had in years...I felt safe there...I knew he couldn't come in my room and invade my body...I didn't give a shit about the repercussions I faced because I was absent for weeks...He didn't ask and I didn't tell...when Mom came home things would just go on as they always had...the motto of our house became "Don't Upset Your Mother!"...

I envisioned and anticipated a time when my life would not revolve around her...one day I would escape this hell on earth and have my own life...a life that was focused on my happiness and my needs...

Several days after Tony ditched my Mom her wacky tendencies exploded into another 'nervous breakdown'...

We had been out at the mall and she started acting really strange...She was buying armloads of clothes from a whole bunch of stores, but she was in a daze...her words were not clear and nothing she said made sense...I tried to pull her arm and yank her out of the mall because I was starting to become really worried and embarrassed by the way she was acting...I finally dragged her out of the mall and into the back parking lot...there was a group of punk rockers sitting in a circle on the grass beside the concrete and Mom pulled her arm free and started running towards them...I couldn't catch up to her in time...she parted two guys with black Mohawks and ears littered with studs and arms covered in tattoos...these were serious punks, not just posers like I saw at school...I was so terrified by what I was seeing that I froze...and then she sat herself down cross-legged in the middle of their circle...they were passing around a joint and didn't seem fazed at all by the fact that there was a forty something year old woman sitting cross-legged in their inner circle...I watched in horror as she started removing her shirt down to her skin-coloured full support grandma bra...her fat squished out and her red moles shone like beacons in the dull sunlight...She started 'spreading the gospel' of Jesus Christ and she told them that she was his chosen one and that 'The Lord Jesus' would accept them no matter what...the punks looked entranced by her and asked her "what she was on and could they have some of that fine shit"...

I shut my eyes tight and then imagined myself becoming invisible...I pushed the punks aside and yanked my Mom up by the arm...she pulled away with so much strength that she hurt my arm and I flinched with pain...I tried again and again but her and the punks started chanting..."leave her alone kid, she's cool...let her say what she wants to say..."I pushed back through the

circle and ran into the mall with tears running down my face...I was scared
and hid in the public restroom...I sat on the food court toilet covered in a oily
residue...staring at the closed cubicle door...I stared at the graffiti splattered
all over the door, entranced by my fear and confusion about what to do next...
"For a good Fuck call Reba at 895-5890!..."

I decided to go back to the parking lot to try and get Mom one last time...
If I could just get her home and give her a cold shower or something, maybe she
would snap out of her trance-like state...I sprinted up the escalator double time
to the back exit door where I had left Mom...the circle of punks were there but
Mom was gone...I asked them where Mom went and one really cute bald guy
looked at me stunned saying "The security dicks got her man...I don't know
where they took her"...Oh my god, now my half naked mother was missing and
maybe getting arrested in her granny bra...I would be the laughing stock for
sure now...I went to the Security office and asked if they knew where she was...
The man at the desk looked up at me with compassion as he pretended to type
something on his typewriter...he was just buying time...I said "I'm not stupid,
please just tell me what you did to my mom?"...He finally looked me straight
in the eye and told me that they called the police who "brought her down to
the station". I was stuck at the Upper Canada Mall, my Mom was taken by
the police and I had no change to get home...I collapsed into a heap in front of
the glassed in security office and started to sob...The kind eyed security guard
asked if I had any friends I could get to come and get me...I called my friend
Jilli Blane and asked if her and her Mom could come and get me...

Mom was in the hospital again...apparently she had stopped taking her
meds a month prior to the mall incident...for the first few weeks I couldn't visit
her because she was in solitary again...I pictured Mom in a white strait-jacket
in a square room with quilted white canvas walls covered in stains from past
occupants...sitting in the corner rocking back and forth mumbling verses from
the Old Testament to her invisible audience...the hospital staff didn't want me
to be 'traumatized' by seeing her that way so after about a month I was allowed
to go, once she was taken out of the locked down ward...When I went to visit
her she didn't know who I was for a while...she just stared blankly at me and
mumbled her evangelical bullshit...as if I didn't hate church enough...now it
was overtaking my mother as though she was brainwashed by it all...

For two months I went from house to house, staying with all my friends
and using up all my favours...I felt like I was intruding on my friends and was
embarrassed by what I was going through...all my friends had such 'normal'
families...I had to hold in the bitter resentment I felt...almost a contempt as
I watched their stable home lives being played out...I was a fly on the wall

and my soul was slowly shriveling up as I watched my friends play the role of another 'normal child' in a 'normal family'...I searched and waited for some sign of dysfunction, but it never surfaced...I silently mourned and felt consumed by melancholy...

Why had I chosen this path for my life? Maybe all the answers would unfold and my bright light would click on revealing all the reasons why? I waited for that day to come and I ducked and swayed trying to get out of the way of the shit flying at me at a steady rate...Sometimes it hit me directly in the face and other times I was able to skirt around it unscathed. I came to the conclusion that as long as I was in my Mom's care that life would not be predictable in any way...I would never wake up with the same secure routine...I longed for stability and tried to mimic it in my own little niche...for a preteen girl I had one of the most clean and organized rooms...My bed had hospital corners and I displayed all my belongings in straight, solid lines...I had a collection of coke cans lined up on my bookshelf, they were these special edition ones that had vibrant graffiti-like pictures...They were facing out and the word 'coke' was displayed in unison with each solitary can...My room was the one and only milieu that I had complete control over...if anyone moved my cans or made a crease on my bed I grew anxious and felt like my heart was going to beat right out of my chest...

After three more weeks in the more normal unit of the psychiatric ward Mom was finally released. When she came to pick me up at Jilli's house her Mom was in the middle of teaching us how to toll paint...I liked how when you placed the tiny dots in a certain order they turned into something beautiful...I was enticed by the way you could paint by steps and in the end have a beautiful flower with perfectly curved petals and a curly stem with perfectly shaped leaves...I wanted to stay in that basement...I wanted Jilli's life...Fantasies of trading roles with her flooded my mind as my mom stood at the entrance of the craft room and talked at warp speed...After two minutes I was already burnt out and embarrassed...I begged Mrs.Blane to let me stay just one more night but Mom was anxious to get me home with her...She hated being alone, maybe that's why she always had such a constant stream of boyfriends...Before we left Mrs. Blane said to mom, "Magda, I was just wondering if I could ask you for a favour. One of my husband's friends, Daniel, is in the psyche ward for a deep depression, since you just spent time there I thought maybe you could go and visit him for us? Maybe you could make him feel better about it, just be a listening ear, someone who can relate to what he is going through? Mom had a quizzical look on her face, like as if it took a few seconds to register... then she blurted out "Yes of course, what is his room number?"

"He is in Room 3A on the Blue Ward, just to let you know he is suicidal right now, I just want you to be aware Magda. Oh! And thank you, he really needs a friend."

We said our good-byes and Mom and I went back to our tiny bungalow with the plastic on top of the carpet. As soon as we walked in the door I said to Mom, "This plastic shit on the carpet reminds me of Ross, I fucking hate it!!!" Mom replied, "Oh, Hannah, I do wish you would not swear dear, it sounds very garish! We can rip it off right now if you want?" I looked at her, we both grinned and got right to work, ripping every last piece of the thick plastic overlay off the plush off-white carpet...As we ripped we screamed out every profanity we could think of, laughing hysterically the whole time...Mom even let me shout the lord's name in vein out since it was an extra special night... Next came the venetian blinds, we ripped them off the windows...we ripped apart the house getting rid of any reminder of Ross and threw everything out the side door onto the driveway until there was quite the pile...Mom and I stuffed each load into the trunk and drove to different apartment complexes around town filling their consecutive dumpsters with Ross debris...It felt liberating to be rid of him in every way...It was about time we took our house back...

Mom still wasn't due back at school for another few weeks, she was on "hiatus"...Much of her "recovery time" was spent back in the psych ward with Daniel the Depressive...Again, Mom just brushed me off for a man...After a few days of trying to get her to do things to straighten out our lives, like pay the overdue bills and buy groceries, I gave up..."Mom give me some money to buy groceries?" "Mom let's clean out that storage room today!" "Mom shouldn't we be paying this bill that has a past due stamp on it before our power is shut off?" "Mom" "MOM"...

All of my comments fell on deaf ears and a placid face and in another reality...I got so frustrated that I gave up after a while...I was used to fending for myself...I just thought now that Mom had the Bipolar Disorder diagnosis and she was on Lithium that she would straighten out, maybe be normal...

Mom was at the hospital during all the visiting hours and I could tell by the look on her face that she was feeling more than compassion for Depressive Daniel...Here we go, does this woman never learn? When she would finally come home at 9:30pm we would sit and eat Neapolitan ice cream squished between two warm toaster waffles and she would talk endlessly about this new mystery man...I pretended to care just because if I listened to her yap about him I would at least be getting some attention...Apparently the nurses were saying that Mom was a 'miracle worker' a regular Anne Sullivan...Since she had been visiting, Daniel had done a complete turnaround...he was starting to crack the odd smile again, and Mom could get him laughing on her visits... Again Mom was saving the world one person at a time, and I was shoved into the background to fend for myself...I was happy for her and him I really was, but in my own selfish way I just wished for once I could be the key person in her life for longer than a few minutes...

After Daniel was released, Mom would go 'visit' him at night...she wouldn't return home until morning, and sometimes she would be gone for days at a time...One day when she was home briefly to get a change of clothes I complained to her that I didn't like being home alone so much...I was scared to fall asleep by myself night after night...That night she took me to Daniel's place...This was the first time I had actually seen him, he opened the door and said "Hello Hannah! I have heard so much about you!" He was a large man, about six foot something, he had a heavier build with a large protruding belly, greasy grey receding hair, his smile was very kind, I tried not to seem like I was staring at the large, oil filled blemishes that covered the surface of his face...He had a big two storey with five bedrooms and a big screen colour television...I thought to myself "At least he doesn't live with his parents"...His two sons were there...Tim was scrawny and about seven feet tall with long wavy blond hair and ballooned lips like the lead singer from Aerosmith...Conner was five months older than me, about five foot nine, short, brown hair and the same blemishes as his Dad only smaller... The two boys didn't say much to me...Tim quickly retreated to the basement and Conner asked me if I wanted to watch <u>Hellraiser</u>*...I said "OK!" and teetered on the very edge of the snot green, velour couch, crossed my legs and said nothing...Conner and I only spoke in between movies...when we heard the squeaking noise coming from upstairs we looked at each other in disgust and he turned up the movie...Did Mom just bring me here so she wouldn't feel guilty for leaving me home as she fucked Daniel the Depressive right upstairs?...How revolting, I hadn't even spoken to him really and they were screwing right above our heads...Gross! After Conner had played three movies consecutively he was starting to doze off...I think he stayed with me all that time out of pity, because he knew our parents weren't coming down... He finally got up to go to bed at 2am...It was a school night and I had an English test the next day...I was pissed off, because I had none of my school books there and I had no way to study...Conner threw me a Mexican blanket and gave me quick tutorial on the TV remote...I watched Much Music and fell in and out of sleep ,fucking freezing my toes off sitting up on the snot green couch, waiting for my Mom to come downstairs and take me home...*

After the sleepover, I decided I would rather sit alone at my house all night than sit on Daniel's old couch and freeze while I listened to my Mom have sex right above me…So Mom and I started seeing less and less of each other…I started to rebel and break the rules but Mom was so wrapped up in her new romance that she didn't even notice the shit I was getting involved in…Again I was invisible…

Suburban Streets

After moving in with husband number three, Hannah gave up her fantasy of becoming the most important person in Magda's life. She had no penis between her legs so there was no way she could compete with pock faced Daniel. Magda said he was due to go get surgery to get those bumps removed, so on the day of his surgery her Mom told her to smile lots and give him lots of encouragement. Magda always had compassion for everything and everyone; she was the most non-judgmental person and was always trying to work hard at making the underdogs of the world feel 'special'. Daniel was a bit of a pet project for her, something to distract her from the chaos that was going on in her mind. His ex-wife had been a whore who would flaunt her lurid affairs as though they were precious gems. She would sit in front of her vanity mirror caking on thick cover-up that was two skin tones too dark, and then she'd draw layers of thick, black eyeliner on the top and bottom lids so that it looked like her eyes were about to jump out of their sockets. As she sat transforming herself from housewife into cheap slut she would drink "Peach Boone's" and talk about her hot, passionate sex with anonymous men to her lonely, depressed husband as he perched on the edge of their marital bed overflowing with murky melancholy. He said nothing, but the silent tears that slid gently down his bumpy cheeks expressed more than words could have.

Magda was trying to make up for the horror his ex-wife had put him through by being the most dedicated housewife. She would come home early every night and make a nice meal for him while he took his permanent spot at the kitchen table, drinking 'near beer' and flipping through gun magazines. There in the dated kitchen she would prepare a different rendition of the ground beef delicacy every night. She would throw mysterious contents into the large crock pot in the morning and for supper she would proudly present the family with her weekly ground beef fare; Monday was chili night, Tuesday was sloppy Joes (a.k.a. chili on a bun), Wednesday was spaghetti (noodles with chili on top), Thursday was Sheppard's pie (chili with instant mashed potatoes on top), and the weekend was a free for all. After a few months of this Hannah felt her gut starting to rip apart from all the cheap ground beef so she announced to Magda and Daniel, as they were in their delegated spots in the kitchen, that she was now a vegetarian and would need some grocery money to go and buy vegetarian food.

Daniel's two sons and Hannah fought with their parents about having to move into one house. Daniel had the larger house so it was a no brainer that they should just move in there. Magda and Hannah had bad memories of the 270 Currey Cres. house, leftovers from Ross, so Hannah didn't argue when Magda told her they would have to move on. You could remove the plastic covered carpet protector but you couldn't remove the nightmares. Magda and Daniel made a promise to the kids; as a wedding gift, each child would get a new waterbed and could spend two hundred dollars on decorating their rooms. Hannah picked out a soft white leather, full motion waterbed with a half circle, pleated headboard. Her sheets were a delicate, baby pink satin. She spent an entire weekend painting her room the same pink as her sheets and she placed a wallpaper border with black background and pink and white roses. Her room looked so grown up. She spent weeks perfecting every detail in her room and was very excited about it. The first few weeks she sought refuge in her room with her three cats. Sometimes when no one was home she would also sneak her 'new families' black lab "Oden" in there too. Oden became her confidant and friend; she would stay awake for hours telling him about the secret, underground life she was leading. Her room was like a shrine of collectibles. Like her mom she hoarded things; but it was controlled chaos, everything was chosen and everything had to be put obsessively in its place. Her bed was nicely made at all times, she made it before she even got out of it in the morning and then set the pillows and throw pillows in a perfectly 90 degree angled display. Before she left she would straighten everything up, do a 360 degree check and then close her door.

A few weeks after we moved in Mom told me that Daniel was going to go in to get plastic surgery to remove his face blisters…He wanted to look nice for the wedding that would take place in two months...He left on a Monday morning and Mom said when I returned from school that I should not say anything about it...When I got home, I knocked on the door...Mom came and opened the door a crack, she whispered, "It is pretty gruesome, so Daniel is hiding in his room...He wants to come down but I need you not to stare or comment in any way...just act as though nothing is different...I tried to imagine how horrific it was, I had just seen "Hellraiser" for the second time, I wondered if he looked like the guy with a trillion pins stuck in his face, but without the pins...

I sat in the living room, talking about stupid school things with my soon to be stepbrother Conner...we whispered about what we thought he might look like...When we heard his feet padding slowly down the steps we stopped talking instantaneously and waited in anticipation...

Daniel walked by the entrance to the living room and I strained not to look at him...he mumbled "hello" in a muffled voice...Mom said it was OK to come in, that we would have to see him sooner or later...When I saw his face I almost passed out, the first few layers of skin had been completely removed, exposing a fleshy bloody surface, caked in dry, shades of brownish-red blood coagulating all over his face...there was also a light sheath of a transparent type sheeting covering his exposed face, it looked like a thin layer of melted candle wax...I asked if I could be excused and I went to my room and just sat, petting my cat Misty for about an hour...

This surgery took place during Mom's report card time so she was really busy, staying late at school...She gave me the job of washing Dennis' hair when it got so greasy it stunk...I never understood why I should have to do it...I said nothing and tried to act normal as I bent his head over the green, imitation marble, shell shaped bathroom sink...I tried to choke in my disgust as the soapy, blood-streaked water, chunky with scabs and dried pus swirled down the drain...Daniel was embarrassed that I had to do this for him, but apparently I was helping the family out...By the time the wedding date came around, Daniel' face had scabbed and healed and his eyes shone with happiness in his new skin and the prospects of a new life with my Mom...

Things were OK for the first little while...I obeyed the rules and I kind of liked having a nuclear family again, or for the first time, I really didn't know...Daniel also had hiatus hernia which was some problem with his gut that made him projectile vomit without warning...After having my meal interrupted with Daniel spewing second hand, sour, ground beef puke all over the kitchen table and our meals, and the floor and the dog and my Mom, I decided that family dinners were not all they cracked up to be and I went and ate my vegetarian TV dinners in my room on my wooden TV tray as I watched "Saved by the Bell" on my beat up old black and white TV...

The tides started to change though when Daniel replaced his 'near bear' with Bud Light...He sat at that table all day, I never saw him move unless he was trying to make it to the bathroom without hurling on the floor...By the time I got home from school he would be drunk...Mom acted like nothing was wrong and stifled any of my attempts to tell her what was really going on...I put up with enough, I just saw my life starting to slide slowly down the toilet once again...Mom needed an award for the worst man magnet...

One day I came home fresh and excited about a fun day at my new high school with my friends...I was in Grade Nine and I had just found out that I was voted in the top ten of the hottest grade nine girls (a list compiled by the Grade thirteen boys)...I felt important, I had always been the ugly duckling in Elementary school...I had bad clothes, bad bowl haircuts and holey shoes...But now I was a working woman, with better clothes, long sun bleached blond hair and I had a great new body, slender with small perky breasts and long legs...I hid my new puberty stricken body with baggy sweaters and pants that were a few sizes too big, but at night when I was alone I would look at my naked body and admire it's beauty...Soon I would start to feel shameful and filthy, like a pervert so I would throw my baggy clothes back on and avoid the mirror for the rest of the night...I never wore make-up or styled my hair because I wanted to blend into the background...I had a natural beauty that was noticeable no matter how hard I tried to hide it...Boys were starting to notice me...including my stepbrothers and...well I felt pretty vulnerable...Like I was a large T-bone steak and all the men in the house were viciously hungry lions trying to snap at the fresh, raw meat...I wore two sets of pajamas every night to bed and I locked my door (even though I knew how easy it was to jimmy the lock with a bobby pin). I asked my mom several times in confidence if I could please get a deadbolt or a padlock for my door but she just responded with, "Oh, you're just being silly dear!" It took everything in me to not slap her hard across the face to clue her in...I held back realizing that I would never be able to gain access into 'Magdas World of Oblivious Gaiety'...

My fears came to a head when I came home one day from school and placed my school bag on the kitchen table...Daniel and his sons were at the table scribbling something on a yellow, lined legal pad and they all fell silent as soon as I walked in the room...Tim pulled out a chair and told me to sit with a facetious smile spread across his puffy lips...They said they had a business proposal for me...I could tell Daniel was drunk because he slurred his words when he said "We haf a great idea, how we can make sssome exdra money on ya!" *My body froze and I moved my chair back in case I needed to escape…"On Me?" I responded breathily…They looked like vultures about to ravage a kill, and I knew that look…Daniel showed me the pad of paper and said "Look at these figurs'. If you become a stripper and dance three nights a week, we can take fifty percent and split it equally between the three of uz and you can walk away with the other fifty percent? We could clear like, I don't know about free hundred dollars a week! That's like twelve hundred a month! How's bout it Em? Are you in?" My face, in an instant, like an etch a sketch that's half completed and someone has just shaken it vigorously, became devoid of expression, I stood up, stunned and horrified! How could they? HOW FUCKING COULD THEY??? I ran outside in my socks and kept running…I ran with my eyes directed at the pavement…I ran across intersections without looking both ways…I ran until the sun started to set…I had nowhere to go…I just knew that that house was no longer safe for me…I was too embarrassed to tell my friends so I stayed out all night…Running…My exhaustion overtook me and I crawled into a tube slide in one of the parks in a safe neighboorhood… It smelt of stale urine and I tried not to inhale as I eventually drifted off to sleep shivering…*

The next day I wanted to go to Mom's school and tell her what had happened but I knew there was a large chance she would believe them over me…

I walked to school in the same clothes; still shoeless…I opened my locker and breathed a sigh of relief when my grubby white gym shoes tumbled out, tied loosely in the middle. Silently, I put my thrift store Ked's on and went about my day with a blank stare on my face…

After school my friend Sheila Lander introduced me to one of the most popular boys in Grade thirteen, his name was Shane Irvine (a.k.a. Icabod, Finnius, Diadam). He was the one who had put me in the top ten. He invited me and Sheila to his acreage that night…I had no ties, I waited for Mom to come looking for me all day and she didn't…Sheila told her Mom she was staying at my place so we were free for the whole night…Shane said his dad was cool and he didn't come home much so we'd have the place to ourselves…I figured my life had exploded in my face again, why not just throw caution to the wind, what did I have to lose…

Shane met Sheila and I in the student parking lot after school in his beat up old mint green Ford truck freckled with copper patches of rust. He pulled up fast and stopped with a loud skid, flung open the squeaky old door and said, "Hop in gals!" "Who in the hell says that, Gals, come on!" I thought to myself silently…I slid in next to him and my leg brushed up against him…I

*felt a surge of warmth slide through my body and gather in between my legs…
He was ugly, with crooked buck teeth, a crooked nose and a small dark patch
of hair just lingering on top of his head…something about his confidence and
presence lit a fire inside me…As he drove he slid his left leg up the door of
the truck and rested his foot on the arm rest. His tapered, faded jeans were
so tight; I noticed the bulge between his legs stretching the worn fabric of his
jeans to their limit…*

*I wanted him to throw me down on the hood of the truck and smother
me with his passionate kisses…I wanted him to rub his bulge against my thigh
and the warm place between my legs…As we drove down the bumpy gravel
roads to his acreage every bump inched me closer to his heat…I had nowhere
to turn anymore…*

*We pulled into Shane's gravel driveway and I noticed a tiny, weathered
wooden shack to the left of us…the shack was surrounded by fields of tall
dandelions and wildflowers that grew organically in patches…I figured it must
be a shop or garage…We pulled up and Shane confidently announced, "This is
it! C'mon girls." Sheila and I walked carefully through the overgrown brush…
we reached the door…I was shocked when we walked up to the entrance of the
shack…"It's cozy girls, but it's all ours for the next twenty four hours, Dad's on
nights and he works a 30 hour shift"…sadness washed over me as we walked
into the tiny house…It had to have been no more than four hundred square
feet in total…the door opened directly into the makeshift kitchen…There were
two upper, wooden cupboards painted in a thick dark brown enamel paint,
one was crooked so it didn't shut completely…the sink was the big white kind
that you see in laundry rooms with a garden hose attachment, smattered with
droplets of different colours of paint…the counters were raw plywood boards
nailed down in a haphazard manner…on the wall above the sink there was
a bare light bulb illuminating a naked lady calendar from the seventies…
Shane must have seen the look on our faces because he quickly stated that "this
ole' shack was here on the land when we bought, Dad and I have the plans to
build a really nice, swanky place with all the fixing's…I, I, like I said, this is
just temporary"…He asked if we wanted a beer and we said "sure" in unison
to break the tension, this got us giggling as we said "Jinx, you owe me a beer!"
By then we were all laughing…*

*As strange as his little shack was, I felt more at home there then I did at
my large, 2000 square foot suburban carbon copy house on London Road…I
found it refreshing that there was no pretentiousness about the place and
I could just kick back and put my feet up…Old, beat up stuff was always
attractive to me, that is probably why that night I fell for Shane…*

Five Grade thirteen guys burst through the door and took their places around the table in the next few hours and as they all piled into the tiny dining area I had already gotten drunk…Shots of different, unfamiliar fluids were being handed to me and I just kept pounding them back…We started to play drinking games and some of the guys had to stop because they had too much…I just kept going though, I couldn't get enough, this was my first tango with the hard stuff and it was making me comfortably numb…All those horrors started floating further away with each shot that I inhaled…A few of the boys kept repeating that I needed to stop or I was going to get alcohol poisoning…having no home to go to…no one searching…oblivion sounded like a welcome place and I ignored their persistent warnings…

Once inebriated I learned that this troop of guys were the originators and authors of "the list of hot Grade Nine chicks." Shane looked me straight in the eye and said "you can have your pick of any guy here, just so you know." I felt slightly under siege and though Shane was definitely the least attractive but I felt comfortable around him, like I could be real…I felt like the other guys were out of my league, or too mainstream…that just wasn't me, it wouldn't work…I kind of felt sorry for Shane too, maybe he needed someone in his life. The room started spinning so I ran sideways into the tiny bathroom and slammed the hollow core door…I felt a huge surge of relief as all the booze came out of me into the snot green toilet…All of sudden a door opposite the main door, one that I thought was a closet opened and there stood Shane staring at me with my head in the toilet…After I got myself up to standing he looked me straight in the eye, held my face with his hands and kissed me hard on the lips…It was sloppy, but nice…I was really too drunk to know or judge…We forgot about the rest of the people there and ended up in a dark room with a double bed… We fumbled around in the dark groping at each other…the room was dark and I hated making out when I couldn't see his face…my muscles became rigid as fear filled me…I was too drunk and too weak to fight it or ask him to turn on a light so the foreplay continued until we were lying intertwined, naked…I asked him where we were and he said it was his Dad's bed, that his was a single and we wouldn't fit…I asked if he had a condom because I wasn't on the pill…he said, "I don't have one, but I can get a Ziploc, is that OK? I mumbled "whatever" and he threw on his dad's brown velour housecoat and went to the kitchen…I heard voices but they sounded like a distant buzzing…I was embarrassed that everyone knew what we were doing, that they probably thought I was a slut, even though this was my first time, and that they may know why he was getting a friggin' Ziploc…this was not how I imagined losing my virginity…but I thought "Fuck it! I won't even remember tomorrow…"

It hurt, all I could feel inside me was the hard corner of the bag snagging at my insides, he moaned and groaned with pleasure as he slid in and out but I just winced and waited for it to be over...If this was what 'love' was I could live without it...I pretended to enjoy it when he asked me if it felt good and of course I slurred "Oh Ya Baby!" cause I didn't want to hurt his feelings or make him mad...

For weeks I stayed at different people's houses and waited for Mom to come and apologize or look for me, but she was brainwashed by another dysfunctional man and I was laying in yet another pool of neglect and abandonment...What would it take for her to see me...would she notice if I died? I started drinking hard every night at different people's houses. People I didn't even know. Most of the time I could drink any of the guys under the table, girls too...I had just turned fourteen and was already an alcoholic...I felt lost and unloved, the drinking became my trusted companion...at least it would make me forget... some mornings I would wake up alone and fully dressed laying in a pool of my own vomit and other mornings I would go home with Shane and share his single bed in exchange for craggy sex...I didn't know where else to go, Mom still had not tried to find me...I began to wonder what heinous thing Daniel must have told her for her to write me off like this, but in my heart I knew, her addiction to men was stronger than her commitment to me, that was something I could be sure of...

I was lucky to get meals because I rarely showed up for my shifts at McDonalds...my check would just barely pay for some booze, a pack of DuMaurier Lights and a few plates of fries in the school cafeteria...I was sinking deeper and deeper into my hole, suffocating and trying listlessly to scrape and dig my way out towards the light...The vision of the man without a face and the two little ones was so distant now that when I tried to summon their faceless presence in my imagination all I saw was a colourful mist...something that was fading more everyday...I was drowning in alcohol and meaningless sex with people who cared nothing about me...I wasn't sure if I would escape or when...If Mom would just come find me, everything would be OK, I would straighten out if we could be a duo again...I needed her so bad, she was all I had and I was losing her again...After spending weeks getting drunk and hanging out with strangers and borrowing clothes off friends I thought I would try and go back to Daniel's and see if Mom would take me back...I would have waited forever if it was up to her, so I had to suck it up and go knock on the door of the house on London Road...Mom answered the door and I fell to the ground in a heap sobbing like a baby, Mom brought me upstairs and we both said nothing...She said, "I love you honey, me and Daniel and the boys were worried and we're really glad your home."...I contemplated telling her what had driven me away, but what was the point, I didn't want to know her reaction, in case it would devastate me, it was better not knowing, and I wasn't going to tell...telling would make my life even more hellish then it already was...

I still haven't told my Mom what Daniel and his boys devised that Spring day, I don't know if she'll ever know...

Lavender Butterfly

Psychiatric Ward
Winter 1989

She rubs the sleep out of the corners of her eyes and faces the sterile wood veneer cabinet with its rounded stainless steel handles. The bedroom is a tiny cubicle with its walls a muted shade of green, the colour of sickness, and triple paned glass windows. She hopes that this was a nightmare and eventually she'll wake up in a different skin, with a different life, maybe 15 years into the future. She reaches into the drawer of the dresser with the rounded corners and takes out the tiny change purse whose fabric is a cheap rendition of an Asian tapestry. She folds back the fabric and runs her fingers over the round metal hinges, they are as sharp as she fantasized them being. Like an 'Exacto' knife penetrating cardboard, she pushes a frigid hinge hard into her ivory skin, her crimson blood seeps out from under the surface of her wrist, first the left, then the right.

Denial...

Opening the tiny drawer inside the closet she runs her hand over the lavender angora sweater, inherited from her elderly Scottish neighbor Moira. It is cozy and the arms are long so they will cover up the fresh wounds on her wrists.

Hide your pain you weak Bitch!

An old woman, with a face as weathered as a genuine leather wallet that had sat in its owners back pocket for 30 years, sat outside her door slumped over in a snot green vinyl chair with stainless steel arms. Her fat squished threw the openings on each side of the chair and she reeked of

55

sour body odor. She was dressed in a loose polyester housedress that was plastered in abstract shapes in various neon colours so it was not difficult for Hannah to notice her very large, round protruding belly.

Hannah casually chirped "Good Morning" to the woman.

The woman stared blankly at the battleship green linoleum as though Hannah did not exist.

Hannah repeated her greeting this time tapping the strange women on the shoulder.

"Um…Good Morning"

"The aliens are coming to take my baby" sputtered the strange frizzy haired woman.

Hannah sat down beside her with interest replying "When is your baby due?"

"In one week, but they will take the baby before I deliver it, this is my ninety-ninth pregnancy and they have taken all my babies."

"Oh!" Hannah shuddered curiously.

A nurse quickly shuffled over in her bleached white runners and yanked Hannah back into her cubicle.

"Listen Hannah don't go around trying to encourage the patients!" she spat as she forcibly sat Hannah down on her cot with the rounded corners.

"Gertrude out there is really far gone and she doesn't need anyone leading her on."

"Is…I mean is she really pregnant? You know she really looks pregnant."

"Well, she has all the physiological symptoms of a pregnancy, her belly even grows as you could probably see, but it is a phantom pregnancy."

"Oh, weird."

The nurse turned and left the room, leaving Hannah to ponder the strange phenomenon. Hannah always made sure to say "Good Morning" and "Good Night" to the 'pregnant' woman. It seemed to everyone that was the only time the woman would respond to human contact.

Hide your Joy Bag in the closet!

Hannah leaned back on the tiny cot, running her right hand over the fresh wounds on her left forearm, she closed her eyes…

> *Scrub, scrub, scrub, the dried on black hash, from all the hot knifing, won't come off the element on the Shane's friends filthy stove. I can hear them in the next room, laughing, laughing while I am here scrubbing, scrubbing and it's not even my fucking apartment. They will think I am really cool, me being in grade nine and them in grade thirteen, I*

am lucky to even be here. I'll keep scrubbing; scrubbing it is worth it to look cool.

Grabbing, grabbing…hands that are unfamiliar…hands that are not my boyfriends. My body seizes up, seizes up, I can ignore it…this uncomfortable feeling in my chest will go away. My boyfriend comes in and I feel his hands, but their eyes…eight pairs of eyes watching, wanting…

Thrown down, down to the filthy, greasy smelly floor that has not been washed in months. Rip, rip, rrrrriiiiipppp, clothes are torn, I reach to cover myself and eight sets of hands, so strong from all the football, basketball, arm wrestling played… clamp down my hands, feet, arms and legs. Trapped, trapped, my boyfriend is thrusting himself in while his friend forces his penis into my mouth…

Blind rage, blind rage, a super human strength… suddenly I am outside the house, shoeless, sockless, standing in the hard packed snow, clothes dangling from my bruised body…scrape, scrape, scrape…my skin detaches as I rub it swiftly down the stucco on the side of the house. Laughter, laughter, hideous laughter coming from inside the house. I thought he loved me…

Home, home, this is not even my home, it is my house where no one knows I even exist or what just happened. I run up to my bedroom and slam the door, blocking it with the cheap glossy white bureau, 'No more pain, I'm gonna end this pain now!' Searching, searching for something, anything to inflict pain…a dirty butter knife, encrusted with old peanut butter…'that'll do!'

Breathe, breathe, I can't breathe, I am hyperventilating. I need AIR! I wedge the frozen window open and punch the screen off with my bare hands. I sit out on the icy two-story window ledge, scraping, scraaaaping, cutting my flesh, trying to release the demons in my head. Rock, Rock, rock…back and forth…

Hannah awoke with a start four days later in a room she could not recognize. If only that had been a nightmare and not the reason she was on the psychiatric ward of the town's only hospital. That horrific night she had tried to freeze herself to death. She had blocked her door with her heavy bureau, and had been out on the ledge for five hours. Magda had seen the back of Hannah's torn white t-shirt and the steam from her daughters breath out her front bedroom window…her screams filled the tiny hallway as her and Daniel tried to push the bureau backwards and get in through Hannah's door…Finally Daniel moved the bureau back enough that Magda could squeeze herself into the room.

> *The next thing I remember is trying to run out the hospitals two steel gray doors, but being caught by the five dollar an hour security guy and the cheap alarm system. All my friends at school are going to find out, this is a **small** town, and they're going to say I'm just like my mother, **crazy**.*

She takes a deep breath and plasters on a smile as she walks out into the common area. As she sails through the corridors, she chirps "Hi" or "Hello" to all the other patients. One man is silently weeping in a chair over in the corner of the cafeteria. He has short, dark chestnut hair and Hannah cannot help but notice his face is almost turtle-like. He is dressed in a deep blue velour housecoat (you know the cheap kind you can buy at K-Mart for about $9.99) and brown leather clog slippers. Hannah bends down and touches his arm gently asking "What's the matter?"

He continues to weep. Out of the corner of her eye, Hannah notices a Kleenex box,

"Wait a sec, I'll be right back" she coos. She returns with a handful and places it gently in his half-opened hand.

"Thank You" he says in a very weak, almost child-like voice.

"Did you need someone to talk to?"

"Oh, I'm alright, just sad," he is barely audible and is shaking slightly as he speaks.

"What's making you sad?"

"Well, you see that woman over there?" He points to a large woman (about 450 pounds) with dirty blond hair, transparent blue eyes and heavy make-up. The woman is sitting alone at a table eating the toast that is available to all the patients twenty-four seven.

"Yes" she replies

"She stole my pudding at dinner time…she steals my dessert every time we have a meal." His cry turns into a sob.

Hannah puts her arm around him and rubs his shoulder. His sobs are soon succumbed by her gentle, loving voice and kind words.

A few hours later Hannah spots the large predator sitting outside her cubicle, so she walks over knowing that there is good within everyone and she must have had a reason for behaving this way.

She pulls up a chair next to her and her strong perfume assaults her nostrils; it is mixed with a pungent body odor. She tries to stifle her coughs and breathes through her mouth. She realized that the woman was not wearing make-up at all but magic marker all over her face, made to mimic make-up. Hannah asks the typical question all patients on the floor ask one another, "What are you in here for?"

The woman gruffly responds "I threw my husband through a plate glass window!"

Hannah begins choking on her words, "He must have really upset you."

She replies "He is a little man, only about four foot nine. He said my roast was undercooked! Asshole!"

"Oh. That must of 'er made you feel really mad and underappreciated."

"Ya. I guess. What do you want?" She spat at Hannah.

Shaking Hannah replied in her gentlest voice "I was just wondering if you could stop taking that guys pudding at mealtimes?"

"No, I don't get enough food around this place THEY"RE TRYING TO STARVE ME!"

Hannah replied, "Just have my puddings from now on O.K.?"

So it was, Hannah just sacrificed her dessert to the giant woman from then on. The sad, gentle man no longer slouched over top of his meal tray sobbing while he ate, but would take a moment to force out some semblance of a smile in Hannah's direction after eating his pudding every day. The large woman, Penelope, also befriended Hannah after they met by accident in the 'get ready in the morning' common room. Hannah was giving some of the ladies make-over's. Penelope walked in and all the other women straightened up and quit talking. Hannah introduced Penelope to all the ladies and asked her if she also wanted a make-over. Penelope threw her 12 pack of Crayola's on the counter and squished herself into the vinyl chair next to Hannah. "Well, no one has ever done my make-up, I guess it's o.k. Just don't make me look like a freak,eh!"

Playing pool and racing wheelchairs through the halls became pastimes that all the teenage residents on the psychiatric ward enjoyed. Occasionally Hannah and her new friends would also sneak out on the smoking deck for a cigarette. Hannah had been smoking since she was eleven years old. Her friend at the time, Tanya, was a real bad ass and had bought a pack. She enticed Hannah to have a puff. Since her first inhalation in the school playground...the rush ...the light-headedness...she was hooked. Her mother had caught her smoking one out on the back porch one night but that didn't stop her in the least. Her new found rebellion had just made her want them all the more.

Joe was the first friend she'd met on Ward 3A. He was a cutter just like her and had suicidal thoughts. His hair was spiked and dark brown and he was tall and lanky. He was one of those intellectual types who probably didn't have very many friends at school but Hannah was drawn to him because of all their similarities. She would go into his room and listen to Michael Bolton cassettes on his Sony Clock Radio. It got them feeling all melancholy and would induce deep conversation. Hannah told him things she hadn't even told her best friend. Every day was a new adventure as they made their own fun in the sterile ward. They would escape out the steel doors when the nurses were making their rounds at three o'clock and they would run wild touring the hospital. Her favorite place to go was the Obstetrics Ward; her and Joe would stare and wave through the glass at the fresh faces of the tiny newborns warning them to enjoy life now. Of course, they would be caught eventually, but they got away with it because they were 'mental patients' (there were some fringe benefits to having this title).

Every morning at ten o'clock, they all had to go down to room 204 for 'group therapy'. Hannah noticed one girl; she was from Ward 3B, where the extremely psychotic patients resided. It was right across the hall behind where the telephones were. Hannah had peeked in there while talking on the phone sometimes. Once she had seen a scruffy looking man, wearing a stained white cotton housecoat, running chaotically around the floor screaming "I'm God, Jesus is my one and only son". Hannah noticed that everyone in there either looked sad, stoic, petrified or blissful. She had heard rumors from the other patients that the God guy ate cigarette butts and fished feces out of the toilet with a Tim Horton's coffee cup, and then drank/ate it yelling "Tim Horton's coffee, mmm…Tim Horton's coffee, delicious!"

The girl from 3B was about 250 pounds and was wearing a black Metallica concert tee-shirt and acid wash jeans (stretched to their maximum capacity); she was curled up in the olive Lazyboy with her head down, her arm brandishing a white, bloodstained bandage from her wrist to her elbow. She believed that Alice Cooper possessed her and told her to cut herself up. When she spoke it was in a fearful tone so quiet Hannah had to strain to hear her. Hannah always lied in these sessions, just as she did to all the nurses, doctors and even her own mother. She always claimed she was doing "really well" even though you and I know she was just like

Hannah-hiding. Though she was never allowed contact with this girl outside of group, because she was from Ward 3B, Hannah always tried to connect with her somehow during the sessions, be it a warm smile or a quiet "hello", she just felt the need to nurture this overweight rocker girl. It may have had to do with the fact that she was reminded of her best friend in elementary school, Candy Cannel. The only difference was that Candy had flaming orange hair and was about one hundred pounds heavier.

Helping the others and keeping a smile on her face distracted her and made her feel good about herself temporarily but every so often she would breakdown hard. She would sob uncontrollably for hours in her room and when the nurses tried to talk to her she would be totally unresponsive. This would annoy the nurses and they would punish her by taking away her privileges. Her Dad used to make her go to bed without dinner as a child for crying inconsolably:

Spinning, spinning...I feel like I am at the bottom of a ditch covered up to my neck in mud...helpless, exhausted...holding this secret in is tearing a hole through my chest...I can't tell...they'll kill me...they rule the school and I am nothing...I have no one...no one even knows who I am...I do and I hate her... how am I going to go back and face them at school? I feel at home here, no one judges me, I finally feel like I belong...people here are more screwed up than me...it's the first time I have ever felt more normal than someone else...I am so scared they are going to send me home...no one understands me there...no one understands me at school...my friends here in the psyche ward understand me because here we can say anything we want to say, there are no masks to wear...this isn't high school. I also had a secret; a result of that horrid night's event, something that had been revealed to me by the nurses...

A Place to Call Home?

You shoulda put your joy bag at the back of your closet!

When she stepped onto the old transit bus that was transformed into a "school special" she was greeted with silent but daunting chuckles and a few "crazy bitch" spat out. She sat by herself and forced the headphones of her walkman over her ears, tugging at the strands of her bleached blond hair, sometimes tugging so hard she would stare down at her hand, full of platinum hairs. All the way to school she listened to the mixed tape that Joe made her in the hospital, she tried to make time stand still in her mind while Sinead O'Connor serenaded "Nothing Compares 2 U". She listened to the song over and over until the bus rounded the corner and stopped at the main entrance. She expected people to call her crazy but wasn't prepared for people to start calling her a slut too. One boy in her drafting class had even pissed in the corner beside her chair and left an unwrapped condom on her tall chair. This was a guy she barely knew. At lunchtime she got her tray of food and noticed that Shane and his friends were in the Cafeteria too. She sat as far away from them as she could, by herself in the corner right by the exit door. She heard hoots and gales of laughter coming from Shane's table and then he stood up on his table, gyrated his hips and started yelling "Oh! Oh! Oh! Ya!" while darting out his tongue, pointing in her direction. Hannah ran crying from the cafeteria grabbing everything she could off her tray. She ran into the girl's bathroom and closed herself into the stall. Her mouth filled with pungent vomit and she hurled it into the stained toilet. She sat on the filthy toilet and felt nauseous as she pushed her lunch around the blue tray, surrounded by wet shredded toilet paper pieces and the stench of stale menstruation.

One day Hannah got up the courage to pull aside her friend Sheila to see what rumors Shane and his friends were spreading about her. Sheila she had an allergy to the sun and smelled of bad BO no matter how many showers she took. She didn't want to be seen with Hannah at school because of the rumors that were spreading around Huron Heights so they met later that night at PJ's Convenience store.

Sheila said "Shane and the guys have been telling everyone that you had an orgy with all eight of them and then you dumped him, they are telling everyone all the details and making you out to be a real easy slut."

Hannah replied, "It's just not true, it's just not true Sheila!"

Sheila responded, "Well I can't be seen with you, Sorry! If Shane and his friends see me with you I'll just be back where I started."

School was in session for two more months and that stall is where Hannah spent all her spare time, avoiding the comments and harassment brought on by the same group of boys who violated her....

Escape...please I need to escape this nightmare...somebody save me...

Summer 1990

The secret Hannah had been keeping to herself since her stay in the psych ward was bitter sweet. The nurses had given her a pregnancy test while she was admitted and it had been positive. Hannah had lied and said that she told her Mom. She was afraid that her Mom would say it was sinful and take the baby away from her. So two months later when she went to go stay at her Dad's in Edmonton for her yearly summer visit, she was still pregnant and really didn't know what she was going to do. She fantasized that having a baby would fill the constant void that existed in her soul. Having someone to be responsible for that would love her unconditionally. She told no one her secret as she daydreamed about what her life would be like when she had her child. She knew it was a girl and that her name would be Lela, and their life together would be beautiful.

One night as she sat in her sister Lou Lou's room she confided in her and told her all the details of what had happened to her that horrific night in Ontario. There was no mention of the baby that was a result of that night. Lou Lou held her as they both sobbed uncontrollably.

Lou Lou whispered through her tears "I am so sorry I left you in hell, I should have let you come live here with me and Jory. I am never letting you go back there again. Mom has her dicksmack husband to look after her now. Come and live here with me and Dad and Kim."

Ceremoniously the girls tore up the return airplane ticket and threw the pieces into the air giggling. With that a wave of complete relief came over Hannah as she knew maybe now there would be some hope for her and her unborn daughter. She decided she would wait to tell her parents for fear of what her Dad and Karen would do.

She never looked backwards and felt such power in the fact that all of those shitheads back in Newmarket would be wondering what in the hell happened to their punching bag. Hannah just hoped that they would feel guilty for what they had done and never do it to anyone else.

While she was riding the bus to work one day she was reading all the illuminated ads above the rows of seats adjacent her. One of the ads was a large white sign with the words 'Planned Parenthood' scrawled in a bright purple block font; to the right side was a shadow of a purple pregnant teen; at the bottom was a phone number. She grabbed a pen out of her cheap brown hemp purse with an embroidered peace sign on the front and wrote the number on the back of her bus pass. She thought her waitressing shift at Humpty's Egg Place (a job Lou Lou got her a few weeks after ripping up the ticket) would never end; the minutes just clicked by at a snail's pace. With each cup of coffee she poured, along with a plastic smile and some idle conversation to the regulars, she got more and more anxious. She needed to let this secret out of her soon. She desperately needed some advice or sympathy or something. Some days she forgot and would just go about her day, but all of a sudden a wave of fear would wash over her and she would remember just how desperate her situation was. She had always wanted to be a Mom but she knew in her heart that this wasn't the time. Her wounds were as raw and exposed as they would ever be.

Her shift finally ended and as soon as she walked in the door she was relieved to see that she was alone in the house. She took a few cleansing breaths but felt the tightness constrict around her heart. She was a master at holding everything in but now was a time when she really needed help. The monotony of the tones as she dialed Planned Parenthood soothed her in some strange way, there was some relief knowing that the stranger she was about to confide in would be there for her and knew just what to say. The voice on the other line was a gentle older woman whose name was Rosalie. Her explanation to Hannah that this child was going to depend solely on Hannah and that expecting this child to fill her void was not an accurate belief. After purging her soul to Rosalie she felt confused and scared. Abortion was out of the question, now her fear started to seep to the surface and her anxiety level rose.

Two nights later Hannah was reading *I Know this Much is True* by Wally Lamb and she felt a searing pain shoot through her belly. At first she thought it was gas pains but they didn't let up for a half an hour. Terror ran through her body as she felt something wet seep out into her underwear. She ran to the stark white bathroom and yanked her purple, flannel pajama pants off. Doubled over in agony she felt so alone. No one was home and she felt like her insides where being ripped to shreds. She felt clumps sliding out of her and was terrified to look into the bowl. In her heart she knew it was not the right time for Lela to be her daughter and this was her body's way of telling her. As the fetus of her daughter swirled down the bowl of the stark, white toilet bowl she felt a deep sense of loss. She held vigil as she shook with despair and relief. She never told a soul about what had happened to her that day. Her feeling was that if she told no one than it didn't really happen. Her future changed in that instant, the physical remnants of that terrifying night had been erased.

Candy

Elementary School

Years spent trying to conform in order to fit in to the groups allocated by the many public schools Hannah attended had left her confused about who she really was deep down inside her soul. Never feeling normal she was left to flounder in and out of stereotypical youth cliques. A majority of the world fit nicely and comfortably into those cliques, but for Hannah it was a very stifling and inhabitable existence. She had no clue how to put on fronts and play the role of someone who she was not internally. The rare times when she did show glimpses of her true personality were challenged by the many individuals who led the conformation movement; in school, in clubs, at the playground and even within the walls of her humble home. Adults were in on it too, they singled you out if you were different or unusual in any way. Creativity and individuality were stomped out in the public sector at every level. Hannah migrated to people who were different as well. Her friend Candy Cannel had been close to three hundred pounds in grade six had flaming orange hair and a violent temper to match. If anyone got in her way she would lash out as a way of protecting herself. Her sense of humor is what attracted Hannah to her and the fact that Hannah felt safe in Candy's presence. The girls connected instantly and no sooner they had a label placed on them by the rest of the kids: "Laurel and Hardy". Getting through the school days was easier alongside Candy because she protected Hannah from the bullies that had preyed on her in the past. Candy always had a comical yet equally as cruel comeback for the tauntees in the schoolyard and it gave both the girls a great amount of satisfaction to take back their power now that they were no longer one vs. the playground.

Dear Diary:

It is so hard to be yourself in this world. People rarely celebrate one another's differences, and if they do it's usually fake. I want so much to be myself and be celebrated and admired for the amazing qualities that I do possess. It is a rarity to find someone who accepts everyone without judgment. I think "Oh, they must be justified in treating me this way, maybe I am a freak." I have no self esteem whatsoever. Is it true that you teach people how to treat you, or is that concept all wrong? People want you to conform because they feel they have to in order to "fit in" to societies mold. They don't want to face the consequences if they unleash their true identity to society. Those of us that refuse to conform are then stomped on and abused by the individuals that want us to be like them and stifle who we really are. The happiest and most beautiful people I have met in my life are truly themselves. Even though I feel like I don't know who I am, I can't help being myself. Lying doesn't come easy to me. There have been periods in my life where I have conformed, but it sucks the life out of me and I have to stop because it is literally destroying my psyche. Maybe I'm just weird and everyone else is normal, but I doubt it. When people are alone with me they come out of their protective shells. They know I won't judge them, so they unleash their stifled souls while in my presence. I can see their bodies relax and the colour return to their faces. I know when I am seeing someone's true self, because at that moment, the moment they reveal themselves to me they look stunningly beautiful. Their features soften and the corners of their mouths lift up in a gentle smile. Maybe that is why people can't be around me too much, because they are so used to hiding themselves, they don't want to look at what's buried deep within them.

When I watch a movie with a protagonist that is a free-spirit, I fall in love with her ability to just announce to the world, "This is me, if you don't like it, FUCK YOU!" I instantly connect with these bohemian characters, I see myself within them. The majority of the population must also admire these characters because if they didn't these roles would not exist in films so often. People that conform are aching to release themselves…to dance in the rain…to sing at the top of their lungs in public places…to shout hello to passers by…These people seem resentful and bitter most of the time. They gossip and complain about life and the people in it constantly. Oops, now I'm being judgmental, or am I just making an observation?

There was a period where Hannah broke away from Candy and started hanging around with a group of the more "popular kids" at school. Candy was enraged at Hannah for betraying her and leaving her alone again. One day they were standing in the ravine and Candy spat "Hannah, you are just a product of everyone else around you!" It was true Hannah was like a chameleon, she just adjusted herself to fit with whoever she was around. If green was your favorite colour, and she adored orange she would sacrifice her true love for orange and say that her favorite colour was green as well. What an exhausting way to exist. People saw through it and would soon start to disrespect Hannah because she didn't have a mind of her own. It was only with people that loved her for who she was that she felt comfortable stating her opinions and being less wishy washy. This is why her time within these groups was both limited and unsuccessful. This was the blueprint that her life journey would follow. She felt almost homesick but really did not know where her true home was.

More Than an Arts School

September 1990

The most unforgettable and comfortable time in her life was the three years she spent at Victoria Composite High School in Edmonton. On her first day of school her and her sister Lou Lou walked down the stark white hallway on the second floor and laid their bags down in front of a set of pale grey, weathered lockers. As they were stooped down putting their books and bags down they heard a very friendly effeminate voice sing out "Welcome! Who may you two be?" The girls turned around to be welcomed by an overweight, Caucasian boy with golden hair and the friendliest blue eyes. Hannah and Lou Lou fell in love with him instantly. The girls struck up a conversation about where they came from and how they had ended up there by accident because all the other schools were full and this one was the only one with space for them to register so late. Lou Lou had already registered at her old High School but wanted to be in the same school as her little sister.

Other students started to arrive: some leaping down the hall in their pajamas, holding hands as they sang show tunes; some wearing cheerleading uniforms with their hair pulled in a tight ponytails; some doing pirouettes in their unitards; some sitting cross-legged playing their acoustic guitars and harmonicas while their entourage sang along in folksy notes. The scene mimicked the cafeteria scene in the musical film *FAME*. The magic was that they all hung out in a cohesive group; there was no bad blood amongst students who were different. Differences were honored; celebrated and encouraged in this aged Arts School.

The boy the girls had met, Trey, introduced them to his partner who was a six foot tall Goth guy with jet black hair and skin as devoid of colour as bone china. In fact the girls noticed that all the students with lockers in that front hallway were homosexual. Their new friends welcomed them with open arms even though they were straight; they nicknamed Hannah "Little Hoopster" and Lou Lou "Sista Hoopster", Trey was "Big Hoopster" and his partner was "Vamp- Hoopster". For Hannah and Lou Lou, everything felt right:

Every day was an adventure at Vic. It was a school that was very focused on the arts and every one of the students was encouraged to express their individuality; no one's character was ever suppressed. Principal Haskell knew each of the students by name and cared genuinely for each and every one of them. It was so refreshing for Hannah and Lou Lou to come to a school that admired them for their uniqueness.

Hannah's days there were spent in various art classes; keyboarding, modern dance, drama, and of course all the required courses. Her teachers were just as unique and beautifully different as her new found friends and she learned so much from all of them. They truly cared about her. Her experience there was like belonging to a close knit extended family; the kind of family she dreamt about as a kid.

The friends that she made were genuine and innocent, unscathed by the mainstream world. Her days of partying and drinking vodka slurpies until she passed out were over. Parties with her Vic friends consisted of sing alongs, slumber parties and elaborate dramatic plays that they would put on. It was not that they all had simple lives, they all had their own individual struggles but they used their time together to heal and nurture one another and help each other. Her close friends formed a dance troop called "Kiss My Beat". They had two performances; one at the Edmonton Centre Mall in the food court and the other was at the Fringe Festival. The group sadly had to disband when the leader Malannia got too pregnant to perform. At their last performance her engorged breasts were literally falling out of her polka dotted halter dress.

Malannia and Hannah had become very attached to one another, very quickly. Both had difficult pasts and had grown up very quickly. Malannia had been dating a guy that was a bit of a prick and he had gotten her pregnant. While Malannia was trying to put herself through school and make a home for her and her child her baby daddy was off screwing everything with breasts and a hootchie. Hannah saw her friend struggle but also drew strength from her friends' resiliency.

I lived with my dad and his wife when Malannia was due to have her little baby. She had been having some Braxton-hicks contractions for the past week and her baby was slightly overdue. Our little 'Kiss My Beat' gang had become a close knit group and we had been getting together quite often. One particular gloomy late fall day I had invited the group over to go for a swim in my dad's pool at his fancy downtown condo. The six of us were swimming around singing at the top of our lungs and imitating one of our drama coaches who was a little bit of a twat. All of a sudden Malannia started to grimace and moan. We all swam over to her and she said, "Ohhhhhh...I think I just had a contraction." I felt scared for her, being sixteen and having to go through something a woman should have to endure, a woman who is by the side of her supportive husband and family (in a utopist world maybe!)

I had been to all of her Lamaze classes with her and had learned the breathing exercises, so we began, all six of us: he, he, he, who...he, he, he, who...And so on for the next ten hours straight. Our other friends had curfews to comply to but I could not leave my friends side. She had been there for me all the times I needed a shoulder to cry on and she needed me. Her puissant boyfriend was nowhere in sight.

We had been at the hospital for about 12 hours and she had been having very frequent contractions for at least 24 hours...Things were not progressing quickly and my sweet friend was beginning to look pale and exhausted. I was angry that her mother was not here, or her grandmother, or her boyfriend... These people should have been there... I was standing beside her holding her bluish, bloated hand when a nurse came in and shoved me aside. She took out a needle, removed its sheath and was about to jab it into my best friends arm without even asking or advising her of what she was about to do...I shoved her back and asked what she was doing. She replied, "I'm taking her blood." I replied, "I'm taking her hand and holding it, thank you very much!".

By this point Malannia was hooked up to a bunch of suction cups with wires hanging down all over her. Due to the length of her labor and her tender age the hospital staff wanted to keep an eye on her vitals. I watched them tap my friends mid inner arm to try and find a beefy vein...I watched as they jabbed the needle in several places with no result...I watched as they finally found one and...I watched as the blood was so sluggish to come out I could see each cell make its treacherous climb up the transparent needle...BANG!

I woke up on the floor beside my friend, littered in all of the chords that I had ripped off of her as I collapsed on the floor. I had forgotten to eat, sit or drink since her contractions had begun and apparently blood makes me faint. Who knew? I cried as they wheeled me out of my friends' semi-private room.

They were making me go home and sleep, against my will, for the safety of myself and my friend. I yelled, "I'M COMING BACK MAL!!! I'M COMING BACK!" as they wheeled me out on the wheelchair they had shoved me into involuntarily. When I had looked back at my friend I saw tears rolling down her cheeks as she laid there in her white polka dotted gown, swollen, scared and alone. After arguing with the hospital staff for a while, and begging them profusely not to make me leave my best friend alone, they ensured me that Malannia would not be having her baby any time soon, her cervix was still only 4cm dilated. They said to go home for a couple of hours, sleep and eat a sandwich and to come back when I had some energy to really be there for my friend. They promised they would take good care of her but I didn't believe them. They had been snide and disrespectful to us since we had walked in the door. I didn't want my exhausted friend to have to deal with those self righteous bitches alone!

I took a cab to Malannia's modest apartment and forced down a few pieces of peanut butter toast. While I was shoveling it down and thinking of some things from her home I could bring Mal to make her more comfortable I heard a key turn in the outside door. In stumbled negligent baby daddy, drunk as a skunk and smelling like he bathed in an ashtray. I heaved and forced out a "Hello!" He said "What's up, PHlanna?? Ha Ha.." I said, "Well Malannia has only been in labor for twenty four hours straight! Where have you been?" He said, "All right! I'm gonna run to the store and buy some stogies to give out to the guys!! Right on!" And with that he walked right back out the door...D.U.M.B.A.S.S.!

I found a blue duffel bag in Mal's hall closet and grabbed her a few things she might need after the baby came; her red and black Michael Jackson flannel jammies, her red leopard print housecoat, some panties, some clothes for her to come home in, the clothes and diapers to bring the baby home in, and the car seat she had received from her Social Worker. Then I sat in Malannia's chair and drank some lukewarm tea as I watched the minutes pass slowly until 6am, when I was allowed to return to the hospital without getting bitchslapped by the hormonal nurses. Dumbass had not returned when 6am came so I cabbed it back to the hospital without him. Malannia didn't need the drama anyway!

When I finally got to the hospital I lugged the bag and car seat up the stairs double time to get to the maternity ward. "I whispered to myself..."please don't have the baby alone; please don't have had the baby without me!" When I reached her room she was not in her bed. It was made and she was gone. I checked the number, 305, it was right but her name was no longer on the name plaque. I rushed to the nurse's desk with the bag thrown over my shoulder and

I asked where she was? And if she was O.K.? The nurse told me that they were prepping her for an emergency C-Section and that I could say Hello but that I was not allowed to go into the Operating Theatre with her. I asked why and they told me the father was going in with her. That fucker had not been there for her through most of this pregnancy, except to cause her grief, and now he got to go in! FUCK! So I gave her a kiss and told her to be strong and watched as the nurses rolled her into the O.R. She looked back at me with her funny matching turquoise cap and mouthed "Thank You Girl!" While her cocky baby daddy gave me a thumbs up and widdled his phallic cigar in between his pencil thin lips.

Just as we all thought, Chip, the baby daddy took off soon after the delivery. Our group of six looked out for her and her new baby boy .I stayed with her for the weeks following the birth and helped her recover from the surgery, so did our other friends. We became a family, always being there for one another. Malannia named her baby boy Jaguar and he was the most loved little boy in town. She brought him to the school regularly to visit all of the students and teachers. He was one of the sweetest, most loving souls and he enriched us and taught us so much about humanity and what was important in our worlds. He gave us all a focus that brought us to a whole new level of closeness.

Hannah fantasized about never leaving Victoria Composite High School and the people that cared about her so deeply. She had never felt so secure and connected before and she was like little chick afraid to take its first flight away from the warmth of its mother's nest.

Sister of Sacrifice

Winter 1990-July 1992

During Hannah's High School years in Edmonton, Alberta she lived in one of the cities dingiest back alley neighborhoods. It was commonplace to see hookers propositioning every passing car. There was one hooker that Hannah found most intriguing; her name was "Bunny". She chain smoked Benson and Hedges Deluxe Ultra Light Menthol 100's and would sit on the sister's dilapidated, old front porch chatting with Hannah about day to day occurrences in her very extraordinary life. Hannah thought she was really nice; a comfort to be around; Hannah never felt like Bunny was judging her.

The front rooms of that house were never bright with sunlight. The kitchen at the back of the house was bright early in the mornings and at night the shocking brilliance of the fluorescent lights lit the way for dumpster faring vagrants till the wee hours of the morning. Any light that did filter through the dingy windows of the front rooms sun porch was filled with sprinklings of tiny dust particles. The architecture of the front portion of the house was pretty; tall baseboards (*ruined by thick coats of clumpy, high gloss, shit brown paint being applied by previous owners*), high ceilings (*endowed with water stained cheap ass ceiling tiles*), a curved staircase (*with nails and wood coming loose and stabbing you on the foot, and paint that peels off like scabs*); and textured walls (*walls were formerly white, transformed to a cloudy beige from years of being smothered with second hand tobacco or pot smoke.*) The entrance always felt dreary to Hannah when she walked in the door. The kitchen was where the action was. She loved that old, dingy, single, iron sink covered in stains from years of shitty cleaning.

Standing there doing dishes in the hot, sudsy, water. That was where she and Lou Lou would catch up on their days of school or skipping school, boys and gossip about friends and co-workers.

Lou Lou sacrificed so much to make sure Hannah had a "normal" life. She woke her up for school and drove her everyday even on the days she skipped out. Even though Lou Lou and her roommates smoked pot she wouldn't allow Hannah to get involved in it. There was one night that she let Hannah try hot knifing some hash in a safe environment. If Hannah was going to experiment she better do it with Lou Lou first; this was Lou Lou's rationale. They all stood huddled around the tiny, old stove (definitely original to the house) with their blackened knives cradling the chunk of hash; smoke rising up filling their lungs with thick, sharp smoke.

I think I need another toke...I don't feel any different than I did before... nineteen...twenty...."O.K. Lou I'll stop now"...cookies...mmmm...Oh, oh I need to microwave them so they taste home baked...ya...oh they taste amazing..."Here guys try these they're so fuckin' awesome, they're like the best thing I've ever tasted, so oatmeally and gooey with raisins...Oh I'm so hot, I've never been this hot before in my life...

Hannah ran outside and leapt into a snow bank in the backyard headfirst. It took a while for the other stoners to realize she was missing in action or they were just too far gone to care. That was a long night for Hannah; she never thought she was going to come down. After she warmed up and Lou Lou finished telling everyone off for letting her little sister jump in the snow, she and Lou Lou sat in the dimly lit living room surrounded by the buzz of her friends chatting about the meaning of life and things of the sort. Lenny Kravitz came on the stereo singing "Mr. Cab Driver" and Hannah and Lou Lou connected with one another from across the room. They sang the whole song in unison with so much heart and love for one another. To them it was like no one else in the room existed, just their voices singing together in complete joy. There were many other moments like that while they lived together. Moments of absolute connectedness in a way no two other people in the world could connect.

There is no relationship like the one between siblings. Lou Lou and I shared a bed growing up, we shared joyful experiences and experiences made from the stuff of nightmares. Together we were always there trying to pick each other up and brush each other off. If it were not for Lou Lou and her strength I would not have survived our childhood. She has always been my hero, the person I could laugh and cry with. I'm so glad she let me live with her. I need her right now more than ever. I thought Dad and Karen would take care of me like parents are supposed to, but it just felt like I was in the way. Maybe it was just hard to get used to having all these kids around, with so much baggage. I probably never gave them a fair chance. I couldn't take all the rules. I'm not used to having rules. I listen to Lou Lou though. I respect her, more than anyone in my life.

Hannah and Lou Lou lived with an artist from high school named Ariel. She was Métis and her hair was flaming red. She had a little baby who constantly puked all over what little furniture they had. Ariel was sleeping with one of the stage managers that worked at their artsy high school.

Hannah would lay in the next room listening to them fornicate till wee hours in the morning. When she passed the teacher in the hallways of the Drama wing, where she spent the majority of her time, she would smile, nod, rushing by. She kept their dirty little secret to herself. Ariel's rent was paid by the government (i.e.: welfare), while the sisters worked until two o'clock in the morning almost every night of the week to pay the bills. Trying to fit in projects, homework, and the odd dance or drama production made for quite a lot of stress for the two girls. They were trained to be very responsible from a young age, so it was almost second nature to them. When the sisters were home, laughter always filled the walls of the obscure home, even when times were particularly difficult. One afternoon the girls cranked up their favorite DiVinyl's song "I Touch Myself", and then proceeded to gyrate, and pretend to touch themselves on cue while they sang the lyrics at the top of their lungs. Their laughter turned to hysterics when the bed they were performing their routine on, complete with castors began to join in the dance as it shimmied to the motion of the dancing sending it on a rampage around the makeshift bedroom...

I love myself; I want you to love me... When I feel down, I want you above me...I search myself, I want you to find me... I forget myself; I want you to remind me... I don't want anybody else, when I think about you I touch myself, ooo, I don't want anybody else, oh no, oh no, oh no no...

That song carried so much meaning for Hannah as it was her goal to love herself. She knew if she could just accomplish that goal she would be set free. There were chains that held her captive, the chains of the past and torment brought upon her by preying pedophiles, aggressors, and people who found joy in torturing those with vulnerable spirits. One saving grace though, the one that would lead her to her goal in the future, were those individuals that saw her shining light and nurtured it throughout her life. They planted the seeds in her mind that would eventually grow into self-assurance, strength of spirit, wisdom and the gift of connecting with other like-minded individuals. The sisters would grow to be fantastic women and this stage was yet another stepping on their journey up towards the sun.

September 2008

It has been a week now since she went missing, we are all still holding vigil at the house, doing Lou Lou's chores and caring for her kids, crying and feeling an unbearable heaviness on our backs. As I stand out in the frigid, cold night, trying so hard to light my damp cigarette with this crappy dollar store lighter, I can feel the freezing cold rain drops soaking into my tangled, unwashed curls. I stare out in the direction of the black reservoir as the rain starts to accelerate and choke my thick woolen sweater. It is unfair that I am standing here warm and my sister is out in that dark abyss somewhere, lost... Is she somewhere in that vicious body of water? I sob as I scream questions into the frigid air. I want to suffer too, so that she is not alone, I am guilty sitting in her warm house, with her family when she is out there, missing and alone... out of control...helpless. I don't know what to do without her...the thought of it is tearing a gaping hole in my soul...

Crazy Love
Little Black Book

"A symptom of mania is hyper sexuality. Victims of sexual abuse have a tendency to be promiscuous."

With all the odds against her, Hannah spiraled in and out of reality, and had fleeting encounters with anyone who offered her their attention. When she was in the presence of a boy her body responded like a ravaging temptress as her simultaneously mind froze in revulsion. The two were in a constant state of juxtaposition, but in the end her body always won the race. Her mind became brainwashed by her body and got used to hiding in the shadows while her body satisfied its uncontainable hunger for sex. Her body was Hyde and her mind Dr.Jekyll, and with each encounter the emptiness in her soul deepened.

Ten years later, once the aftermath of her rampage of meaningless sex was over Hannah and her sister, snuggled up in the warmth of the imitation glowing embers of the false wood stove in Lou Lou's shed, exposing the sexual exploits of their pasts. Lou Lou, having been married at the age of nineteen, had a shorter list, but it felt good to get the names out on paper. It was like pulling off a Band-Aid and revealing a wound that has finally scabbed over, a wound you have tried to resist picking at. Hannah was the first to reveal her list…

Steve .G.

We met when I was thirteen and he was seventeen, at a carnival. His appearance was peculiar and he dressed like a forty year old man heading out for a day of golf, donning brown, pleated corduroy pants and pastel golf

77

shirts with the collar standing straight up (all freshly ironed by his mother, including the white, cotton briefs). He didn't ask for sex for the first month we were dating. Our dates consisted of necking in the playground; drinking blue slurpees laced with vodka; or hanging out in the McDonalds parking lot waiting for something to happen. He brought me to the United Church in his town at dusk one night and we sat on the front steps. I was casually chattering away about my friend Sheila when I heard him unzip his pants…Suddenly he forcefully grabbed both sides of my hair and pushed me down hard onto his lap…Apparently he had already taken 'it' out so he forced me down on him…I wouldn't open my mouth, but he kept pushing me down whispering hoarsely, "suck me off!"… I felt bile rising in the back of my throat and I winced as I opened my mouth…I put it inside and bit down on it as hard as I could…He screamed and pushed me backwards onto the cement sidewalk…I was laughing hysterically as my head struck the cold ground…he looked like such a fool standing there holding his package, in front of the church with his pants down around his ankles…He was mouthing some curse word at me but I couldn't hear him with my ears ringing the way they were and the sound of my own laughter…He called me a crazy bitch, yanked his pants up and said, "You can fuckin' walk home!" I felt a throbbing pain where the back of my head had cracked against the pavement, as I placed my hand on the pain I felt the thick, syrupy blood adhere to my hand like glue.

I walked the twenty kilometers home in a fuzzy daze, unfathomably calm. You know when a bad situation occurs and you let it happen without standing up for yourself. You relive it like a video clip in your mind playing it over and over, reacting in all the variations of ways you wish you could have responded? I focused on the stretch of pavement ahead of me; the night sky darkening and the stars beginning to reveal themselves, twinkling as though they were winking at me…

Mark .V.

When I was thirteen and a half my friend Sheila and I snuck into the private Catholic School, <u>Sacred Heart</u> one day when we skipped school. We heard from some friends that the guys there were really cute, so we snuck into the hallway and ran into the girl's bathroom. Our friend Julie went there; she met us during her third block and give us uniforms to change into so the teachers wouldn't know we weren't from that school. After we changed into the crisp, white button down shirts, kilt-like miniskirts, and knee high black socks we walked casually through *the hallways and had lunch in the cafeteria with Julie and a few of her friends. Like chameleons we were high from the adrenaline, hormones and the illicitness of it all. While we were sitting in the cafeteria I had my head down, I was stirring my mound of ketchup with my warm, salty French fry and I heard the squeak of a chair being pulled out in front of me. I looked straight ahead and I was staring into the lap of a very tall guy with platinum blonde hair and a striking face like one of those guys from "GQ Magazine". There was an instant chemistry between us which led to an invitation to meet at his place after school. His name was Mark. We hung out in his basement with a few of our friends who finally got the hint and all went home. It was just him and I, alone in his basement. He sat down on a narrow, wooden window seat and told me to hop up. Perched carefully in his lap, we necked for a long time. His kiss was tender, no protruding tongue like with Steve.G, .(fucking toad!). I really liked this guy and I didn't want to lose him. My mind raced as our lips connected tenderly (why would this hot guy want to be with someone like me?) I rushed things along out of fear. I placed my hand in between his legs and felt him, warm and hard. I had a flash of my babysitter and my mind wanted to run away…but almost automatically I unzipped his pants and started stroking him…That's what boys wanted right? If I don't do it he'll throw me away…I was repulsed when I slid down his lap and put my mouth around it…He was so huge I felt like I was going to choke…I didn't know what I was doing, but I was holding back my vomit and squelching in my tears…He must have felt my discomfort because he pulled me off and zipped up his pants…We sat, silently beside each other for a long time…*

He turned to me and said, "You didn't have to do that, I liked you!"

"I think you should go home now."

I stood up and walked out the door knowing I would be too embarrassed to call him again, that that was our first and last moment. I left confused and unsure.

Steve .W.

The first boy that caught my eye in High School was a blond, husky weightlifting, football player named Steve. I met him during the first month of Grade Nine. He was a year older than me and had the face of a child attached to his large, pumped up frame, like a mismatched puzzle piece that someone crammed into a different puzzle with an unsuccessful attempt to make it fit. The innocence in his eyes drew me to him like an inescapable magnetic force. He was my first boyfriend at Huron Heights. Once we met we started skipping school and running across the street to his low rental apartment to hang out while his mother was working. An obsession with his body image made him seem vein... As a child he was beaten by his father because he was 'chunky' and he was on a rampage to have the most defined physique. That goal was placed at the top of his list and anyone getting in the way of that would quickly be exterminated. Things were great for a long time, connected by our tainted histories, we felt comfortable unraveling our inner secrets to one another. Months passed and he started taking me the gym he worked at, Weight Works. He put me on a strict weight lifting regiment that was far too challenging for my 85 pound frame; pushing me hard every day after school. I would try and impress him by bench pressing more than my body weight, while my body begged me to submit.

We tried to be intimate a few times but Steve was never able to 'get it up'... so small I couldn't feel him. He started to become more aggressive with me as his body inflated more and more each day. Slowly I started to shut down, putting some distance between us. A few of my friends mentioned the fact that they heard he was taking steroids. As I researched things began to crystallize...Steroids caused aggressive behavior...impotence and shrinkage...inflated ego...One day when I was in his apartment he stepped out to the store to get me some Haagen Daaz, coffee flavor ice cream...While he was gone I searched his apartment for his stash...I dug around in his black and red Adidas bag until I found a pocket that was camouflaged...I reached in and shuffled around until I felt a small pill bottle...ah ha!..."Steroids 50 mg"...I fidgeted to get the child proof cap off, but it was difficult because my hands were vibrating...Finally I smashed the durable blue plastic against the edge of the marble counter and the lid flew off and landed on the floor... tiny, white pills, shaped like the Pillsbury dough boy, came spraying out covering the cold, slimy tile of the bathroom floor...I bent down and scooped them all up in my right hand and then I dropped them in the toilet and flushed...

The realization of what I just did hit me after I saw the last pill swirl around in the toilet bowl until it disappeared into the dark feces stained drain hole...As the toilet muttered it's last belch I heard the door handle turn..."Hey! Baby, I got you some Haagen Daaz, coffee flava!" I walked sheepishly into the kitchen and pulled out the padded, silver speckled vinyl kitchen chair...as I sat down I heard the air escape and I was lowered down, fixed to the chair... As I played with the container I looked up at Steve as he stood looking down at me with a grin spreading ear to ear...

"I have something to tell you." I whispered raucously.
"What's that Han?" he piped up lovingly.
"I flushed your steroids down the toilet." The words spilled out of my mouth like dirty, bath water.

A wash of white slid down Steve's face and then it was flooded with red…His head looked like it was going to burst and spray chunks of brain all over the peach melamine cabinets.

"I was just trying to help, they're making you sick."I choked.

He ran to the end of the kitchen, took a decorative cast iron frying pan off the wall and flung it Frisbee-style directly at my head as he screamed, "YOU FUCKING BITCH!!!!YOU HAVE NO IDEA WHAT I WENT THROUGH TO GET THOSE!!!"

I ducked to avoid being knocked out by the frying pan…as it whizzed by me and landed hard on the floor behind me…My legs were paralyzed even though I was desperately prompting them to RUN!

He started picking up anything he could reach and flinging at me…I ducked, my legs responded eagerly and circled the kitchen of the tiny apartment as he chased me…As I ran I yelled behind me, "It's them or me, you decide!" I felt a Corel plate smack the side of my head and then bounce off the linoleum floor and as I looked forward I noticed the back, sliding door was open ajar…I waited till he was preoccupied with trying to take a picture off the wall and then I made my escape out the side door…

Steve called me one last time to tell me he quit the steroids and that he missed me and wanted me back. I rejected him for fear that his aggression would eventually lead to my untimely end. He hung up the phone and relief saturated my psyche. I didn't think it would be that easy…Hours later he called and said he had just slit his wrists because he loved me so much and didn't want me to leave him. I hung up the phone and called 911, then pulled the cord out of its cozy socket. The next day at school I found out that the ambulance got to his house and he refused to let them in. When they eventually broke down the door and he was sitting in the corner of the living room, crouched down, holding his knees snug to his body and rocking himself back and forth; wrists fully intact; pride, not so much . He didn't come back to school until the rumors cooled down. Other than trying to start a gang war with my new boyfriend Shane, which didn't go over well…he didn't surface much after that.

Brian

I had just turned fourteen when I was kicked out of Magda and Daniel's house for the second time, this time for breaking too many rules. While touring Newmarket late at night with a slurpee spiked with cheap vodka, I met a homeless boy from Barrie at "Mr.Sub". I could tell he had been on the streets for a least a few weeks because his clothes were dirty and torn and he had a layer of filth covering him. He was cute though; with his scruffy, mid-length, platinum hair and brilliant, baby blues. My desperation for some sort of attention took precedence. For the first few nights we slept in the park together, holding each other in a lean to we had built out of our coats and some twigs we'd gathered from the ground…We drifted off to sleep to the far and heart wrenching cries of the coyotes; a sign of the delicate overhaul suburbia had on nature. While awake we made plans about where we could stay and how we could scam food. I had been skipping work lately so my money was drained out. I decided that I was going to approach Mom at her school about coming home in exchange for Brian coming to live with us temporarily. Mom was wearing her rose coloured, coke bottle glasses and a three piece banana pant suit when I popped my head in her room. As usual she acted like nothing had happened, as though I never left her house. She said "Sure you can come home, I would just love it, and I'll just ask Daniel about having your friend stay too, I don't see why not!" Mom drove us home in her beat up brown Chevy Nova, she was in la la land on the drive and didn't even ask where I was or who I stayed with for the last few nights. She doesn't ask, and I don't tell…

She told us to wait outside while she spoke to Daniel. After a few minutes she opened up the door and said, "I'm sorry Brian, but Daniel won't agree to let you stay with us, you're welcome to call your family and stay until they come and pick you up. Brian shook his head and said "No! Thanks anyway, I'll be fine."I winked at him from behind my mom and then said, "Mom, could you go back in the house? I'm just gonna say bye to Brian."

Mom said, "Toodleloo Brian! Nice to meet you!" and bounced cheerily into the house.

Brian and I began scheming our master plan. When my mom and Daniel went to bed I would sneak him into the house. Hours past and finally they went to bed and turned the lights out. I had to wait a bit longer until Conner and Tim went to bed as well…

Brian was hiding behind a bush, beside the house and as he stood up he stretched his tired body out and cracked a tired stare, one of a man many years older than fifteen. We made the trek up the squeaky half spiral staircase; our black lab excitedly panting and padding close behind us. I snuck him into my baby pink room and he was about to sit down on my nice, satiny bed…"STOP!" I spat raucously, "Why don't we have a shower first and then go to bed. I snuck him into the bathroom after I made sure the coast was clear. Daniel's nasally snores resonated in the dankness of the shadowy hallway. Conner and Tim slept downstairs and came upstairs only to pump iron in the *graffiti covered weight room. Brian was first, I turned around while he took his grimy clothes off and climbed into the shower. I passed him a towel when he was done; he was transformed into a vulnerable boy with an innocent face. I felt my body tingle with excitement as he turned around dripping while I undressed and got in the steaming hot shower. As the warm water pounded me I escaped into the blissful moment. It had been at least a week since I'd had one, the freshness of the Irish Spring soap lathered across my weary body refreshed and delivered. After we were done I checked to see that the coast was clear and we ran from the bathroom to my bedroom, stifling our giggles. We reached my smooth, white, hollow core door at the end of the hall. It clicked as I twisted the imitation crystal knob ever so slightly. We turned our backs to one another as I slid my baby pink nightgown over my head. I passed him an oversized t-shirt and a pair of my size 2 white sweat shorts to wear to bed. As he changed I snuck a peek at his muscular back in the reflection of my vanity mirror. We turned off the lights and slid between the pink satin sheets of my waterbed. There was a cloak of silence as the warm waves of the full motion waterbed mimicked a cozy slip and slide, igniting the hormones within us as we brushed innocently against one another. I had never shared my bed with anyone; my girlfriends had always slept on the bunk beds that were beside my bed. A nervous comfort enveloped me as I felt him next to me; we lay on our backs speechless for awhile, saying nothing, feeling the moment, resisting urges. Casually I inched closer until we were holding each other, we started to kiss passionately, with only two thin layers of fabric between us, and my desire insatiable. I rolled on top of him and…CREAK, a door opened in the hallway…the heavy plastic mattress sloshed as I yanked it up with all my strength…my door knob started to turn and I spat "You need to climb into the crack!" stunned, he followed my orders, squeezing himself into the four inch crack that I had made between the soft silver plastic mattress and the frame of the bed…he left his face out so he wouldn't suffocate…mom padded into my room and whispered, "Han, Han, can I sleep here? Daniel is snoring and I can't fall asleep."*

I pretended to sleep and stretched my arms and legs out so that I was covering as much of the queen sized bed as I could…

I heard Brian gasping for air so I moaned,"Oh! Huh!"

Mom tried to crawl into the bed and as she did I heard Brian stifle his groans. I knew if I didn't get Mom out of my room soon he might asphyxiate. When Mom tried to move me I flung my arms and legs back into place, making it impossible for her to have enough room to lie down. Exasperated she gave up the fight and went back to her room. I waited until I heard her door close and quickly yanked the heavy mattress up. Brian squeezed out of the handmade crack dumbfounded, sweaty, half naked and breathless. I tiptoed over to my door and turned the lock until it clicked into place. I tried to climb into bed silently but the water sloshed as the weight of me hit the mattress. It took awhile for Brian to recover from being trapped in the side of the waterbed, so we just laid there and talked. We started making out again and just as we were in the throes of teenage ecstasy we heard Mom's door open again…SHIT!…This time our actions became automatic, Brian slid into the crack and I had barely pulled my nightgown down when Mom began jiggling my doorknob, eventually the lock unclicked, she snuck over, sat on the ledge of the bed and shook me until I pretended to wake up."What! What! Mom!",

"I have to sleep with you, I have a big day tomorrow, report cards are due and Daniel's snores sound like a chainsaw!" she whined.

I felt like I didn't have a choice so I told Mom, "You can sleep here, but you have to sleep on the bunk bed!" She climbed onto the bunk bed adjacent my bed and I kept pulling the mattress aside so Brian could breathe. Eventually her breaths became patterned and deep. I pulled the mattress aside and Brian squeezed out. I threw a couple extra blankets over him so no one would see his form if we didn't wake up in the morning; exhausted we soon drifted off holding hands. Brian decided the next day that it was time for him to go home and make amends with his family. I never saw or heard from him again…

Elliot .M.
Summer 1989

Elliot and I had lived in the same neighborhood since Elementary School. He was gorgeous with his pretty face, blond hair, preppy clothes and hairstyle. He went to "Sacred Heart," the same Catholic school I had snuck into in Grade nine. Sometimes him and his friend Mike would play with me and my friends after school; frolicking on the jungle gym, teasing each other so that it seemed on the outside that we couldn't stand one another. Once we became old enough to express our emotions in a mature and honest manner, we ran into one another outside the "7-11 Convenience Store". I had just broken up with Shane for the first time and had just turned fourteen a few months prior to seeing him again. He wore street clothes and he must have been about six feet tall. His manly air and his soft persona struck me instantly. We spent the next couple weeks together hanging out as friends. He was the first guy to take me out on a 'real' date. He brought me a bouquet of red roses on our first date *and took me to a real sit down restaurant, "The Village Square". They had real glass wine glasses on the tables and Elliot pulled out my chair, picked up the soft, blue linen napkin from beside my seat and spread it out on my lap. He' saw' me; the inside parts that were usually overlooked. He listened intently to what I had to say. For about a month, he never asked me for anything in return. All the money from his job as a stocker at the A&P was allocated to shower me with Van Halen CD's, treats and flowers...*

We had been dating for a month and had not gone past first base. I tried to seduce him a few times but he stopped me, quietly commanding respect and expecting me to respect myself. On our one month anniversary he slipped me an envelope. I slid my hand inside and my fingers touched three, thin, soft, red rose petals and amongst them were two movie tickets, for "Jungle Fever". Amidst the petals was a gracefully written note on baby blue paper:

Dear Hannah:

> *This is a coupon good for:*
> *One night at the Best Western Hotel*
> *We can celebrate our love for one another*
> *There will be many surprises and new experiences*
> *I Love You*
> *Elliot*

I contemplated a long time about whether I was going to tell my mom the truth about where I would be spending the night. Not wanting her to say no, I made up an elaborate excuse. So wrapped up in her own fantasy life, she was oblivious (one of the perks of having a flaky mom).

That night Elliot and my nervousness lay heavy in the air, the silence unbreakable. While we sat through the tense Spike Lee Joint movie, a forbidden romance between an Italian woman and a black man, I wondered as I watched the movie if Elliot had ever been with another woman, or if he knew I had already lost my virginity. Was my tainted history written on my face? Or was my 'pure' and 'virginal' façade victorious.

Elliot turned the key and opened the door. He asked me to go in the bathroom for a moment while he 'set up'. The cold porcelain seat sent chills through my thin gauzy tie-dyed mini-dress. What did he have in store? I knew that the likelihood of us consummating our relationship tonight was fairly high, so I had some preparing to do...I grabbed a handful of toilet paper and pulled up my skirt. I plucked open my satin panties and washed myself so that I would feel fresh for him. Pulling my orange canvas purse open, I pulled out my think brush and ran it through my long, wavy

85

platinum blond hair. I applied a fresh coat of light pink Bonnie Bell gloss on my ripe lips (mmm…smells like cotton candy) I was nervous, excited but ready for him.

After a lot of rustling around he tapped gently on the door and said mildly,

"Close your eyes" as he led me out of the bathroom and into the tiny hallway. "Open them Hannah!" There were tiny candles decorating the entire room, giving the room a luminescent heartbeat. Elliot stood before me in nothing but a pair of white "Joe Boxer" undershorts with a black band. His chest was defined and rippled with understated muscles; his skin was a creamy, ivory smorgasbord of delight. I realized that my mouth was gaping open and I wasn't completely sure that I wasn't drooling. (Snap out of it girl!) The delicate fabric of my dress caressed my fingers as I slid it up over my head and laid it gently on the mahogany chair in front of me. I stood before him in my salmon pink lace bra and panty ensemble. We stood across the room from one another for a frozen moment in time, soaking in one another's fresh, mysterious forms. Caressing each other with our gaze, our hungry eyes remained focused and sure. Slowly we started to move toward one another in a subtle tango of passion. Reaching his arms out to me, he pulled me close. His body was hot and smooth against my almost naked form. He laid me tenderly down on the crisp, cool hotel sheets and began kissing me ardently. There was something peculiar about the sheets that coupled with my flesh. Something cool and smooth, like tiny raindrops against the crook of my back, blended with the overpowering scent of baby powder and roses. Sensory candy was mingling with the heat of our bodies. He brought his hand over the top of my head and swept up a handful of delicate pink rose petals, slowly sprinkling them over my fierce body. Elliot could not have been a virgin because that night we took one another for hours at a time, over and over again as Van Halen serenaded us on the portable tape player that Elliot carried in his arsenal. Things were so nice and calm with Elliot, I was happy and relaxed with him.

Shane came back into my life and brainwashed me with his dynamic charm and damaging passion. He was very, very bad and I think subconsciously I felt that I didn't deserve someone like Elliot. So I broke Elliot's heart just weeks after our night of numinous passion…I often wondered what would have happened had I stayed with Elliot. That horrific night with Shane and his friends would never have happened…

Abraham Or Joe?
Summer 1990

Abraham was a boy that I met as soon as I arrived in Edmonton. I had just turned fifteen and felt like this was my second chance to make a new life for myself. Life in a large metropolis allowed me to be anonymous. Abraham and his brother Gabe hung out at the local arcade "Coin Castle" where Lou Lou and her friends hung out, letting me tag along. We would spend hours in the tiny black store with black lights and neon graffiti scrawled along the walls. Filled with all the classic video games; Ms.PacMan, PacMan, Cosmic Wars, Final Fantasy, The Adventures of LoLo, Future Wars, Street Fighter and numerous pinball machines. Hours were spent trying to beat the high scores of our favorite games. One evening Lou Lou's ballerina friend Nikki introduced me to Abraham. He was short, cute and funny and my trust for him materialized instantly. At the time I was staying with Jory and his roommate Joe. I had a long-term secret crush on Joe. When I was in Grade Six I came out West for my summer with Dad and Karen and he came to our Grandparents a-frame cottage overlooking Blind Bay in the Shushwaps. We spent part of the summer there every second year. I would wait until him and my brother were out on the boat and I would look through his luggage and put his clothes against my cheek, breathing in his boyish scent, and feeling my body respond in unfamiliar ways. He didn't notice me before, but lately, since I had breasts I had noticed him looking at me in a different way... Like he was really hungry and I was a slice of rich, chocolate cake that he wanted to relish and devour... He had a fierce girlfriend who he'd been with for a couple years and I knew if she ever saw him look at me she could take me down hard...

One night Abraham said he would come over to Jory's place and hang out. Joe knew he was coming over. As I was making a trip to the bathroom he pulled me into the entrance to his bedroom and whispered hoarsely in my ear "If you want to experience a real man, meet me in my room tonight." Fearful yet mysteriously enticed by his licentious proposal I told him "I'll see!"

When Abraham came over Joe and Jory each had a couch so Abe and I went outside and sat on the hood of his white, rusty 1982 VW Golf. I was distant and aloof with Abraham and my emotional state was recognizable and new to him. He tried desperately to make small talk or incite me into one of our usual lively conversations, but to no avail. As the sun began to go down and the night masked the sky in its darkness, Abraham started to come on to me. Turned off and anxious about Joe's offer I clumsily went through the motions. Finally after about twenty minutes I made a lame excuse about " needing to go to sleep, so I wouldn't be tired for my early bird waitressing shift at "Humpty's Egg Place." Eventually Abraham gave up his advances and went home filled with an obvious glance of disappointment on his face.

I walked into the dark basement suite and noticed that both Jory and Joe were in their rooms, seemingly asleep. Petrified and excited simultaneously, my body fought my mind and soul. Joe represented danger and I had just thrown away a gentle, safe boy my age for him. I slipped into the bathroom and all there was to clean myself was a dingy old washcloth, full and stinking of bacteria and grime. Instead I scooped my hands and gathered a pool of water and soap then I sloshed it between my legs and wiped myself with the only, limp beach towel hanging from the solitary rusty, towel rod. I paced back and forth from my couch bed to Joe's door only in my imagination as I lay on the warped couch bed in my black, strappy velvet nightgown. I snuck down the hall and put my hand up to the door to knock several times, but chickened out and slid my socked feet back to my makeshift bed. Finally I gave up, realizing that it was not a safe idea. I tried to quiet my racing mind as I went over every scenario. Then a door opened, I squinted my eyes shut, feigning sleep. I felt and smelt someone's hot beer breath on my back. "Han...Hannah...Are you awake?" It was Joe's voice hot on my exposed shoulder. I hesitated trying to pin down a decision at the spur of the moment.

"Yes." I responded with some trepidation as I turned to face him.

He took me by the hand, helped me up and took me to his bedroom. I was blinded by the enveloping darkness, trying to feel my way through the maze of furniture in his room. He shut the door and pulled me close to him. I felt his naked body up against the velvet of my nightgown. I could feel his excitement pressed against my bare leg. The scenario terrified and enticed me. What if his girlfriend found out? Or worse, what if Jory found out? I felt guilty at the thought of betraying my brother but it was too late to turn back because he had me kneeling on the floor in front of him and he had already entered me; there was no turning back.

He lasted all night, his refractory period lasting mere minutes, just enough time for us to share a cigarette. By the morning my delicate womanhood was sore and moaning. The last time he tried to enter me I pleaded with him:

"I have to get back to the couch bed before Jory wakes up. The sun is starting to come up so it must be like 7:30, he'll be waking up soon."

I put my clothes back on and shuffled back to my couch bed wincing at the pain that shot through my body. I laid there and silent and tears started to flow down my face...

Moving On

After my move to Edmonton and my summer rendezvous with Abe and then Joe I took a hiatus from men. Feeling jilted and betrayed by the friends I left behind in Ontario I found it surprisingly easy for me to move on. After the miscarriage I focused on building new friendships at school and at work. I was proud of myself, for enduring a whole six months with no men, no sex. My dangerous addiction seemed to be latent and my hope was that it would stay that way. That addiction, that hunger was what always got me into trouble, my nemesis that could consume my soul and overtake it in the instant I got reeled in by a man boy's hungry stare. I promised myself I would refuse to get sucked in again. Each morning I worked hard to mask my natural beauty as much as possible, reverting back to my old regiment; make-up free, baggy jeans and large, formless t-shirts, hair that was air dried and uncoiffed. My transformation into an invisible, untouchable woman was a success. I had friends, most of whom were gay men. There was a relief in knowing that they didn't want anything from me...

Love in the Tropics
Christmas 1990

About a year after I moved to Edmonton Dad and Kim decided to take me to Honolulu, Hawaii for Christmas. The excitement of getting away from the supremely frigid temperatures and misery that Edmonton brought with her in the winter months was tangible.

Upon arrival in Honolulu, we got leid by two beautifully exotic local woman, dressed in beautifully rich floral muumuu's, with fuchsia, orchid crowns. The heavy, tropical air, thick with heat and humidity enticed my willing senses. I walked with a bounce in my step as I breathed in the sensual aroma of my amethyst orchid lei pooled with the fresh ocean scented air...

Earl .J.

Dad and Kim trusted me and therefore gave me tons of freedom to roam around Honolulu on my own for the duration of the trip. During the day I would find a small private spot facing the ocean. As I gazed out at the turquoise expanse of it I imagined I was far off in the distance, invisible, waltzing in the glow, far above the surface, as bright as the sultry air. The sea and sky were almost identical, bleeding into one another, making love horizontally in the sky.

Dad, Karen and I would meet up and share meals at restaurants that were painted bright blue with gigantic fish tanks covering entire walls. As we ate our surf and turf the giant, tropical fish would swim by and look at me with their large bulging eyes as they preformed their water dance with grace and charm. Honolulu was littered with carbon copies of this formula of restaurant; there to amuse and entice the tourists. Locals would be dressed in black slacks and crisp white button down shirts, loyally serving the gluttonous, half Caucasian, half Asian customer base. As I snuck peeks at them I felt twangs of pain and compassion for the local people, having to make their living catering to middle and upper class tourists, putting on their plastic smiles and making sure to say "Please" and "Thank you", "Sir" and "Madam". I wondered if they dreamed of a better life for their families because it was obvious that their smiles were pasted on. Would any of these people escape? That I didn't know but I tried to be super, extra nice and warm with our servers because I didn't want to be grouped with the plague that occupied their treasured island paradise.

Every night I walked up and down the main strip which was by day a one stop shopping locale with tourist traps peppering the entire street; shops full of baby blue cans of "Mauna Loa" macadamia nuts, shells with "Aloha Hawaii" carved into them, t-shirts with "Hang Loose Hawaii!" written on them, and other plastic local gewgaws with tiny golden "Made in China" labels adhered to their bottoms. At night the streets became a red light district; a cesspool of newly formed couples intermingled with horny middle aged men and prostitutes dressed in skin tight, shiny imitation leather and garish polyester animal prints; their engorged parts squeezing out of the clothing like toothpaste from the tube. They fearlessly propositioned generic, solo men of all genders and ethnicities as they walked by, eyes down to the ground, trying not to think of their cookie cutter families and their mini-vans.

One night at dusk as I was sitting on a wooden bench, watching the prostitutes drum up business, I simultaneously heard a deep, smooth man's voice and felt a firm tap on my naked shoulder..."Hey girl!" I spun around to meet the deep brown eyes of the most stunning African man I had ever laid eyes on. He was over six feet tall and had flawless skin as rich as dark chocolate. He was stunning in his navy blue uniform with a gold encrusted crest with "U.S.Army, Corporal" written on it and a collection of numbers. Being so lost and struck by this man that I didn't notice that he wasn't alone. His friend held out his hand and said, "My name is Carter, nice to meet you girl!"

The gorgeous one said, "What's a pretty girl like you doing sitting on a bench in Hawaii at midnight all by herself?" I told them that I was here with my parents and I didn't really have a curfew. They invited me to come to the basketball court by our hotel. In the middle of the concrete jungle there was a brightly lit basketball court filled with young, African army boys. Corporal Earl Johnston was the boy that my eyes were glued to. I sat on the bench, squinting from the brightness of the floodlights and watched Earl's cut body become speckled with perspiration as he sprinted and hopped naturally around the court, his chest rippled with muscles formed from years of athletics and army training courses. I wished I had worn something nicer than my jean cut offs and my plain black tank top and pink and purple striped flip flops.

After the game, Earl told his friend to meet up with him later; he wanted to "make sure his girl got home safe". I giggled internally at the fact that in the matter of two hours he was already calling me "his girl". We walked back to my hotel hand in hand, the humidity and perspiration acting like glue, adhering us for the duration of our stroll. He was assertive with his feelings for me! Funnily, I was OK with it, I trusted him. When we reached the promenade in front of my hotel we sat side by side on the ledge of the ornate concrete fountain marking the entrance. First we talked for a while and then he pulled me close to him and kissed me passionately; his hands discovered all the curves of my young budding body and I gently ran my hand up and down his thick, hard thigh. Our passion was insatiable; I had wanted him so hungrily right at that moment...

I spent all day the next day searching for a dress to wear for our date the next night. He planned on picking me up after training when the sun was beginning to go to sleep. While I was walking down the strip I noticed a few tents full of clothes, accessories and the work of local artisans. A sundress straight ahead of me pinned up on a felt divider in a dimly lit corner of the marketplace caught my eye. It was form fitting and had a white background with large stripes of tiny different coloured daisies; blue, pink, orange and purple. It was perfect, size 2 and everything. I found a strappy pair of purple sandals with a small heel and I went home to try the collection on. I started getting ready at about 4 O'clock, just to make sure I had enough time to prepare. I skipped dinner with the parents and focused on presenting myself to Earl with the utmost potential. As I stared at the slight curves of my young body adorned with this revealing cotton dress, the daisies enlarged at the places where my assets were accentuated, making them slightly obscene. At that moment a bolt of fear shocked me into half removing it. It looked spectacular and I feared that Earls would not be the only eyes on me. In the end I took the gamble and went with the revealing ensemble, placing a light lavender sweater on top of the ensemble in case I lost my nerve.

As I was choking down a piece of honey toast I heard the buzzer ring…I felt like a girl on her sixteenth birthday waiting to see what her parents were about to give her as a gift…Would it be a Camaro or an Oldsmobile, a sparkly fuchsia cell phone or an old snot green phone with a coiled up cord…Earl ended up being a Camaro: fast, smooth and sleek…He treated me like a lady, opening doors and using his manners. We went to the early showing of "Boyz in the Hood". The movie was so emotionally intense, especially for Earl who had grown up in the hood in Chicago, and at the severe moments we were both in tears. He had been stationed in Honolulu on assignment with the Army one week after his eighteenth birthday and had been here for three consecutive years now. His family had moved with him and he was supporting them all on his meager wages. His mother, sister and her young son were his sole responsibility. When he spoke of his reality the tension in his eyes was palpable. After the movie he let the floodgates open up and we sat on the beach and had a heart to heart about all the hardships he had endured living the life of an impoverished black man in America. He said his friends weren't very supportive of him dating a white chick, so we would have to keep the relationship a secret. Since I was only there for ten days, we knew our time together was scarce.

After our talk we walked along the beach and watched the leftover sunset in its Clementine coloured brilliance. His thick arms were the largest and smoothest I had ever been enveloped in. Being in his presence flushed me with tenderness and an aching that was voracious. As we were walking we saw in the dim distance a hut a few dozen feet from the water's edge. We stared at one another with silent knowing. It was an old, rickety change room by day and a safe haven for young lovers and homeless people by night. Earl ducked as he led me into the musty building, its walls masterfully adorned with graffiti art. To the sound of the waves crashing desperately against the shore, Earl held me and guided me backwards until my barely clothed back was pressed up against the cold, damp concrete. I felt the rough texture covered with years of salt against my delicate skin as Earl hiked my daisy smattered dress up above my hips. He slid down my pink satin bikini panties as I searched hopefully in the dark for his zipper. I unzipped it savagely as our groans belted out of us in unison. He entered me and our bodies slammed against one another in untainted passion. We reached sensational bliss in unison and afterwards I shook with satisfaction and then fell limp in his arms, unable to take a breath. He was terrified and started to shake me yelling, "OH MY GOD, ARE YOU OK? HANNAH WAKE UP, PLEASE!!!!" I gasped and drank in a guzzle

of salty sea air as I looked up into Earls dark eyes half giggling, half sighing.
"Wow! That was amazing!"
He said, "You passed out! Are you OK?"

I replied, "I think so, it was just so amazing!" He pulled my underwear
back up and slid my tight fitting dress down over my slim, teenage form, zipped
his pants up and held his hand out to me.
"Let's go to Jack in the Box and get you something to drink. Maybe you're
dehydrated too."

For the rest of the trip we were inseparable. When he was not doing
his training exercises he showed me the 'real' Hawaii. Stepping outside the
'touristy kitsch' to see the stunning countryside was a gift. He took me to a
pineapple field a hundred miles from the city, its vibrant salmon coloured sand
nourishing the symmetrical rows of spiky green leaves. Like a dream, the island
called to me, it wrapped its arms around me and held me close. I could hear
its heart beat and feel the warmth of its breath stroking my cheek. As we drove
we sat in silence, comfortable with the lack of words.

I fell hard and fast for Earl and the island and the days were slipping away
too abruptly. Fantasies of how I could escape the flight home and visualizations
of how sweet life would be if I could stay there tempted me. For some reason I
felt more like myself there than I did at home. I had no mask hiding myself, I
wore clothes that hugged my body and I felt more beautiful than I ever had.
Being a complete stranger gave me a freedom that was new and comfortable.
At home, even in Edmonton, I felt as though I had to act a certain way, passive
and humble, with no opinion about anything, fearful of being rejected for
having a conflicting point of view, blending and transforming to suit my circle
of friends. I would always be a people pleaser, but not here. The island was a
refuge…I felt like a captive animal that had finally been released back into its
wild, natural, capricious environment…

The day of my departure I put on my daisy dress and walked down to the
beach. Earl was coming to say good-bye that afternoon and our flight would
be leaving at dusk. I fought back the sorrow and tried to resist the sobs that
rose up in my throat like sour bile. As I sat on my beach towel watching the
children dip their toes into the water, run away giggling and whoop with pure
joy back to the secure arms of their parents; I was lost in the monotony of the
lapping waves. Out of the corner of my eyes I noticed someone approaching,
not wanting to be disturbed I maintained my linear focus. A man smelling like
weed reached my vibrant, rainbow beach towel and tapped me on the shoulder.
"Aloha, young lady!" I turned to face a Caribbean man with a weathered, sun
kissed face, dreadlocks hanging down to the middle of his back, a red, black

and green bandana wrapped around the top of his head, and a bright yellow t-shirt with a faded, black silhouette of Bob Marley with his arms crossed… He said "I'll draw a picture of you for ten dollars, and you give it to your boy." "What do ya say sista?" I had twenty five dollars and fifty cents American left so I said "sure, I would love it!" He took a fold-up easel out of his backpack and unrolled a burlap pastel holder full of well used worn out pastels. I sat with my back shielding the hot morning sun as he studied me with a genuine smile on his face, like a man that was totally content with his life and was not constantly wishing for more. The pastels moved with such grace and abandon, possessed by his inner vision. When he was done he presented me with the most stunning portrait of me. I handed him a crumpled up twenty and gave him a hug. "Thank you for making my day, and giving me a gift to leave with my boy!"

He said, "No problem my girl, have a nice day!"
Earl was picking me up outside the hotel at three and the anticipation was too much to handle. I went down to the lobby of the hotel and sat on the edge of the fountain waiting for him; as I waited I listened to "Diamonds and Pearls" by Prince over and over on my little pink walkman. As I listened I sang the words quietly to myself and felt overwhelmed with love…

> If I gave you diamonds and pearls
> Would you be a happy boy or girl?
> If I could I would give you the world
> But all I can do is just offer you my love

I was so caught up listening to Princes syrupy voice that I didn't realize that two hours had past and it was now five o'clock. Earl was supposed to be there at three. It was our last time together and he was late. I ran into the hotel and slammed my finger several times against the tiny round elevator button. It seemed like it was taking forever so I sprinted over to the door labeled "stairs" and I ran up the six flights to our floor. When I got to the room Dad and Karen were just leaving to go for supper at the chintzy aquarium restaurant. "Has Earl called?" I sputtered, short of breath…
Karen said, "No, I don't think so." And asked if I would be joining them and I said "No, I need to wait for him; I don't want to miss seeing him…"
"Well then, we'll see you later, please be back at seven sharp so we can leave for the airport!" "OK, thanks have a good supper." I huffed through my desperate words. I still had the rolled up portrait of myself in my hands and desperately wanted to give it to Earl before I left. I wanted to be lost in his soft, smiling eyes and feel his smooth warm hands discover my body. Tears were streaming down my

face and thoughts started firing like daggers through my soul, "What if I never see him again? What if he is stuck and can't get to a phone?"

For the next two hours I ran up and down the stairs waiting and searching for some sign of him, checking to see if that red beacon would be flashing on the phone letting me know there was a message waiting. There was no answer on his phone and I never received that beacon that would save me from heartbreak. Dad and Karen returned and waited for me with compassion for fifteen extra minutes, but he never called or came to the hotel. Dad and Karen left as I wept alone in the room for a few extra minutes of solitude. I slipped the portrait in the night table drawer and scrawled out one final note to Earl...

> Dear Earl:
>
> I waited as long as I could. I tried to call but I had to go home. I don't know if I'll ever see you again, but please take the portrait that is in the night table, it will give you something to remember me by. I'll miss you terribly and it is ripping my heart out that we couldn't say good-bye. You're in my heart always,
>
> Love Hannah XOXOXOXOXOX

I never heard from him or saw him again...

Coming Out
Dane, Chris and Terrance

Speckled throughout her numerous, sordid love affairs were a few gems that Hannah fell hard and swiftly for. These were the only men that shared Hannah's intense sensitivity about life and experiences. She built strong friendships with them. These young men were going through a transition and for some reason Hannah kept colliding with them on their search for their true selves. During her moments of clarity and self love she was attracted to healthy, safe, gentle men. Men that would never threaten or hurt her, men that would cherish her for her true self and ask for nothing. Men that felt safe wilting in her arms and letting her nurture them.

Dane

During my grade twelve year at Victoria School for the Performing Arts I was kicked out of my dad's house for dissing my stepmom on the phone. I had moved back in after feeling overwhelmed with all the responsibility of trying to hold down a full-time job and finish High School. I had been back for only six months. Karen had overheard a phone conversation I was having with my Mom and a fight ensued. Once again I was homeless. Dane was a good friend that I had been hanging out with. We danced in a show together for dance class. He was pure of heart and had the most stunningly beautiful face with perfect square bone structure. His body was cut and defined from all the years he had spent dancing. It was impossible not to fall in love with his gentle, loving personality. The more time we spent together the harder I fell. His mom let me stay with them while I sorted things out at home so we spent an entire week together. I began fantasizing about the life we would have together, but never let my feelings out for fear of being rejected. He was too beautiful and perfect for me and he would need a stable, woman that was free from all of life's baggage. I was damaged goods; I couldn't see why he'd want me...

For months we spent all our time together, talking endlessly about our dreams for the future and rehearsing for modern dance pieces that we were both in. We never crossed the sexual boundaries in any way, which made me want him insatiably. He was the first man I had truly been friends with; he respected me and never even tried to cross the line. I was very content that to him I was not just a piece of raw meat to be savagely consumed.

After three months wanton and in limbo I decided that particular day, while we were in Churchill Square, I was going to tell Dane that I had fallen in love with him. That morning he too said that he had something to tell me. He was dressed in tight fitting, faded cut-off jean shorts and a fitted white t-shirt and the blue in his eyes was complimented by a perfect, cloudless sky. I had dressed in my light denim strappy sundress adorned with a large embroidered sunflower. I imagined what the strangers walking by us were thinking."What a stunning couple! Those two kids were made for one another! I would love to have a man like that on my arm!" As we walked to the concrete pavilion Danes electric energy was drawing me to him like a magnetic force. Here was my chance, now I just needed to say it..."I have something to tell you too Dane!" The walk to our spot by the cascading fountains seemed to take forever...the time extended by the fact that we walked in complete silence...

He laid his sweatshirt down and motioned for me to sit on it. Once we were comfortable he said, "Do you want to go first or should I?" I told him he should go and waited with anticipation for him to profess his love to me. Looking straight ahead he said in a hushed voice "I need to tell you something that I have never told anyone...I trust you with it...I need to tell someone or I will go crazy..."

"You can trust me Dane, I will keep it to myself...You can tell me anything..."I responded as I brushed my hand down his forearm (my body tingling with the impact of my soft fingers against his flushed buttery skin)

"Hannah, I think I am bi-sexual or maybe even gay...I feel attracted to another man and I'm just so confused..."

As his tears rolled down his cheeks, I tried to hold in mine.

"It's O.K. Dane, you have to be true to yourself. Does this guy know you have feelings for him?" "Well, I don't think so, he's gay but he doesn't know I might be..."

I swallowed my desires like a thick, chunky mouthful of regurgitated phlem.

I listened as he told me what the last few years had been like, hiding who he truly was and what a relief it was to have finally found a friend he could trust enough to reveal it too. Though my heart was breaking in two I realized that he had been there for me and now he really needed me, my selfish desire to be with him shrunk away into a dark spot within my soul where it would lay dormant. His friendship meant more to me than anything and I didn't want to ruin it...just having him in my presence was a gift...

Over the next few months I distanced myself from him because my hunger would not subside and containing it was like trying to stop a brushfire from feeding on dry brush surrounding it...

Chris

Eventually Hannah's time at friend's homes ran out and she moved back in with Lou Lou. She had put off telling her sister that things didn't last with her Dad and Karen because she knew her sister felt so much responsibility for her. When Lou Lou heard of her situation she welcomed Hannah back with loving arms. Lou Lou had invited a few friends from work to come and live in their ratty, inner city house while Hannah was living with the folks. One of them had a peculiar face, with a crooked nose that looked like it had been punched several times and broken; a lost look in his eye and had a scrawny figure adorned with freshly pressed, preppy attire. His name was Chris and Hannah never really liked anything about him. He was sheepish and strange; he looked uncomfortable in his own skin and hardly ever cracked a smile. Life was too short to be taking things so seriously at the age of twenty. They lived in the same house for months before they actually spoke two words to one another. There was always an uncomfortable silence that hung between them like a thick curtain.

Lou Lou had strict orders that none of the three new male roommates lay a hand on her little sister and if they did they would pay the price. None made an effort for a long time either. One night Hannah came home and had a couple strawberry vodka coolers. Chris was the only one home so he joined her in the kitchen and they struck up a conversation for the first time. The hours collected and the two still found themselves there, tipsy and blurry eyed connecting with each other for the first time. They ended up falling asleep, head to head, talking on the soft, oatmeal coloured sectional. When they were alone in the house they looked forward to talking and flirting with one another, their secret relationship starting to blossom. They had kissed one another lightly on the lips a few times but their physical relationship had not moved on. When they kissed Hannah noticed Chris pull away as though her lips were in flames and were scorching him. They decided to make it official and go on a date. He came into her room to see what she was wearing on their date and made a few minor adjustments. Apparently she had no sense of style and he had to 'fix' her before leaving. She felt uncomfortable with the red bandana wrapped around the top part of her head and the crisp, white button down shirt tucked into her second hand jeans. As she glanced over at him in the car she realized that he was dressed almost identically except he had on a baby blue button down with delicate white stripes. They looked foolishly like those old married couples that wear the same blue, velour track suit with the names "Vern" and "June" embroidered on the pocket; heading out for a long, smoky night of bingo.

On the drive to the Italian Eatery Chris pulled the car over on an old tree lined side street and looked down at the floor in front of me. I forced a smile, half excited, half feeling foolish in the matching clothes he had made me wear. He looked me up and down and his eyes became transfixed on my ratty, brown loafers. He said, "I can't be seen with you in those shoes!" I felt the anger rise up in my throat, burning hot. He knew my financial situation and why I was unable to buy brand new, fashionable Converse runners that matched his vibrant red ones. What the hell did he want from me? Was he trying to turn me into him? Fucker! I retorted, "Fine then, you don't need to be seen with me anymore, you stuck up prick!" I got out of his shabby, grey car and slammed the door with as much passion as I could muster. I walked home shaking with anger and feeling completely insulted and that was when I realized that Chris was trying to deny the fact that he was a homosexual and no matter how hard he tried to change me, I was not going to grow a penis anytime soon…

Terrance .K.
Winter 1996

Hannah's years at the University of Alberta were a whirlwind of work, sex, and friendships. Being alone terrified her so she latched on to anyone, male or female, that would give her the slightest bit of attention. One evening after class Hannah and her friends decided to meet at a quaint little café called "The Library". They took a small table in the basement that had antique mismatched chairs and a rickety table that wobbled if you leaned on it too much. Colourful light, from dozens of tiffany chandeliers, danced along the deep rust walls giving everyone a sensuous glow and the walls were adorned with antique books. That was when they first noticed one another. He was sitting directly across from her and wasted no time "My name's Terrance." Everyone at the table became invisible as he held out his slender, manicured hand to Hannah. As she gently grasped his hand she felt a surge run through her body, "I'm Hannah." She hung on his every word and for once did not try to be the life of the party. The formal way he spoke and his use of intelligent conversation intimidated Hannah slightly. Inside she felt like a little child afraid to say anything stupid. She took the time to organize and censor what she was going to say before she said it aloud. By the end of the evening Terrance sat next to her, they broke off into their own intimate conversation ending in him asking her out on a date.

Terrance was an avid water polo player and needed to train so he asked Hannah to join him at the campus pool the next afternoon in between classes. She wondered if he had ulterior motives in asking her to go swim before going on a "real" date. Questions like; "Does he want to check out my body before he moves any further?" and "Does he want me to preview his package?" ran through her mind. Oh well, she was willing to do anything to be close to him. She had been unable to focus on anything but him since seeing him at the restaurant. Every time he entered her mind she felt moist and giddy. He would be her new conquest.

Hannah had contemplated long and hard on which bathing suit she should go for; the hot pink bikini with padded push up bra or the plain black one piece. No matter which one she picked she would be self conscious of her body. Being tall and slim was a positive but having small breasts and the pubic hair of a cavewoman made her self-conscious. In the end Hannah chose the safe black one piece. She was shocked when she came out of the change room and he was standing there waiting for her in a tight red Speedo. All the other guys were wearing shorts. As they walked towards one another Hannah felt a little embarrassed but extremely turned on by the bulge beneath the Speedo. Jory used to wear Speedos when they went to the beach as teenagers and her and Lou Lou would laugh hysterically at him because they were so "out". The memory made her stifle a giggle. She had an incredible urge to run over to him and tackle him with her fluffy pink bath towel and wrap him up tight like one of those tiny 'pigs-in-a-blanket' they give out a cocktail parties.

The pair frolicked in the water swapping flirtations as they swam around the pool. She tried hard to contain herself when he bounced up and down on the diving board, clenching his firm butt cheeks as he sailed aerodynamically through the humid, air, heavy with the scent of chlorine. This would be the script for her wildest dreams for months to come.

For the two weeks they dated, Hannah felt so happy and light she was sure her feet were going to lose contact with the very ground she walked on. They did yoga together in her living room at the "Happy Hippy House" (a home she shared with seven other University students) after eating vegetarian creations that she whipped up in the galley kitchen. One Wednesday night they baked chocolate chip cookies by the dim red twinkling of her plug in chili pepper lights, surrounded by the sweet, sensual smell of melted chocolate he slowly pushed her body up against the counter and kissed her with concentrated passion. The intensity of this long awaited kiss brought her close to orgasm. When she reached down and brushed her hand across his tight buns he pulled away and said; "Let's go for a walk!" It must be true that women can get blue balls too…

They walked through the forest, her floor covered with inches of soft, delicate snowflakes, the trees bending with the weight of snow on their branches, luminescent in the dim first evening moonlight. They danced through the snow, kicking up piles of it and throwing clumps of it at one another as they laughed hysterically. Terrance's voice strong and confident, from years of being in a chorus group, began singing Broadway tunes. Hannah joined in when she recognized the words and they linked arms skipping through the forest like Dorothy and her friends in the Wizard of Oz.

So this is what it feels like to be madly in love. I adore the fact that he gets me, he really does. He has so many similar interests and it is so easy to be with him. Not only is he gorgeous, he is passionate, musical, intelligent, and he really, really digs me...

He invited me to his house one winter evening...I rode my bike down Whyte Avenue, through the slush with a huge smile on my face...We had never done anything more than kiss and I wondered if that night our passionate love affair would progress...

When I came in the door I felt the mood of the room drop like a heavy drinking glass and I visualized our picture perfect love smashing into tiny, glimmering shards...Terrance held me close and whispered "We have to talk!" I felt his hot tears roll down my cheek as he held his face next to mine...He sat me down on a hard, red milk carton and told me why it was impossible to be together..."It's me, not you...I feel so much love for you, but I am in limbo right now about my sexuality..."I couldn't fucking believe it, this was the third guy that had come out of the closet while in a relationship with me...I felt like making up a flyer, covered in rainbows, advertising my services:

Date Hannah for a couple weeks
And find out once and for all
If you are gay or straight! Call me @ 555-8332

We both cried hard that night, we told each other all of the hidden secrets that lay beneath the surface. He told me we would still be friends, but in my heart I knew this would be the last time we would spend together. I was jealous of the man he would eventually fall in love with and I felt jilted knowing that it may be close to impossible to find a man that was gentle, nurturing and straight! At three o'clock in the morning I realized it was time to say good-bye; we held one another for a long time. When I left he put his neon safety vest on me so that I would be seen while riding down Whyte Avenue on my bicycle. That ride was painful both physically and emotionally. As I rode past mobs of drunken partiers I hid my tear stained face. I just wanted to get home, blow dry my frozen wet hair and put on my warm, flannel pajamas. When I got home, luckily none of my seven roommates were awake to hear my stifled sobs. I collapsed on my mattress, studying the poster of the naked, golden haired woman holding her black, haired baby up to her. A montage of Terrance memories flooded my mind and I felt a strong sense of grief. The vision was dissipating like snowflakes on a warm windshield...

Alexis .M.
Winter 1992

After many years of being with men, she came to the conclusion that if they were not gay, they only had one goal, to be fucked as soon as possible and as often as they could. Her desperate need to have control over her sexuality made her 'easy'. When with a man she would perform with confidence and poise. Her body always responded as though it was ready and willing, hiding the fact that inside her exposed inner child was shriveling up into a tiny corner of her soul. Lacking a father figure in her life made her ravenously crave the closeness of a man. Her flesh being the currency traded for the inevitable intimacy she so lacked.

Alexis was her best friend Asia's brother; she met him one day when she and Asia walked into the family room. He sat on the purple velvet couch watching 'Hockey Night in Canada' while he spit foul, brown chewing tobacco glitch into a paper Dixie cup. Hannah acted coy as she sat holding her legs against her body on the orange Lazy Boy recliner beside him. She made idle conversation with him as Asia came in and out of the family room. Hannah snuck glances at her friends much older brother; he was tall and slim, athletic with some muscle, with dark, olive skin, smooth and flawless, and short, soft black hair. His foreign look ignited a heat within Hannah that was so intense she felt like she needed to pour a pitcher full of ice water over herself just to escape.

The three of them sat in the family room all night and had a great time laughing and joking about Don Cherry and the wacky smack that he peddled to his Canadian followers. Later that night in the dark hallway Al passed Hannah while she was alone in the hallway, he whispered, "I think you are stunning, my door will be open tonight if you want to join me after Asia goes to sleep!"

This was the second guy that had propositioned me in this way. Was my sexuality that transparent? I had to stop and wonder if there was a sign on my head that said, "I'M EASILY FUCKABLE!" I didn't know but I wanted him as much as he wanted me. So I hung out with Asia for the rest of the evening. We listened to "Black Velvet" by Alannah Myles on repeat while we danced and talked. Then we went to our favorite heavy metal bar, "The Purple Onion" and drank 'Kokanee' beers straight from the bottle until we were plastered. At last call we had our usual Malibu and milk and took a cab home. When we got back to her house we giggled and ate a whole head of iceberg lettuce with our hands crossed behind our backs (a drunken tradition) as we laughed hysterically. In the back of my mind I was thinking about her brother and feeling a tremendous amount of guilt. We shared a bed so after we finally turned in I laid next to her listening to her soft, heavy breaths as she drifted off to sleep. I went over the scenario a few times in my head. My desire for him outweighed the consequences. Had Alexis slept with other friends of Asia's or was I the first? Did it take one to know one? After I was sure she was asleep I snuck into the bathroom to tidy up a bit. I smelled good and the final net hairspray had held my long, loose curls in place even after being crushed on the pillow for what seemed like eternity.

I stood staring at myself in the mirror, trying to deny the guilt that was swollen across my face. It felt like the time I skimmed the bottom of Mom's purse, gathering all the loose change for chocolate popsicles. At least fifteen minutes passed, with numerous enactments that included me quietly padding down the dark, plushy, carpeted hallway, standing in front of Alexis's door with my hand clenched and held close to the painted wood, ready to knock my way into his bed. After the fifth rehearsal I dove right into the opening night curtain call, I knocked lightly on his hollow door. The sound resounded and I wondered if that first knock would be loud enough to arouse him out of his fresh slumber as it was meant to do. I stood for a few moments and then heard the bed creak, moaning with age as Alexis's heaviness removed itself. This was it, there was no turning back now, I felt like sprinting back down the narrow hall, but the rush of adrenaline and the exhilaration of doing something so taboo filled me. The door began to open and he stared at my thin, young body, still immature and unscathed by childbirth or age, clothed in a baby pink cotton nightdress covered with tiny embroidered tulips with delicate, curly stems. His chocolate brown eyes devoured me as he took hold of my hand and led me to the double bed in the far corner of his room. He sat me down gently on the side of his bed and we said nothing to one another, our hands and the heat of our bodies communicated in a passionate tango of wordless intensity. He was a stranger to me, but I loved Asia and he was like the male version of her... her own flesh and blood...I wanted to change my mind when I thought of how she may react. What if she woke up and the spot beside her was vacant. Had her other friends left her bed to have their secret rendezvous with Alexis too? Maybe she was in on it? I doubted it though, it was against her overprotective nature...I felt like I was acting like a rebellious teenager, going against my parents wishes...She was my world and I couldn't believe I was willing to risk losing her for a night of sexual revolution...

That was the night I let down my guard and unleashed the 'free' sexual being that had existed dormant inside my chastised body. Alexis took me to a place in my mind where flowers exploded with vibrancy and fields of bright yellow and green stretched out to infinity. I lost myself in throws of passion. Even though I was aware of the fact that we would never set foot outside this room as a couple, I was content to be his lover, and he had respect for me. After we spent hours exploring one another's bodies with hands, tongues, feet... we would talk. He was a talented listener and played the role of therapist, father, and brother while I played the role of patient, daughter, and younger sister. Laying naked and talking for hours offered a vulnerability of spirit...I realized that I needed him...He made me feel better about myself...The fact that he wanted me in his bed made me feel important...After each night of partying with Asia I would end up back in his bed, her melodic breaths my cue to go back and knock on his door over and over again...He had on and off girlfriends and he never let them into his bed...He was crucial...he taught me how to be in control when I was having sex...He never mistreated me or was too demanding, he just carried me down my path of sexual discovery...After our time together was over I had my sexual awakening...

Ken .D. Part 1
Winter 1992-1997

Her rendezvous with Alexis had stopped abruptly when she met a new guy at the bar one night. Hannah spent the next six years in a relationship she thought was committed and secure. They had met at "The Gas Pump Bar and Tap Room" where Hannah and Asia were permanent fixtures several nights a week. He was one of the first men to ask Hannah to dance. Most nights she spent her time hiding at the bar, in oversized clothing and little make-up, her dated bronze rimmed glasses perched on her face, camouflaging her organic beauty. Her look was intentional, a way to protect herself from the hungry looks of men. If she blended into the static environment she could just stand at her usual spot and nurse her beer or Bloody Caesar; wiping the crunchy celery stick along the ridge of the thick, transparent glass, and running the salt along her tongue, squinting with pleasure as she sunk her teeth into the moist, crunchy treat, enjoying the burst of Clamato juice on her tongue. The bartenders all knew her name, so did the regulars. She was more comfortable standing at the bar talking to them. If a strange man came up to asked her to dance she refused, feeling like they had just invaded her sacred space at the shiny, mahogany bar, covered in round, rust-coloured, blemishes.

Ken was the first man she agreed to dance with. He had a friend named Devon with a blonde mullet and a beer gut; his eyes friendly and trustworthy. *Asia pulled my arm after they offered their proposal to dance with us. I decided if Asia was coming too I would be safe. We ended up dancing with the two men the rest of the night. I felt liberated with a sense of wild abandon. I finally let my guard down and released my true self onto that gleaming dance floor. Ken sucked me into his world and it was comfortable and safe. He cared for me like a wounded child for the next six years. His family treated me like I was their own flesh and blood. Finally I felt like I had found my place in the world. I fit and I was loved unconditionally by a large, close knit group of people.*

His family spoiled me with gifts and love. They treated me like I was a stray cat that they found close to death on the side of the road and it was their mission to nurse it back to health. His mom, sister and aunts welcomed me into their circle of pure, nurturing energy. We talked, we cried, we ate fresh baking and drank tea in a backyard gazebo covered in ivy. My love for Ken was strained, but I stayed with him for his family. His inflated ego and undying hunger for sex was the price I paid for a 'family'. I put up with his explosive temper and spent entire nights sobbing myself into exhausted slumber alone, curled up on the cold, slippery linoleum floor of our tiny, basement apartment bathroom, waiting for an apology or for him to scoop me up in his arms and carry me back to bed.

During our time together I began having intense flashes of the sexual abuse I had suffered in my childhood. I hid my horrific memories and tried to smash them deep into the centre of my grotesque intestines. Eventually the toxic images were taking over me all throughout the day. They would haunt me in HD quality in the middle of menial tasks, lectures at the University or quiet moments. They became impossible to contain. I spent entire days weeping uncontrollably for the child that was damaged and violated so brutally, so many times, by so many men.

I grew more uncomfortable as Ken began asking me to "spice up our sex life" with toys and movies. I agreed unwillingly and begun to feel like I was being violated again. My need for a stable family that loved me unconditionally outweighed my desire to have 'safe' sex so I stayed with him and his increasingly warped sexual needs. My instincts taunted me, begging me to run far away, but his family was providing me with something that I had desired and longed for so drastically in this lifetime.

I had begun the healing process and was involved in a sexual assault group therapy session. This session brought all of the memories back to the surface in order to eventually clear them out. I lost my insatiable desire for sex as it brought out horrific images and emotions that were crippling.

When he asked to bring another partner into our bed I was stunned and horrified. It seemed like the more revelations I had the more he wanted to warp our sexual relationship.

One night he came home with his best friend Devon. Both were drunk and had spent a night gambling on the VLT's, drinking beer and smoking cigarettes. I was sleeping in our bed with our two Jack Russell terriers, wearing my flannel two piece pink pajamas', covered in red hearts and cartoon monkeys. I spooned the smallest puppy and began to shake violently as I heard the two men stumble through the door. Barely able to breathe I clenched my eyes shut to feign sleep. After some drunken episodes of laughter I heard the doorknob turn. Their forced whispers sent a chill through me, "Let's wake her up, she'll do it!" Ken haphazardly flopped down on the bed beside me causing the larger dog Cody to tumble off her little corner of the bed and onto the plush floor with a muffled bang and a breathy whine. An elbow stuck into my rib cage, piercing me, I clenched my eyes together, holding in my painful reaction, pretending to be asleep. I heard them moaning as they kissed one another sloppily, the smell of beer and cigarettes souring the sweet air in the bedroom. Ken started to call out my name desperately in between kisses. "Hannah, Han…Han…Dev's here, we want you baby…" What was I supposed to do, paralyzed with fear and burning with anger that the man who knew what I was going through would spring this on me…I felt like I was back in that old house, vulnerable and exposed surrounded by hungry teenage boys, cheering for more…I held my breath as they began groping me and each other…this time there were two, strong, athletic men that were drunk and unpredictable…I had become a master at going through the motions with detachment…I had lots of experience acting and played the role with so much believability that if I was being reviewed by a critic I would have received stellar reviews…A five star, award-winning performance…My heart was ripped out that night…Ken had destroyed me without even realizing it…He hadn't protected me from violation, he had been the ringleader and he was now the enemy…

After Devon left I told Ken that I was uncomfortable being a sex toy for him and his buddy. Devon was married with three small children and I thought what we had done was immoral. He agreed lightly that they would never do it again, but he might as well have said it while waving his crossed fingers in front of my face.

A week later I came home from an afternoon shift at Thorncrest, the group home that I had been working at while studying at the University, and

I opened the door to our humble apartment. Ken was on all fours and Devon was kneeling behind him, Ken was moaning like a teenage girl and Devon was ramming himself into Ken, grunting with pleasure. I stood there, invisible. As I watched I saw flashes of my past with Ken: the night that he sent a dozen red, roses to my hotel room in Ontario the night before I awaited being put on the stand to testify against my stepfather Ross for stripping away my innocence as a child with his evil; the day his mother presented me with my grandmothers ring, the empty space where a diamond used to be filled with the diamond from her engagement ring; the night he held me in his arms as I wept after he got me to stand in front of a mirror and tell myself "I Love You!" The flashes no sooner materialized when all of a sudden, as if being sucked from my very soul, dissipated into a thousand shards of sharp, jagged glass, spinning around in the air, exploding into tiny bullets. My world was rapidly deflating and I found it difficult to breathe…

They didn't notice me, so I snuck into our bedroom and hid under the covers with my work clothes on. I held my flimsy pillow over my ears to mask the animalistic grunting sound of the two men, that I considered friends for so many years, that I trusted, reverberating off the walls of my living room…

Revenge with a Lesbian
Winter 1996

Danika was one of those husky, butch lesbians who wore extra large, shapeless t-shirts and jeans from a thrift store. She had long, straight, red hair and green eyes. Her face was round and free of make-up or the femininity of years of plucking her eyebrows and wearing green clay masks for an hour before she went to sleep. She was a woman trapped in the vortex between masculinity and femininity. When she looked at Hannah there was desire behind her eyes and Hannah could sense it. Revenge hung like a heavy vest of chains around Hannah's chest and she began thinking of ways to get back at Ken for what he'd done. He had shattered her world and committed the ultimate crime by opening Pandora's Box of shameless sex acts. Her wounds were fresh and deep and she wanted him to suffer for what he had done.

She went to a dinner party at her dear friend David's place; her being the only straight guest, she felt honored in some peculiar way. There was a vase of fresh daisies on the table and she was alone. That evening there was a box of white wine that flowed freely and Hannah started to feel giddy.

She couldn't help but notice the intense stares that Danika was sending her way. Danika was struck by Hannah's understated beauty and femininity. When she walked by Hannah she made sure to brush her casually and then touch her shoulder lightly while she apologized. Hannah sensed Danika's flirtation and started to play back in a sensual game of cat and mouse. "Unbreak my Heart" started playing on the stereo and during the second verse Danika cupped her hand over Hannah's ear and whispered hotly, "Meet me in the bathroom in five minutes; I have something to talk to you about." Warmed by her wine buzz and curious about what it felt like to have a woman touch her sexually, she felt a rush of pure adrenaline mixed with a dash of fear.

I saw Danika walk into the bathroom out of the corner of my eye while I was in the middle of a conversation with David. I cut the conversation short so that I could casually sneak into the bathroom behind Danika and enter her current of all female sensuality. I wanted to take a cautionary stroll down the rainbow coloured pathway. There was no darkness attached to women for me...no violation...no threat...I had never considered trying out lesbianism, but I figured it was worth a shot...

I entered the tiny apartment bathroom...the mirror faded and foggy, the shower curtain covered in Egyptian insignias and faces...all of them staring at me and cheering me on...Danika stood, silent in front of me, her flushed cheeks dotted with tan freckles...She took me by the arms and pressed me gently against the plush, decorative towels...I felt the coolness of the towel bar through my purple, satin button up blouse...She held my face in her hands and said "I have been waiting such a long time to kiss you..." My urge to pull away melted when her soft, ivory skin caressed mine...I froze, unable to resist her...She placed her lips with such tenderness on mine and I responded...Her large, spongy breasts pressed against my small, firm ones and at that moment I became enveloped in passion as we explored one another...I felt a rush, like hot lava was pouring out of the delicate place between my legs...The secrecy of our act made me feel every touch with an unresounded amount of intensity...She moved quickly, but with respect and a delicacy I had never experienced with a man...She hiked up my skirt and explored my womanhood with her mouth and hot tongue...no man had ever made me reach my explosive end as quickly or as powerfully as she did in my friends bathroom that night...She had the same parts so she knew how to treat them...For her I would have presented the Women's Choice Award for mastering the art of cunnilingus...

After our next few secret rendezvous I could feel her becoming emotionally invested in me. I was still with Ken and felt that I had to try and save my relationship, terrified to lose Ken's family. They were the centre of my world, making me feel as though I belonged. Losing them may mean losing myself. We had a few more secret rendezvous before I told Danika we couldn't see one another anymore. We continued to work together and every time we saw one another, there was an affectionate shared smile, a brief moment where I wondered what life would have been like spent with her...

Ken, The Sequel
Winter 1996

Her relationship had started on a steady decline of resentment and bitterness after the 'sexual experimentation'. The secure, loving, heterosexual home that once existed was melting away and the raw flesh underneath was being exposed more every day. Screaming matches ensued almost daily and inevitably and would result in Hannah running away for hours at a time or retreating to the basement, curling up into a ball and sobbing with wild abandon. Her internal struggle sent her on a blatant path of destruction. Every time she looked at Ken she wanted to scratch his eyes right out of his sockets with her jagged fingernails.

Dean
Spring 1997

One desperate summer night Hannah went to a pub on Whyte Avenue with her girlfriend Lana. She was in self destruct mode and tried to steady her head so it wouldn't spin right off and fly across the room. As she sat at the table she and her single girlfriend were given complimentary drinks from two guys that sat at the end of the bar. Lana had silicone implants and long, bouncy curls which always drew a tremendous amount of attention to the girls every time they went out. One of the guys was bald, athletic and had a stunning face, the other had dark hair and olive coloured skin. The girls motioned for them to come over and as the men started to approach Hannah slid her hand under the table and yanked her engagement ring off of her finger, sliding it casually into the pocket of her taut embroidered jeans.

The girls ended up going home with the guys and as the night progressed she got more inebriated. She ended up in Dean's bed. As they went through the motions, her desperate raw emotions were regurgitated in passionate yelps. She had stepped over the line and knew this moment sealed her fate. While still naked and covered in the sweat of her act she told Dean through her tears that she needed to use the phone. He said, "Do you want to get dressed first?" "No, I have to do it now or I'll lose my nerve." She choked through her tears wrapping the damp cotton sheet around her tremulous body. She called Ken and admitted everything full stop. His anger mimicked a disappointed father rather than a jilted fiancée, confirming what Hannah already knew in her heart.

The relationship dissolved the following day, all the blame falling on Hannah's shoulders: none of the violations Ken committed showing up even as a blip on the radar of betrayal. His family knew what she had done and they despised her for it. She packed up all the beautiful gifts they had given her over their six years together and set the boxes in the golden Victorian alcove by the front door. The last time she would set foot in 'her' dream house; her gift from Renee, an old man she had cleaned for and loved as a Grandfather for years.

Renee had been her confidant for the two years she cleaned for him weekly and had passed away abruptly alone in his trailer with his dog Bobby. He had no family so Hannah's kindness had touched him and brought some light to his lonely life. They had met while she was working at Superstore one day. When she learned of his inability to get groceries or clean for himself she volunteered to help him out. When he passed he left her an inheritance which covered the cost of a down payment for her little 1928 Victorian in Northwest Edmonton.

There she stood in the doorway and tried to soak in every wall, every baseboard, and every vibrant colour that she had created so that she could hold it in her memory forever. All the fight in her had disintegrated; it was her alone against Ken and his family. She stayed with her girlfriend from Thorncrest Sarina while she looked for a place to live. Because of what <u>she</u> had done she was forced to move out of the house that had been purchased by her in the first place. She moved into a Frankenstein house (an old twenties bungalow attached to a brand new home) with seven other University students. Most of her furniture and other belongings had been stripped from her or given away. When she got into her room at her new place she started opening the boxes. All of the gifts and photos she had carefully placed in the boxes from Ken's family were removed, punishing her by ripping away the only memories she had left of them… She felt like she was standing naked in front of a room full of dirty old men... She wanted to escape and turn back time...She wanted to melt into Ken's mom's arms and reveal what Ken did with his friend and how he had started this war between them.

Proposition

With the chains of stability loosed, Hannah went down a path of explosive sexual reckoning. Her eyes gleamed with desire and her body ached with wanton intensity: an intensity that was impossible to contain. Anyone that fed her attention was reeled into her self-satisfying, self-deprecating sexual spree.

The Return of Alexis .M.
Winter 1998

Several years had passed since Hannah's last night with Alexis. She had met a man that she thought was worth giving him up for. In her heart she knew Alexis was out of her league and that all he had to offer was their secret affair. He remained a distant memory.

While she was walking through the halls of the Hub Mall at the University of Alberta, swarms of people, bright lights, and multi-coloured stimulation assaulted her senses, choking the breath out of her constricted lungs. She felt reality slowly seeping out of her grasp, images of vibrant, chaotic colours spinning and sharp like an angry abstract painting that has come alive and taken up residence in her brain. A tap on the shoulder caused her to snap back into reality. As she spun around she felt like Wonder Woman, transforming for her task. There facing her was an older, more manly version of the man she used to visit on lonely nights after drinking at the bar. Alexis's smile was comforting and familiar, as though he was genuinely glad to see her. Within her she felt a glimmer of hope that maybe they could reconnect and now that she was officially a woman and that he would be interested in starting something more than a sexual affair. He asked her if she'd like to go for supper at "Tiki Tiki Thai" Restaurant on Whyte Avenue the next night at eight o'clock. Overzealous and attempting to flaunt her new found self-esteem she said, "Oh! I think I'm available, just let me check my day timer." She ruffled around in her bag for an extended period because she wanted to draw out the time she was in his vicinity. Just being near him made her blush, his sexuality was insatiable.

The "Tiki Tiki Thai" Restaurant turned out to be tacky, tacky with its red plastic water glasses and scalloped paper menu placemats, educating customers with cheesy diagrams and explanations of the Chinese Zodiac. I was a Tiger, "the supreme emblem of protection over human life, admirable always." He was a Rat, "whose natural charisma attracts members of the opposite sex like wildfire." The overhead florescent lights that littered the drop down ceiling above made Hannah feel overexposed and nauseous. Their silent buzzing seemed amplified by about 100 times. She struggled to contain her urge to run screaming into the frigid winter night. Her fantasy date with Alexis; complete with vases of fresh orchids, linen tablecloths and napkins, wine glasses for water, and tea lights casting a warm glow on her, was as likely as the ticky, tacky thai food being fresh at this place. The mood and content of their conversation was fairly general so Hannah was confused about where the night was leading. Did he just want to be friends? Was he just feeding her so he could have a fuck for dessert? What was the deal?

After they had eaten their appalling processed pad Thai, made with a medley of frozen green giant corn, peas and carrots and spaghetti noodles, Alexis wiped his face with his tiny, transparent paper napkin and came right out with it...

"Hannah, my girlfriend and I have been wanting to experiment sexually with another woman. You used to work with her at Maxwell Taylors, her name is Gabrielle, and she has long blonde hair. Do you remember her?"

The only girl I remembered with that name and hair was a prissy, Mormon girl who used to brag about how virginal she was...definitely not the woman he was describing..."I don't think I remember her Alexis. What are you asking me here?"

"Well, we both think you'd be the perfect woman to join us for a threesome."

I was so disgusted I felt like I was going to melt like a cheap, dollar store candle and end up a steaming hot pool of wax...I felt worthless, yet honored that Alexis was inviting me back into his bed after a seven year absence, in a warped way...The art of saying no had not been mastered by me and the forethought of how it may affect me in a negative way drifted away, far from my grasp..I said...

"Sure Alexis, sounds great!"

Did that just come out of my mouth? I said that as though he was asking me to play tennis with him at the Kinsmen Sports Centre on Friday.

"Great! Gaby is going to be so happy that you agreed to do this; she feels better knowing that it is someone she knows. She thinks you're hot too so it'll be fun." He scrawled his address out with a thin, black Sharpie on one of those cheap napkins, delicately so that it would not tear and bleed. Had his fragility with the napkin been applied to her emotions, her state of mind would have remained stable. To him she was just a good lay who apparently was willing to experiment anytime with anyone. She felt exposed, like a piece of raw meat dangling on a meat hook in the freezer of a butcher awaiting its fate of being chopped into smaller pieces and fed to hungry carnivores.

Threesome night was upon her and she was finding it harder and harder to stay in reality. She wasn't sure what was real and what was hallucination, paranoia or illusion. As if being possessed by charlatans she washed, primped and dressed for her 'manage a trois'. Secretly she felt a thrill just knowing she would be with Alexis for one last night. He was by far the best lover she had ever had. He was so unselfish and aimed to please his women before coming to his own conclusion. Her hunger for sex lately had been insatiable and she couldn't understand it, emotionally it was the last thing she wanted, but physically her body ached for it all the time.

She reached the door and heard a dog barking ferociously and scraping at the door. A couple minutes later Alexis opened the door, holding the panting chocolate lab at his side. He smiled genuinely at her and gave her a one armed hug. If only it was just the two of them…He led her down a brightly lit hallway down a few stairs into a sunken living room painted a deep crimson with bare walls and a large, black leather couch on the left wall. He motioned for her to sit and he called out, "Gaby, she's here!" his voice echoed…

My stomach flutters as I hear her approaching; I am not sure what I am supposed to say, "Hey! Let's get busy?" No that wouldn't work, "Do you have any questions?" As she enters the room I realize that Gaby is an older, swankier version of the Mormon virgin from my old work. I remember her ordering drinks from my mini back bar in the restaurant and being a real snob. She had always treated me like I was a second class citizen because I was working next to the kitchen and my only job was to provide the waiters and waitresses with their drinks for the restaurant patrons. I was later promoted to the bar in the lounge, but whatever…maybe she had changed, she knew who I was obviously…apparently she was no longer the self righteous virgin I had once known…

No time was spent with idle chit chat; they just looked at one another, nodded and took turns necking with me. The only female kiss I had ever had was Danika's; her kiss was more masculine, hungrier. Gaby was gentle and polite with her kiss, there was definitely a difference. It was actually nice. They led me to Alexis's darkened bedroom; the only light was the faint flickering of a taper candle. Clothes were removed slowly and bodies were explored with roaming hands and lips. I felt exposed and scared that I may not be able to perform under this much pressure. Gaby kept climbing on top of Alexis and leaving me to sit on the edge of the bed, naked and uncomfortable, not knowing what to do, not wanting to be impolite or too assertive. Jealousy seeped in over the fact that she was the 'girlfriend' and I was just the third party that Alexis happened to run into. Rapid thoughts of inadequacy consumed my psyche. Alexis noticed when I sat off to the side and would motion for me to come close so he could kiss me or her. He wanted us to make out in front of him and we went through the motions but I could feel her resentment in the abrupt way that she handled me. I'm sure she felt it reciprocated…

Gaby was living with her parents and had a curfew, (strange for a 25 year old) but of course I had no one waiting for me at home. I was a free woman with no attachments, no family waiting or caring about what I was doing. In truth the thought of it made me melancholy. Even though Ken was an egotistical pig at times, at least I had experienced a true family. I insisted on staying the night at Alexis's. He didn't even try to reject me knowing that he owed me at least the façade of what I longed for. We slept naked and I spooned him as tears gently rolled down my cheeks. I stayed awake all night as he slept deeply, free of conscious thought…the demons kept me company that night as I clung to a man that would never let me into his circle…

THE HEALING BEGINS

"The darkness of the cocoon was unfamiliar and confining. It was difficult for her to breathe and her majestic end seemed far out of grasp" Emily Lutze

Regaining Trust

Summer 1995

Hannah entered the dimly lit room with her head down; she raised her head up just enough to see the circle of cushions bathed in vibrantly coloured sari fabrics. With her head bent down it was easier for her to avoid eye contact with the other women in the room. Her impulse was to turn around and sprint out into the fiercely lit hallway, swing open the front door that was labeled "Sexual Assault Centre" in bold, purple, capital letters, and leap down the stairs doing double time. She thought that if she ran she would not have to face her demons and that they could continue to lie buried deep within her somewhere. Night terrors and intensely visual memories of years of abuse haunted her every waking moment over the last few months. It was as though they were trying to escape, or even worse, swallow her whole. The inner demons that consumed her were being suppressed by the illuminated ad that lined the upper portion of the Edmonton transit bus. When she saw it, at first she quickly glanced and then hid her face in her hands. It taunted her with its promise of dissolution. After a few moments she slowly pulled a tiny, lined notepad out of her canvas purse and dug for a pen. She rummaged around in her purse ferociously knowing that if she didn't find a pen her hope for release may be lost forever, Ha-ha! She found a brown eyeliner pencil that would work! She quickly scrawled the number out on the back of her bus transfer and labeled it 'SAC' so that no one would know who belonged to the number.

Her peripheral vision allowed her to glimpse at the crossed legs of a few pairs of women, some slim and some portly, some old and some smooth and new. She had never met anyone who had been through what she had, and now she was in a room full of women that had suffered the same doom. All of these women were there ready to expose themselves to one another. She was terrified to speak, and she was not alone, the room was eerily silent and the air was so thick Hannah found it laborious to breathe. All of a sudden the air was sliced open by the cheery voice of a woman…

"I know that all of you have experienced the worst violation a woman can and I want you to know that inside this room you are safe. No one will judge you or reveal what you have shared here. What goes on here stays within these four walls. If there is an activity or process that you are not comfortable doing, please do not do it. You are only to do what is comfortable for you. All of us, yes, including me in this room have been scarred by sexual abuse and this is a forum for all of you to connect and release the pain that you have buried deep within you. If you keep yourself open to the exercises and try not to fear them you will probably gain more from this experience. You are all here on your own accord, so that is a powerful sign that you want to take back your life. This is your time to regain trust with others, and to rebuild your shattered image of yourself. Use this experience to take you into the pain in order for you to release it into the universe. This room is a safe haven for all of us, and I now ask you to please respect one another and yourselves by truly listening to your soul's voice."

As I sat on the smooth, overstuffed cushion I felt an energy pulling my head back down. I was not ready to look at the other women's faces. The intense compassion that existed within my heart was drifting on the surface and I knew if I looked into the eyes of one of these women, the feeling would be so intense that I would collapse. Collapse with relief at finally finding a sisterhood of women who would share with me my first attempt at revealing all of the pain that was hidden behind my bright, shining façade. The only people that knew the truth were the members of my family, Ken's family and a chosen few friends. Every relationship I had been in was instantly tarnished by horrific memories as soon as it became intimate. Each time a lover touched me I clenched up and felt like I was their victim. The treacherous dance of sexuality was a game of cat and mouse that ensued between my unquiet mind and my soul. Intimacy had become terrifying and extremely unpleasant and my boyfriends would eventually catch on and lose patience with me. In the end I would end up alone once again, left to smolder in the fires of victimhood…

Sharlene, the group leader had a warm, nurturing presence about her; her bouncy, blond, shoulder length curls and her bright red angora sweater made her complexion glow. The first thing she asked us to do was to go around the room and tell everyone our name and something about ourselves. I was not the only one with trepidation in my face, some of the other women were fidgeting and I could see a look of fear spread across their faces. When it was safe I scanned the room discretely and one woman, sitting in the lotus position right across from me, caught my eye. She had long, wavy, blond hair, and she was dressed in a crushed velvet, patchwork dress in jewel tones, with thick beige tights. She was slender and stunning and she was the only woman in the room that seemed to have an air of confidence about her other than Sharlene. She must have sensed me staring at her, so all of a sudden she turned and looked me directly in the eye, I was about to look away and then she smiled and nodded to me, I smiled back and the feeling that we were meant to meet today surged through me...

The introduction circle reached the long, blond haired woman first and she said, "My name is Lola and I am a teacher and a single mother, I came here to try and resolve the pain in my heart..." Each woman had their own story, some chose to reveal more intimate details about themselves, but I gave a choked, rote response, "Hi, my name is Hannah and I am a student at the University of Alberta, I think this is where I am supposed to be..." After every woman had shared, it was time for the next exercise. Sharlene pointed to two blank charts on each of the four walls of the room, she asked us to take five minutes at each chart and write an honest answer. These answers would stay anonymous because we would all be writing with the same, black marker. I tried to squint my eyes and see what the question was on the top of the sheet that was posted directly in front of me, but the dim lighting made it difficult to make out. Before writing Sharlene led us through a relaxation exercise that grounded us and reminded us to stay in the present as much as possible. She told us to open our eyes and then choose a chart. I walked to the one across the room, and it read: "Did your abuser(s) use any threats to keep you from telling? If so, what?" I was scared to write the answer down, because I had never told anyone before, but as I wrote the answer down I felt a flood of relief rush through my body and soul: "He threatened to kill me and my family." The next question was, "How has the abuse affected your intimate relationships?" This answer was one that came easy. It was almost as if these questions were designed to show us what the abuse has done and that abusers use the same techniques to keep you down. Sharlene told us that these were the same techniques that torturers used. With each question that I answered I felt like tiny pieces of the abuse were flying off of me, floating into the atmosphere to be swallowed up by the universe. I still averted my eyes from the other participants answers because

I felt that it would be a huge violation to peek at them. Then I accidentally saw an answer that would haunt me for years to come. The question was, "Who was your abuser (abusers)?" The answer was scrawled in hand writing that was tiny and barely legible…"All the male members of the cult took turns with all of us girls, each night was filled with horror…" Her answers were all over the room and I couldn't stop myself from squinting my eyes and trying to read them. This woman was an astounding person; she had come out of that situation alive and seeking help today with me. For the next ten weeks I tried to figure out who she was. I had a lot to learn from her, and the more I did learn the more my situation felt paler; not insignificant, but a little less horrific…

After each exercise we were given time to discuss problems, concerns or comments we had and then we were given a break. There was a tiny smoking room down the hall with a tiny square fan on the roof for ventilation. The walls were covered in a thick layer of pale yellow nicotine from all the years of abused woman exhaling out their pain in the form of a tobacco haze. I looked forward to our breaks because in that tiny room we instantly connected, even though we were very different women, we had the same experience and that made us sisters.

My first night of sleep after the first session at the SAC was riddled with nightmares about my stuff intermingled with the other participants stuff and I woke up in a cold sweat more than once. My relationship with Ken was still in the Honeymoon stages and I tried not to let all that overwhelmed me come into it. Whenever he tried to get intimate with me I would well up with tears and pull away. Flashbacks of the repeated abuse would invade my mind and strip me away from reality. He tried very hard to be understanding but the turmoil that I endured put a strain on our relationship. I just knew that this was what I needed to do at the time to move past it. My journal became my confidant, my best friend. Every time I awoke with terror I would sit up, turn the free standing lamp beside the couch and scribble out my feelings and memories in my journal. Writing became a vehicle, releasing the past, clearing out my mind and soul for the future…

My second week at the SAC was one of the most poignant because I decided if this therapy was going to work I would need to expose my wounds and head in full force. Our first exercise sounds simple, but it was the most difficult thing I have ever been asked to do. Sharlene announced our first exercise for the day, "I want you all to stand in a circle and say "NO!"We all stood in a circle and Sharlene said, "OK go!" There was silence that was so thick you couldn't have cut the air with a chainsaw. As I stood there waiting for someone to say it, I felt my body start to tremble. None of us could say that one innocent two-letter word. We had all been paralyzed by our captors and forced into the lonely world of silence and submission. Finally I heard someone whisper, "No!" We all lifted our heads slightly, in unison to look and see who it was, it was Lola and she had tears rolling down her face. Other women started off by whispering the word and then gradually the sound of all of their unique voices saying "No!" in different tones, and at a range of volumes shook me with elation mixed with paralyzing fear. I was the only one left in the room that remained silent. My mouth was forming the word but all that came out of my mouth was a pulse of forced air. I tried to join in the chorus because I knew by looking at the other women in the room that they were finally being set free. I so wanted that for myself. Women were wailing and screaming "NO!" all around me and I still could not get the word to escape from my lips. I never thought I had enough worth to be allowed to say it and now I was being given permission and I couldn't do it. Sharlene was looking at me and tears started to roll down her cheeks, as I looked at her sheepishly she mouthed the words, "It's OK, I give you permission to say NO! You can do it Hannah!" I collapsed onto the floor in the middle of the circle of women whooping "NO!" and wailing and I squeaked out the smallest "No!" I felt a gush of relief exit my body through my mouth and I felt a power surge through me. I stared up at the ceiling and I yelled, "NO!" and then I sobbed uncontrollably until the exercise was over and everyone sat around me saying words of encouragement and patting me on the back, "You go girl, good job Hannah! You did it!" If I didn't know it before, I knew now that these women would change the path of my life forever...

Court

Spring-Summer 1995

Group therapy at the Sexual Assault Centre liberated me to a point where I was ready to fight back. Ross had stripped my soul and destroyed me at such a young age. He had turned four years of my life black. I had no memories left of that time that were not tainted by his evil. The women in that group offered me the strength to take my stepfather to court for what he had done to me.

On the eve before my twenty-first birthday I was in a hotel room, back in Newmarket, Ontario awaiting one of the most difficult days I would ever face. My siblings were there with me and my mom came to visit. My sister had brought her first child, a ten month old baby boy, because he was still being nursed. We had gone to my mom's to stay but had gotten in a fight with Daniel over what we were going to say about mom. He asked us to leave and we had to go find the hotel room late in the evening. His only concern was for my mom's reputation in that town. She was still there, we were gone and we were supposed to protect her. We were aghast at the fact that all he cared about was protecting my mom, with no concern for how we may have been feeling. This had been the formula throughout our childhood and the reason mom stayed with Ross for as long as she did. Why should I have expected more?

In the morning there was a knock at the door, a housekeeper walked in with a bouquet of long stemmed, deep crimson roses from Ken. On the card the florist had scribed for him said: "My heart is with you, you are doing the right thing, we all love you, be strong, and Happy Birthday Emily, xo Ken."

I walked into the courthouse, my legs wobbling from the terror I felt growing deeper inside of me. Lou Lou had one hand and Jory had the other. They tried to keep things light but inside I was dying. From the corner of my eye I saw him. Ross was wearing the same pale blue suit he wore when my mom married him. I heard his nasally voice and collapsed in my siblings arms. They half dragged and half pulled me into a hidden hallway and helped me gather myself. I broke into tears and they consoled me saying, "You don't want him to think he's won, stay strong."

After four years and three trips to Newmarket to face the man that destroyed me we received the verdict. He was charged with the crime of Sexual Assault but let off on what they called 'Compassionate Grounds'. The grounds being his parents had both died and he was penniless and apparently the trial had incurred a deep depression. The court felt he had been punished enough by life. BLECH! BLECH! BLECH!

After the sentencing Lou Lou and I wrote a letter explaining what had occurred and sent it to over 200 government officials; MLA's, Lawyers, Judicial Boards, even the Supreme Court and we received only one response. It was a form letter stating that this was not in her jurisdiction and was signed by an Edmonton MLA who I can't name.

This is something that I never speak of to anyone. My blood boils when I think about all that he put us through. Not only did our mother betray us by keeping us in that hell, but so did the very 'Justice System' that is supposed to protect the victims of these heinous crimes.

My Journey into Madness

A Letter to Professor Walsh, University of Alberta

Introduction

March, 20, 2000
Dear Professor Walsh:

It has taken quite a while to write this piece. After meeting with you several weeks ago I started it. After one and a half pages I lost the ability to spell words, a skill that has been as natural to me as breathing throughout the years. Even simple words like: *terrible* and *strength* felt foreign as I scratched them down on the page. My doctor explained that this is part of the healing process, relearning skills and starting from scratch again. I must say I was quite discouraged by this so it took a lot for me to come back to it (sleeping 23 hours of each day didn't help matters either). I have also been experiencing tremors in my hands similar to someone with Parkinson's due to the Lithium Carbonate I am on; this side effect makes it very difficult to type. When I finally was able to write this piece it was a very therapeutic and enlightening experience as I have not spoken about what happened to anyone. You may wonder why it is you that I chose to share this information with; you will receive your answer upon reading my story...

Sincerely,

Hannah Rush

For as long as I can remember I have lived at mock speed; holding down multiple jobs, volunteering, going to school, being in relationships and having numerous hobbies as well. I never stopped because every time I stopped it felt as though I was being suffocated by depression, paranoia and self loathing. There was always darkness within me that I hid from the rest of the world. This darkness revealed itself only when I was alone. If I was busy every second of the day those dark undiscovered crevices of my mind were not revealed to my conscious mind.

Over a month ago when I was in your APT class, preparing myself for my final teaching practicum, I was starting to fade in and out of reality. I began retreating from social situations and avoiding friends and family for fear they may notice something peculiar. I stopped speaking out in class because the room would start spinning and I felt it took all my energy just to keep my bearings enough not to start screaming. My ability to focus on readings and discussions was nonexistent as the words just swirled around on the page and even upon multiple readings the information would not be absorbed. My sensitivity to noise was unbearable; voices were loud and words took on a cacophonic quality. Background noises blended with chatter and became overpowering and exhausting to listen to. I lost the ability to sleep…food made me gag…and fluids took on a bleach-like aroma and an arsenic taste.

During the last week of class, my mood all of a sudden shifted. My brain would race so fast at night that I would hold onto anything that was adhered to the earth and try to center myself. None of my usual stress relievers; yoga, meditation, hot baths, relaxation tapes would put my mind to rest. After witnessing my mother's 'nervous breakdowns' my instinct told me this is where I was headed. I knew I needed to seek help but I was too afraid that my brother and sister would compare me to our mother; so I resisted that one final rational instinct.

On Wednesday, January 27, 2000 everything finally came to a head. I had a final exam the next day and still had ten chapters to read and learn. When I was reading my textbook the words just blurred and bled together. The fear started to spread throughout my body and panic took over. With only ten hours until the paper was placed in front of me there was a huge sense of urgency. Persistent, I read the same page over and over for more than an hour, nothing sunk in, I still had no idea what it was about…

Then I received the phone call that would send me over the edge…It was my University Facilitator and she was very cruel on the phone. She said that I would be transferred to a different school and got frustrated because I had to get her to repeat the information several times. Due to my incoherence she thought I was under the influence so thought she could get away with being verbally abusive. After slamming down the receiver I raced around the house franticly sobbing, I called several friends to seek counseling and try to make sense of what had just transpired. When there was no one left to call, still terrified, I had a hot bath, smoked five cigarettes and tried to get ready for sleep. The sound of the innocent bubbles popping close to my ears, amplified, mimicked the sound of fingers down a chalkboard. I hoped that I had enough information absorbed from my course that I could do some cramming the next day prior to the exam.

As I lay on my mattress, shivering as my sopping hair bled into my pillow, my mind refused to stop racing. I attempted to seek solace by reading my 'Spiritual Journal'. Those words were crystal clear; it felt as though the words were directed at me. Yearning for more I gazed at the mirror above my bed searching for answers. As crazy (no pun intended) as it may seem, your face was reflected to me in my headboard mirror whispering, "The time has come for you to go to Africa." You said that the yearning I had been having my entire life was about to come to fruition. This mystical country had been in my dreams and fantasies since childhood, some magnetic force pulling me towards it. It was at that moment that I knew the themed "Africa" curriculum you had been sharing with the class for the past few weeks was directed at me. You were like a mentor prepping me for my journey there. As your spirit spoke, pushing me to pack up my belongings and go, anger rose up in me like stale vomit that rises into your mouth when you've overeaten and you bend forward abruptly. I sobbed "I am scared to leave my friends and family." You responded by insisting it was the right time, you said "you're one of us now Hannah, you must go."

I was so terrified by this that I got dressed, threw on my wool sweater and haphazardly gathered my sopping wet hair and strangled it with a thick, blue elastic. I staggered around the dimly lit neighborhood stifling my sobs, talking to myself, laughing sporadically and contemplating what to do for about two hours. I started to walk towards the University hospital with a visualization of admitting myself into the Psyche Ward. I reached the florescent beacon highlighting the glass doors of the Emergency entrance, and then I spun myself around sobbing, unaware of what to do. Fears of what my brother and sister would do if they diagnosed me with the same disease as our estranged mother rose up in my scattered mind. Questions like: "Will they stop loving me and see our mother in my eyes? Will they stop respecting me? What if they abandon me and leave me all alone?" Screamed and invaded my psyche: "I don't need to go to the hospital. I'm just having a bad day. I can do this, I am pretty resilient." Denying my strongest instincts I turned in the opposite direction of the hospital, my walk turned into a sprint as I re-entered the unpredictable twilight.

I ended up at the Mac's on the corner of 109 Street and 82nd Avenue. As I approached the store I had a sinking feeling that there was an evil presence close by. I ran hunchbacked into the store with my head down. A pleasant looking man was behind the till and noticed my fear. He said "Is everything OK Madam?" I hid behind the chocolate bar rack and whispered hoarsely, "there is evil lurking in the parking lot, shhhhhhh, shhhhhhh, don't tell anyone I'm here!" Looking at me with the most peculiar look he said, "Well, OK, did someone hurt you?" I responded with, "shhhhhhhh, shhhhhhhh, please don't talk to me, they'll see me!" When the coast was clear and there was no one left at the gas station the man at the till said, "Madam, everyone has left, are you going to go now?" Sheepishly, still whispering warnings to myself I skittered out of the gas station and sprinted home as fast as I could, running from the tangible fear.

I walked home and filled my suitcase with thrift store clothes I had been collecting for years but had never worn. Subconsciously, I had been saving them for my trip to Africa. These were vibrant dresses in beautiful jewel tones covered in whimsical patterns and designs. Consisting of translucent fabrics and eclectic design principles, these dresses were perfect for my journey; they were the dresses my spirit self always yearned to wear but my rational self had been too shy to wear; clothes that would announce to the world that I was different or unusual.

The remainder of the suitcase was filled with all my spiritual texts, pictures of my family, candles, 'Nag Champa' incense, and my most beautiful writing paper. I quickly scrawled out a note on my desk stating:

> I Am Well,
> I Am ALIVE!!!
> Take Whatever You Need.
> Everything Will Be Taken Care Of.
> You All Gave Me The Tools I Need.
> It Is Time For Me To Go On My Journey.
> THANK YOU, I Love You All,
> *Hannah*

I then lugged my suitcase down the stairs, trying to be as quiet as possible as the suitcase scraped against the sides of the narrow stairwell. On my last trip of several from the house to the car I looked down and noticed one of my books, *Wouldn't Take Nothing for My Journey Now*, by Maya Angelou, lying face up on the icy ground. I picked it up, dusted off the delicate layer of fresh snow and held it to my racing heart. As I stood outside in the crisp, dark night; I stared up at the moon and said, "I am doing the right thing. There are so many signs." As I reached the car I started to frantically search for my keys, finally realizing that I had locked them in the car. Frustrated, I started to sob uncontrollably yelling, "JUST LET ME GO!" I thought that all those who loved me were somehow holding me back. Instinctually I knew that if I left I would never return. Yearning so badly to say good-bye, but knowing they would never let me leave. Or worse, my fate would be to rot in a Psyche Ward somewhere. All of a sudden I realized I had a spare key in a miniature folk art dresser on the kitchen counter. When I finally got into the car, I turned the key and the car refused to respond to my urgent requests to leave. After spitting and struggling, the sleepy ignition choked loudly and ignited. I laid my head on the steering wheel, partly excited and partly terrified and began to sob, "JUST LET ME GO! I LOVE YOU ALL! KNOW THAT AND LET ME GO!" I still had a deep sense that a force was holding me back, so the sobs transformed into shrill screams. Finally when I regained control, I left...

My home...my family...they did love me...my career...my passions...my need to help everyone...the children at the group home...my dear friends... my kindred spirit...

Thoughts of leaving these things and people caused a mixture of intense emotions. One second I'd be laughing over a memory and the next I'd be screaming and sobbing over the loss of those precious to me. As I was driving I felt as though someone else had taken control of the vehicle. I kept trying to head west but a strong subconscious influence would take over and I would find myself doing a U-Turn in the opposite direction, back towards the city. It seemed like the car was on auto-pilot and was taking me on a circular journey of discovery. As if in a hypnotic state I drove to everyone's house and sat outside in my little, brown, 80's Honda Civic, where upon I would cry and pray for them. I even ended up at my ex-fiancée Ken's brother's house in Sherwood Park (I had never driven there myself so I still don't know how it was that I ended up there). Divine intervention was the only explanation for these circumstances.

After stopping in the cul-de-sac (by now it was dawn) I stepped out of the car and walked onto a meridian in the centre of this suburban circle, I took down my weathered blue jeans and purple panties and urinated right there.

Twelve hours later, something changed. I could not understand why I was unable to leave the city, so I tried to make sense of it. I quickly changed the focus of my purpose; it must have been to stay in Edmonton, drive my car all over the city without being seen, doing good deeds and helping people. I truly believed that God had sent me on this mission.

For the next ten hours I drove around searching for someone in need of aid. If I was thirsty I would stop the car abruptly and shovel a handful of snow from the side of the road into my mouth.

All of a sudden I came across a school bus stuck in a ditch, so I stopped, got out of my car and walked directly onto the opened bus. There was a little boy with large, round, wire rimmed glasses on the bus, I looked at him lovingly and said, "Come here child I will guide you to safety!" He backed away from me with a frightened smirk on his five year old face. So I walked towards him and said, "Don't be scared, I'm an Angel." From behind me I heard a women's voice urgently say in a strained tone, "We have help coming ma'am, we don't need your help, please leave!" I turned to look at her and she was pointing to the door. I asked no questions, I simply turned around and walked off the bus. When I got to the car I felt an undeniable sadness wash over me, I questioned my purpose and yelled at the sky, "Is this all there is, I didn't even help anyone!" I received no reply, so I sullenly continued on my way.

Knowing that I should probably drink something and go pee again I looked for some kind of rest stop. After looking for about 20 minutes I noticed a rundown gas station on the side of the road. The clapboard building was leaning slightly and was a faded paint chipped white with red trim; there was an faded old west mural of a buffalo standing in an infinite field of canola painted on the left side of the building. A sign dangling over the wood trimmed screen door with rusty hinges reading: *Hobbema Gas and Food Stop.* Noticing that mine was the only car in the parking lot I wondered whether this place was abandoned. The interior door was open and I heard the sound of muffled voices. Feeling paranoid I came to the conclusion that I would just walk in and walk right to the bathroom so I could avoid talking to anyone. I wasn't sure how comprehensible my speech would be.

With great hesitation I walked into the store with my head down, I noticed a group of feet gathered in front of what must have been the checkout counter. Poking my head up just long enough to see that the bathroom was directly in front of me I quickened my pace and reached for the grimy handle. I turned the knob, but it wouldn't budge, I wiggled the stubborn knob several times to get it to open and felt the panic starting to rise. Tears started streaming down my face when the lady at the counter hollered, "Hey you! Lady, da door's locked, you need dis key ere." I slowly turned around and walked towards the group of Native men and women. They all looked at me as though I was high or a nut, so I grabbed the key quickly and said, "Thanks." A foul smell wafted towards me as I opened the creaky door of the unisex bathroom. The dank blend of stale urine mixed with a pungent, strawberry air freshener assaulted me as I entered the bathroom. Trying not to vomit, I yanked my pants and panties down and sat on the dingy toilet with the smallest section of my ass as possible. I pushed the urine out at lightning speed, got dressed, ran out of the store yelling "Thanks", and peeled off in my little brown car.

Day turned into night once more. Time was full of holes as I drove down a barren dirt road. I saw a whole bunch of towers with brilliant white and red lights twinkling on them in the distance. I drove towards this place as it was drawing me in. As I pulled in I drove down a long gravel driveway. There were numerous service vehicles and a group of men in multicoloured hard hats standing in a group. I got out of the car, walked up to the men and said, "I feel that your souls are lost, is everything O.K. here?"
They looked at me and each other in a strange, uncomfortable way and said, "Yes, were fine!"
I replied, "Are you sure no one is hurting; everything is O.K.?"
They began to stifle their laughter as they looked at each other quizzically, one husky, black haired man with a goatee said gruffly, "Um…Ya lady, we're O.K., now go back to where ya came from."
A feeling of discomfort rose up in my throat and I spun around and sprinted back to the safety of my little brown car. I skidded away leaving a trail of gravel dust in my absence.
My journey resumed, but by that point I was beginning to feel very let down. I could not understand why no one was responding to my offer of help. I began to aimlessly drive around, unsure of where I was, sticking my head periodically out the window to gaze at the full moon that was following alongside me.

After about an hour I drove by a sign that said *AQUALTA* and had an arrow pointing down a hill on the right. I headed down the hill robotically. At the bottom there were large iron gates and signs stating "No Unauthorized Vehicles, This Gate Is Monitored by Video Surveillance." There were also several signs stating "ENTER AT YOUR OWN RISK!" I got out of the car and yanked the heavy gates open with all the strength I could muster, then drove through and parked my car in a parking lot in front of the building. I got out of my car and headed towards the door. I noticed that no lights were on and the door was locked, so I was confused to why I was brought there. I walked around the building looking in the windows, only to find nothing, so I returned to my car and exited the gates. I drove for a while, not even knowing where I was. Suddenly I came upon the *AQUALTA* sign again with a feeling that there must be something outside myself directing me here; so I repeated the previous routine. I drove out the gates and around the area again for about 20 minutes and for a third time I came upon that sign. I repeated the procedure once again curious as to why I subconsciously kept coming back there. After getting out of the car and banging on the windows, I realized that there was no one there. I didn't really know what time it was, but my instinct was telling me to get out of there.

After exiting the gates a third time, frustrated and unsure I resumed my aimless itinerary. I ended up on Calgary Trail Southbound. As I drove towards the end of Edmonton my radio turned on and bits and pieces of some of the most meaningful songs in my life started playing; I was not even turning the dial. I never heard any song in its entirety, but each one had a message from one of my family members. It felt as though each person that meant something to me took turns relaying a message; the most powerful being the song *Angel* by Sarah McLaughlin. She was telling me about a journey and her words comforted me:

> *In the arms of the angel*
> *Fly away from here*
> *From this dark, cold hotel room*
> *And the endlessness that you fear*
> *You are pulled from the wreckage*
> *Of your silent reverie*
> *You're in the arms of the angel*
> *May you find some comfort there...*

I was touched by the words and began to sob uncontrollably. The meaning of that song was not yet apparent to me.

Noticing the tourism building at the southern entrance to Edmonton, I suddenly felt the urge to urinate. I had driven for what seemed like days and not stopped for gas, yet mysteriously there was still ¾ of a tank left. Night melded into day in my oblivious stupor. I went into the A-Frame Tourist Centre parking lot and began to hear the voices of all my loved ones dead and alive; they were telling me that my purpose was to take their journeys for them. As I walked into the reception area I noticed a colourful display of travel fliers. As I began taking them one at a time out of their holders voices in my head were accompanying each flier; Ken wanted to go to Kananaskis and ride horses like we had done together years ago; Jory's wife Lily wanted to go to Jasper and ride the gondola up the mountain; Lou Lou and her husband Eddy wanted to take their two kids to Drumheller to see the dinosaurs and fossils…By the time all the voices stopped I had filed at least a dozen more fliers in my hands. Luckily I had avoided any human contact as I ducked into the bathroom. Taking a long stare into my puffy eyes I noticed an internal glow as I smiled to myself and said aloud, "Don't worry everyone; I'll take you on your journeys, I Love You All! You're all with Me!"

I had only driven two minutes down the highway when I noticed a hitchhiker standing on the side of the road with his grubby backpack slung over his left shoulder and his thumb up in the air. His flimsy cardboard sign had become illegible as the snow littered it with moist flakes. I quickly pulled over to the right shoulder, screeched to a halt and flung open the door. Something inside made me stop; I thought this was my destiny. He ran up to the door and poked his head in, "Where ya headed?"

"Wherever you want to go!" I replied in a friendly tone.

"I'm going to Lake Louise."

"Get in" I replied to the skinny, freckle-faced, grungy, twenty something guy with a head of untamed fiery red hair.

Once we began driving I felt uncomfortable in his presence, I was questioning whether this was a bad idea. He kept trying to make small talk and I just wasn't in the mood for idle conversation. Starting to resent the fact that he had halted the elation I had been feeling earlier, I turned to him and snapped, "Look, I don't want you to talk to me, I'm giving you a ride, if I'm making you uncomfortable your welcome to get out at any time, you just let me know!"

He replied in a meek yet cheerful tone, "O.K. I'll be quiet, I don't want to get out; it's all good."

There was silence for quite a while so I turned the radio back on. I started to tell the hitchhiker about the songs on the radio speaking to me earlier and all of a sudden we noticed that all the songs were about falling in love. The words spoke directly to me and as time resumed I started to tell River my philosophies about life...

The problem with people these days is that they're too superficial...people are afraid to be 'real'...I'm 'real' and it scares people away...people are forgetting what's really important in life...

He began opening up to me, telling me all the intimate details of his life, presenting me with the full spectrum of emotions. As he spoke, I would comfort him and tell him he was wonderful; that he did what he had to do; and that he was deeply loved even though his father had abandoned him at a young age. Suddenly I realized why I had picked him up; I was supposed to help him by being there for him, showing him unconditional love and non-judgment. We began to live out a fantasy in our minds of abandoning the real world and living together in a tiny cabin in an isolated place with only our affection for one another to keep us at ease.

At some point I lost my grip on reality and pulled over with a screech. The car wobbled violently as I made an abrupt stop on the right shoulder of the highway. I told the hitchhiker he had to drive and then I retreated into myself, curled up into a ball and squeezed myself into the small compartment under the dash so that no one passing could see me.

Every time the hitchhiker spoke I responded with a tortured shhhhh... shhhhhhe...He headed west, stopping only once to get gas.

The gas station was located in a tiny town off Highway 2. I drove into a grungy alley by a dumpster. I told him that if anyone but him saw me the world would end. I gave him my keys, my car, my meager belongings, and a wallet containing the remainder of my Student Loan ($500.00 in cash, which was all my savings), then told him to leave me in the alley while he went to get gas and anything else he may need. I hid behind the filthy dumpster covered in graffiti and layers of congealed liquids, wearing only my light grey wool sweater and jeans in the -20C weather. I cradled myself on the icy cement, balancing all my weight on my green canvas runners, and stared up at the sky. I believed that the hitchhiker was not coming back and that I was supposed to die right there, ALONE. I begged God to take me to heaven so I could rest. A resounding male voice responded, "Through suffering only, will you see the light of God." The sound of the voice soothed me. My mind finally stopped racing, and I knelt down on the damp slush covered cement, placed my frigid hands in prayer position and waited to be lifted to my resting place.

I heard footsteps behind me. It was the hitchhiker; he had come back for me. He said, "Sorry it took so long, I couldn't find your wallet. I ripped your car apart looking for it, so sorry." Disappointment ravaged my heart as he pulled me up to my feet by the shoulders. "Your freezing, come with me, the car is nice and warm and I bought three water bottles, a bag of Doritos and some Junior Mints." I stood still and silent for a moment wondering whether I should resist his offer. My desire to be back in the safety of my warm little car overshadowed the faint chance that it was time for me to join my maker in the afterworld. I hugged this young man's warm, slim body saying, "I thought you weren't coming back." He held my face to his and said, "Do you really think I would leave you here?"
It was then that I looked deeply into his eyes for the first time; they were a mixture of vibrant, speckled hues of blue mixed with emerald green. I felt an intense love and trust for him at that moment. As we reentered the car he said, "My name is River by the way."

All my life I had a strong intuition that my life would end at age twenty five, I was now that age and I almost felt comfort in the fact that I thought it was about to end.

Depleted I realized that the journey was not quite over even though I had wanted God to release me from this cruel world. A realization that maybe this was some sort of beginning arose within me...

River resumed driving and I crouched down in the foot carrier of the seat so that no one would see me. River never questioned me or made me feel crazy in any way; he just humbly took on the caretaker role and seemed to derive some pleasure taking this wild ride with me.

Our next stop was Lake Louise Lodge. River said that I had forced him to go there. All I said was that there was something we needed to do. When we arrived in the front curved driveway, we were surrounded by BMW's, Mercedes, shiny SUV's and limousines. My 1982 Honda, 'Brown Betty' definitely stood out, so River suggested that we get outta here go to his friends place. Entering a trance-like state I gazed at him and told him that we needed to make love right here and now. I said that he was the Devil and I was Jesus and if we didn't make love right now the world was going to be at war forever. If we united the world would finally be at peace. He tried to explain that it was not rational, that this was not a good idea. What if we got caught? We already looked out of place as it stood.

I started to undo my jeans and asked him to take off his. He hesitated so I grabbed his jeans and started unbuttoning them. He said, "O.K., O.K., I just don't think this is a good idea." When we had our pants down I sat down on top of him and thrusted in a robotic manner. We kissed messily and hard as I sobbed, whispering hoarsely, "We're saving the world, you'll see." "The world needs us to love one another, it's the only way." He said nothing but looked convinced that my words had merit. When we were done I pulled myself off of his lap and we pulled our pants up and peeled out of the parking lot. He said cheerily, "I can't believe we just did this, you are the wildest chick I've ever met." I swung my head and stared him down as I spat, "This is not a joke, we just saved them, and they'll never ever know it." As we exited my vision was blurry and all I could see were shards of light surrounded by a fog.

Returning to my fetal state on the cramped floor of the tiny Honda, a wave of exhaustion swept over me and I began fading in and out of consciousness. The next leg of the journey was spent in complete silence and a petrifying state of paranoia. An unbearable fear of anyone catching a glimpse of me as "Jesus Christ" in womanly form paralyzed me with anxiety. Blinded and half conscious I followed the curves of the road unsure of where we would end up next and what awaited us there. Sadness overtook me as I realized that this hitchhiker had taken me off my original course which was to step foot on African soil. River's voice and the sound of the engine quieting as it came to a slow pace awoke me from my trance, River said, "We're here." I reached my head up just high enough to see a wooden plaque with large green engraved letters: West Louise Lodge.

The name was both haunting and curious as I always had the urge to migrate west, my middle name is Louise and Lodge rhymed with the last name of the pedophile that terrorized me as a child.

River had to fight to pull me, my few belongings and his backpack out of the car. He said in a strained voice, "I don't know which room my friends are in so we might have to knock on a few doors." At first I was just starting to come out of consciousness and was draped over his shoulder barely shuffling my feet across the icy balconies and stairways. It seemed like we were going around in circles and making the same trip over and over. A loud wail escaped from my vocal chords causing River to jump, knocking me to the ground. "I can't go on River, just leave me here to die, please, I beg you..." River hushed me and said in a strained tone, "You really need to keep quiet or we'll get kicked out, this is a dorm for all the people that work at the Lodge." After struggling to find his friends we finally reached dorm #304. River knocked on the door as I slid down the right side of his body and onto the icy wooden planks of the balcony. He whispered hoarsely, "Your name is Heidi if they ask O.K.?" I responded with a half assed "mmm...", realizing I hadn't told him my name. Quickly he added, "Don't say ANYTHING! Try and act as normal as you can. These guys won't know what the hell is going on and they'll kick us out." Finally the door swung open...

A tall, scrawny guy with shoulder length, scraggly black dreadlocks and a goatee came to the door; a waft of thick pungent, pot smoke hit my nostrils making me perk up for a second. My head started spinning; I pushed past the guys and collapsed on an empty cot, still wearing my slushy boots and winter coat. I closed my eyes and the hallucinations became rapid and vivid...

Faces of demons...snakes slithering up the wall...they were laughing and taunting...something swooping towards me...trying to suck the life out of me...

Shrill screams escaped my lips and I began yelling "NO!" over and over as I rubbed myself forcefully trying to get the evil off of me. I stripped my clothes off, trying to get the creatures off of me. There was laughter and there were voices, men in the room, I don't know how many, one of them River's demanding that I "SHUT THE FUCK UP!" I ran into the bathroom and locked the door. A weak florescent box light flickered and made a slight buzzing sound, the sound was deafening. Crouched on the urine soaked floor, in layers of filth, I started to wail and sob. This was hell and I was going to die here. Feeling myself dying, tortured by the evil that was taunting and assaulting me, I started choking on my sobs. Someone was banging on the door, yelling at me..."SHUT THE FUCK UP, YOU CRAZY ASSED CHICK! WHAT THE FUCK IS WRONG WITH YOU? OPEN THE GOD DAMNED DOOR! YOUR GONNA WAKE EVERYONE UP AND WERE GONNA GET BOOTED, JUST SHUT UP!"

I burst through the door and screamed at the group of guys congregating in their cloud of smoke on one of the beds, "NO ONE CAN HEAR ME! I WAS SENT BY GOD, HE MADE ME HUMAN SO I COULD SHOW PEOPLE HOW TO LOVE ONE ANOTHER. I AM JESUS!"

I grabbed my battered, red suitcase and threw it open, all my belongings tumbling to the filthy ground, "Look at all my clothes, I was supposed to go to Africa and save the people there, I'm not supposed to be here." River threw a plaid, wool blanket over my frigid, ivory shoulders. They all gathered around, eerily silent as I calmly showed them all my belongings and told them the significance behind each object. Soon their faces softened and it seemed like they were almost convinced that I was telling the truth. I held my naked body up against the wall as though I was hanging on a cross, desperate to show them my vulnerabilities as Jesus had done…

My only desire was to die…die of frustration…as no one here could reach me or make my mind stop spinning…I threw the woolen blanket off of me, broke open the door and ran to the end of the long, second floor balcony…I climbed up the icy railing and leapt off into a large pile of snow down below…I screamed, cried and winced with pain as the snow lunged violently at my skin…imaginary creatures were covering my skin and taking gashes out of it…I begged God to take me home to him so the spinning could stop…so I could rest…

I heard hollow footsteps growing louder, heading in my direction but I was unable to see who the dark figured man was. Someone lifted me out of the icy bank and brushed me off. I felt the wool blanket draped around my cold, bare, shoulders and soon I was lifted up off the ground and carried back to the room by River's familiar arms. At the door he put me down and looked into my eyes, he said calmly "Please don't do that again, just lie down O.K.!" The three strangers held me down and forced my clothes back onto my cold, wet body as I laid there with icy limbs, limp, and heavy with exhaustion. Technicolour flashes of that dark night in high school terrorized me. I shook with fear. I whispered, "No, No, No, No…" with strained helplessness.

I begged them to put me back in my car so I could leave. They pushed me out the door, carrying all my things with looks of anticipation mixed with empathy. I told them that I had thrown the key in the snow when I ran out onto the balcony. The look on their faces hardened so I told them not to worry, that I would get it open. So I went over to the car, grasped the icy handle and stared at the moon. As I pulled the handle four consecutive times stammering, "Please God, open the door…" over and over each time I pulled the handle. I quietly pleaded for divine intervention. This continued for a while and as I repeated the ritual, the young men stood watching and whispering, helpless. I eventually collapsed from sheer exhaustion. I was shocked back into consciousness when I heard a loud crack behind where my head and body was crouched against the frigid metal of the vehicle. After the crack I heard the sound of glass shattering and felt pieces of it landing in my hair. Tiny shards snuck under my coat collar and slithered down my back. Someone picked me up and wedged me into the back seat.

I scrunched my body up and slid into the front seat between the steering wheel and the cold, plaid seat cover. When I realized where I was I gripped the steering wheel and began chanting to the universe over and over...

Please take me home...it's time...I've done everything you asked me to do...please take me home...Please take me home...Please take me home...

As I sat awaiting some response I noticed a brilliant light reflecting in my rear view mirror. The light was getting brighter; it looked as though it was coming for me. The universe had heard me and I felt a surge of relief knowing that I would be leaving this place and going home where I belonged...

Toes freezing...fingers numb...losing hope...the light is not taking me... longing to die...longing to rest...I can't hear anything...I can't feel anything... where am I? Who am I? My heart is filling up with love...you are taking me now...I'm ready...

"It's Not Time...I will come for you later...You still have work to do..."

The angelic female voice still rung in my ears as the brilliant light faded and was replaced by spinning red and blue lights. My head felt like it weighed a hundred pounds and fell down hard on the steering wheel. Cold air rushed in as I felt my door being open. Two large men in dark coats grabbed a hold of me and pulled me out of my vessel of solitude and placed me on a long, hard plastic board. I tried to ground myself as I felt the cot get raised up into the air, but was paralyzed by large, leather straps that cut into my wrists and ankles. I was able to turn my head and saw River standing by a large brunette man in an RCMP uniform. The officer was writing something down on a small leather notepad, as the two of them spoke. I couldn't hear what anyone was saying. All I could hear was a loud buzzing noise. The urge to shove my fingers in my ears was unbearable, but my arms felt as though they were detached from my body. Faces kept intruding into my space and asking questions. My eyes closed and it felt like they were glued shut. All I heard were murmurs with slight inflections scattered about. One phrase was intelligible, "Lady, we're taking you to the hospital." My body awoke and struggled to break out of the restraints, I began crying "Please leave me here! I have a mission! I'm supposed to go to Africa!" River walked towards me as they were about to slide me into the vessel with the flashing lights. There was softness and fear in his glistening eyes, he alleged, "I'll never forget you, I'm so sorry!" I sobbed and clenched my eyes shut as they pushed the cot into the back of the white ambulance and slammed them shut, his face erased in an instant...

*Shhhhhhhh…shhhhhhhh…shhhhhhhh…shhhhhhhh…shhhhhhhh…
shhhhhhhh…*

Everything faded away at that moment…

*Barely consciousness, I opened my eyes long enough to see the tear streaked
faces of my brother and sister staring at me as I lay strapped to a new cot in
a stark bright room…They had come all this way for me in a blizzard as soon
as the police had reached them…Jory all the way from Edmonton and Lou
Lou all the way from Calgary…I didn't know where we were or if they were
real…I smiled and then closed my eyes again…The next time I opened my eyes
I was laying on Jory's lap as he drove through the icy back country of the Rocky
Mountains, the bumps jolting me in and out of consciousness…Hypnotized by
the swinging of his red fuzzy dice with black spots and the yellowed satin baby
shoes that hung from his rear view mirror…As though in a dream, echoes of
an Adam Sandler comedy tape and the repetitious squeak of the windshield
wipers provided background noise during the long drive home…Jory held
me close as he navigated his way through the snow storm in the middle of the
night, trying to mask his intense fear with gentle laughter…After navigating
his way through the blizzard the lights of Calgary shone through the foggy
truck windows and Jory pulled into the driveway of my sister's duplex…Jory
scooped me up into his arms like a wounded animal and carried me down
into the basement…I could hear the hollow murmurs of my siblings strained
conversation as he laid me on the musty futon in the corner of the partly
finished rec. room…They were trying desperately to come up with a plan…
In the end the basement door swung open and I was scooped up into the
arms of my brother, his winter jacket still cool from the crisp winter air, once
again…I felt his hot tears hit my cheeks and his eyes glistened as he stared at
me with child-like fear in his face…"We're going to get you help! Don't worry;
everything is going to be OK, Hannah Banana…"*

A week and a half later, I woke up in a strange white bed with stiff
sheets. I stared up at a butterfly shaped water stain on the white tiled
ceiling, a metal track ran around the edge of the bed in a U-Shape, from
the metal hung a set of yellowing, polyester curtains with cartoon bunnies
hopping on them, feigning privacy. Someone shifted next to me. I saw a
shadow move in the dull illumination through the thin curtain wall. I
heard the bed creak as her weight released itself from the plastic covered
bed, and then she poked her head through my bunny curtain,"Hey Girl,
You're Up! My name is Corrine." As I sat up I looked at a blond haired girl
with a crew cut and weathered bandages wrapped around her wrist. She
told me that I was at the Peter Lougheed Centre in Calgary.

She reiterated that I was diagnosed with Bipolar Disorder and I had just suffered a psychotic manic episode and was lucky to still be alive. After listening to her brief explanation I turned away and squinted away my tears, falling back into my semi-conscious dream state.

I slipped in and out of consciousness for a long time. The stark white room was slowly transformed as the vibrant artwork of my nieces and nephews was adhered to the walls creating a paper quilt of hope and happiness. My sister came and held vigil by my bedside everyday and tried to get me to remember who she was, who I was and who our family was. I had no recollection of anything and she wept silently at the loss of her once vibrant, intelligent little sister. Lou Lou insisted performing the nurse's duties, taking me to the bathroom, giving me baths and telling me that she would not let anything bad happen to me. The doctors had suggested giving me several rounds of Electric Shock Therapy to help me come out of my 'coma-like' state but her and Jory refused to sign the permission forms. She feared that I may never return; that I would remain this shell of a person, with no ability to perform even the most basic of tasks. Her devotion to me was heroic and the day I regained consciousness she sat by me with a look of relief and pure happiness. She knew there would be a long road ahead, but she said she would not give up on me…

-Hannah Rush

September 2008

Angels come in many forms…my angels have always been my brother and sister. They always picked up where my parents left off. They define what unconditional love is…

While I waited for some type of news on my sisters' disappearance I remembered how she had been at that hospital every day, each time I had needed her and how she loved me through it all. Here I was now faced with this gaping hole, the walls in her farm house, a tapestry of her love for the natural. I needed to find her; I needed the strength to carry her children and myself through this devastating experience. My mission was to fill her roles as best I could while holding vigil. On the third day after hearing of her disappearance my father and I walked down the long gravel road to the reservoir by her house. The same place they had found her upturned canoe just days before. In leather sandals, walking by my father's side I searched the treacherous, overgrown shoreline for some sign of her.

With no knowledge of what I was looking for, no knowledge of what I might find, I felt helpless and overwhelmed at the sheer size of the murky reservoir that surrounded me. The memory of my flashes of her walking drenched on the side of the road still haunted me as I walked along the uneven shoreline horrified. Three hours into our walk we came upon a gathering of sparse, baby silver birch trees; they were my favorite species of tree. I sat cross-legged amidst them and clenched my eyes shut. I tried to conjure up something, a sign, a message, anything that would lead to me to my sister. How could such beauty mask such a devastating history? My instinct was usually profound and clear, but as hard as I searched, as much as I tried to hold onto hope I came to the realization that my sister may never return. The more days that passed the more distant my hope became. I wanted a chance to pay her back for all she had done for me. I had such a strong desire to pick her up and brush her off for a change. Now I was strong enough to carry her. My efforts became focused on her family and doing my best to reduce the amount of chaos that they were exposed to. On the way back to the farmhouse Dad and I walked through expansive farmers fields, the sticky mud squishing between the cracks in my loose sandals. Dad said without lifting his head, "I always thought Lou Lou would be the one that would be there to look after me when I was old." I said nothing as I welcomed the pain and frustration of our treacherous walk back to my sister's home.

Kindred Spirits

April 2001

As she flipped through the University's Housing Registry the address 10806-76th Avenue

leapt off the page at her. Her intuition told her that this was where they were supposed to live in harmony together.

Fall 1995

Sarina and Hannah had connected instantly while working side by side in the nurturing environment at Thorncrest. The group home housed forty kids under eighteen; half were severely handicapped and the other half were apprehended from neglectful or abusive homes. Sarina, like Hannah had a gentle, loving soul; she also had the sweetest most angelic voice, one that could instantly soothe you. Surviving tumultuous pasts, and their need to make a difference in these kids' lives united them instantly. After working together for a short while Sarina invited Hannah to a quiet park to climb her sacred tree. It was a grand old oak tree that was formed perfectly for climbing. The two women spent many evenings up in that tree tying prayer ribbons of various colours and styles to the branches. On one occasion they noticed that a bird had constructed a nest and several strands of their prayer ribbons were interwoven delicately into the twigs, grass and mud. The women could see the downy heads of the birds and wordlessly watched as the mother flew skillfully over top of the nest nourishing them. Sarina had a tiny stature and untamed wavy hair that resembled spun gold. When they were up in the tree at dusk the fading sunlight would illuminate her hair casting a beautiful aura around her. Hannah fell instantly in love with her new kindred spirit.

The gentle wind blows our tree and it rocks me with its swaying. My connection to it clears my mind; all my thoughts drift silently away with the gentle breeze. I am at peace with her and she gently rocks me telling me that everything will be OK. The solace that I sought for so many years is present right here and now. Thank God for Sarina…she loves me for who I truly am and sees my beauty shining through even though right now I cannot…she is teaching me how to love myself…

Ken's temper had been flaring up more and more lately and these times with Sarina were the moments that kept her going. Hannah's fiancé was so pessimistic and wrong for her in so many ways. She knew there would be no date set and no wedding, she just could not bear to let go of his family. They were her pseudo family for the time being and she had stayed these seven years for them, not because she was in love with their son. She had bought her first home with him just six months ago and she had put her heart and soul into it. In the fall she had planted two hundred tulip bulbs and they had just erupted making the front entrance a sight to behold. Ken's alcoholic dad Eddie spent his days fixing up the house for them; constructing a picket fence for their wildflower garden, building a dog house for their two Jack Russell Terriers Katie and Sally, and renovating the kitchen. She had painted the 1920's walls in vibrant colours like tangerine, raspberry, lemon, and teal, and they popped with the ornate, white baseboards and crown molding. Her evenings were spent soaking in the claw foot tub listening to Bette Midler CD's. Her time alone in that house was so special and precious that she just didn't want to let go. When he was home they would start arguing and she would end up screaming and sobbing uncontrollably. After one night that was particular explosive Hannah called Sarina and asked her new friend if she could stay at her place for a few nights.

As soon as she walked in the door she was greeted by Sarina's two cats, Aishee and Senora. Aishee was a black, short-haired cat with a petite frame and Senora was a fluffy, snow white cat that rubbed up against Hannah's legs upon entry into the dimly lit stairway. The air smelled of patouli and jasmine and it pleasantly strengthened as Hannah took the ascent up the plush stairs. Sarina's apartment just felt right to Hannah. Even though she had never been there she felt like she was home. There were several plants in hand painted ceramic pots of all the colours of the rainbow sitting on the tiny free corners of her mismatched bookshelves, painted in jewel tones, and on her window ledges. There were pictures of some of the kids from Thorncrest blown up and placed in antique silver frames, propped up on furniture and scattered on the walls. Sarina had taken the pictures and all the children in those photographs looked healthy, vibrant and full of love. You could see in their eyes that they were in a moment of pure bliss, and just enjoying their childish existence. She had the gift of wiping the pain out of those children's lives while they were in her presence; this was also a gift she bestowed on Hannah.

While Hannah was seeking refuge at Sarina's she learned many things that she would grow to love and practice for the rest of her life; yoga, spirituality, gardening and activism. Sarina's passion for those things lit a fire under Hannah, a fire that was so strong it would change the course of her life for the better. These elements of life carried over from Hannah's past were the positive reflections she had from her childhood and Sarina was the precious soul who would gently reintroduce them into Hannah's existence. For such a long time Hannah had pushed them aggressively out of her realm due to the anger that she had for her childhood. Any attachment she had in her childhood, positive or negative was a reminder of the pain she had endured. Moments spent with her kindred spirit would set her free from the denial of elements of life that were sacred.

I have always loved the smell of incense…she lights a stick of Nag Champa and the smell of the patouli carries me into a trancelike state…I feel like I'm deeply connected to the moment…my senses are heightened… I am so excited about life…I let all the fear go…the fear of having to return to my life…for now I am here…fully present…as I look at the T.V. screen I hear Hindi music as the black screen transforms into a beautiful, blue sky with wispy, white clouds…there are four people sitting with their legs crossed and their hands clasped between their breasts…one is a stunning black man…one is an earthy brunette…one is an older women with long, flowing grey hair…and the yoga master has long wavy hair the colour of sand…His deep, raspy voice sends chills through my body…I enter their world and feel every movement of every muscle as I practice yoga for the first time… Sarina and I practice in silence…we simply appreciate one another's presence as she shares this incredible awakening with me…all of my stress…all of my worry…all of my mania releases with every muscle that I stretch in unison with my breath…

After completing the yoga, Sarina and I continue to share a comfortable unspoken silence…to speak would taint the essence of the mood surrounding us…she simply leads me to her bed…tucks me in under her white cotton down filled duvet…and hands me a book called Conversations with God, a cream coloured notebook hand painted with delicate freesia's and a pen…I read all night…and write down the thoughts that I don't want to forget…Sarina is breathing quietly on the pillow next to mine and her cats are curled up on either side of me…The delicate flickering of the candles methodically spread throughout the room casting an angelic glow…something has awakened within me and I know I can't return to my life as it was…

The following day Hannah returned to her home. She co-existed with Ken though the tension in the atmosphere was extremely thick. Now that Hannah's connection to her spirit had been awakened she viewed her life with him in a very different light. She knew his pessimism and materialistic attitude along with his need to control her would stifle her; she knew she had to get out. Their sexual relationship became non-existent. The floodgates of obscurity had been opened and that was something that she was unable to tolerate anymore. When Ken was out gambling away the money she earned at Thorncrest, she would tenderly meditate to try and push the negativity out.

One night, when she was home alone, she meditated and something extraordinary occurred…

I need an escape from reality…if I stay I will be reliving my past…I need to go to a safe place…

She lit the stick of Nag Champa that Sarina had given her, and as the herbal smoke enveloped her she entered a meditative state. The candle light preformed a kaleidoscope dance on the lemon and raspberry walls as she sat cross legged on her floral feather duvet breathing so deeply that she entered a trancelike state. She stared into the antique floor length mirror framed in etched mahogany and saw her true beauty for the very first time. She had never had the courage to stare into her own eyes and she was mystified at the experience of doing so. How long she had let her spirit hide within her vulnerable physical form. Once she was fully connected to her soul she witnessed a soft turquoise light emerge from the centre of her naked chest. This energy source danced gracefully around her and caressed her delicately. She never wanted to leave this essence that was her true inner self. Every moment would be etched in her memory of this introduction to the beauty that was hiding deep within her. She heard a gentle voice whisper…

"Hannah, you are a courageous and magnificent human being…you have so much to give…don't let us suffer anymore…we need to be free…to express ourselves…to let go of worry and guilt…we are one…now you know I am here

within you…you have the strength to let go of him…surround yourself with the beauty of all things…be in nature…allow people in that will nurture your spirit…let go of the negative influences…you don't need them anymore…they are holding you back…if you listen you will reach your full potential…"

The bedroom door swung open and as soon as it did her spirit swirled frantically around the room and reentered her body. Ken had returned home early and saw this. For a moment he was speechless. She felt like she had been violated again. Having him see her essence and knowing the way the force had responded was confusing and disturbing to her. Her first moment with her spirit was disturbed by this man that she professed to love in an awkward way for so many years. If he responded to what he just witnessed in a tender, loving way she may have felt there was some shred of hope for their future. His focus was more on her nudity and his physical response was animalistic. He pushed her back onto the bed. She scrambled to grab her turquoise, chenille housecoat and threw it around her body like a cocoon. She stared hollowly at the ceiling as she went through the motions, planning her escape. There was no fight left in her.

Remembering Lou Lou
September 2008

The last time she had visited her sisters farm was the last time the women had seen one another. Hannah remembered fondly how spiritually connected they were:

As I sat across from her in her musty, old barn she stared into my eyes and her beauty took my breath away. Her ease and calm shone through her luminescent blue eyes. Her long, wavy brown hair was backlit by the sun giving her an angelic appearance. The love I felt for her came out in warm, gentle, rolling tears. She smiled and said, "Why are you crying?" I responded in a hoarse whisper, "I can see your soul, your pure happiness; it is so comforting to see you so truly yourself."

Later that night we sat side by side on her old lazy boy recliners in her little shed drinking beer out of a can and rehashing the lessons we had learned from our spiritual readings.

For about a year we had formed our own spiritual book club called, "The Loula May Club". It was at that time that my sister found her spiritual self and began nurturing it. We would choose a book on a spiritual principal, put the principals into practice and then have a meeting about how it affected us.

At about one in the morning, still alone in the shed, she stared at me with such reverence and said "I am going to hug you without touching you, O.K., so tell me if you can feel it." She clenched her eyes shut and I followed suit. All of a sudden I felt a warm rush of tenderness enveloping my belly, a feeling similar to the moment when my babies were first placed on my chest after birth. I whispered to her, "I can feel it Lou, it's working. Oh my god, it feels so amazing."

I tried to hug her in the same manner. As I clenched my eyes shut I conjured up the image of me actually hugging her and she responded instantaneously, "Oh my God, Han, I can totally feel that, it is so warm and beautiful." When we opened our eyes none of them were dry and we sat in silence mutually appreciating the power of that moment.

The rolling hills of tall, wild, golden wheat; the collection of tattered, leaning barns; the huge, organic vegetable garden; the 'car graveyard' full of old rusty, vintage vehicles; the gentle old farmhouse being slowly transformed into a more modern version of itself; the stray animals of various varieties and forms, free to roam the barnyard; the opportunity to allow her children the freedom to go and do as they pleased…All of these things helped my sister to loosen control and relax. She had carried all of us for so long that it had shown in her face, now that stress was evaporating and leaving her looking more serene. Simplicity was the key to her freedom and she had found it there at that farm so many miles away from civilization, in the midst of the prairies with a stunning view of the mountains, candy coloured sunsets and a view of the reservoir…

Transformation

Early Spring 2000

After her stay in the Peter Loughheed Centre's Psychiatric Ward she had returned to the "Happy Hippy House." The only problem was that her friends had no idea what to do with her. Upon coming home from Calgary after her diagnosis she had not left her bedroom for days. She had entered a deep depression and though her friends cared for her, their worry was too much of a burden to carry along with worries of regular University life.

Jory came to the Frankenstein house one day with his beat up old Ford truck, the vehicle of Hannah's salvation in the past, to move her out of that house. Jory carried her once again to the front seat. She could barely keep her eyes open while she stared blankly at the stacks of crinkled, invoices with their curled yellow corners scattered all over the dash. After all her stuff was piled into the back of the truck they made the journey out of town. As they drove down the bumpy, windy roads Jory told Hannah that the family had decided the best place for her was with his wife's parents, the Dalton's. It was difficult for Hannah to accept the help but she came to the realization that at this point in her life she really needed someone. The warmth and loving milieu at the Dalton home was what Hannah had always wished for herself. The gift of knowing that there were marriages that were happy and stable out there solidified her ever present dream of having her own family one day.

Though she was always made to feel welcome in their home, she was beginning to feel as if she needed to move on and regain her independence. She had never felt as safe and cared for as she had in this home and it would be hard to leave Jory's mother-in-law Grace. Their bond had become so strong in her days there. Grace had become a 'mother' figure to Hannah-a strong, stable, loving mother. Grace had all the qualities Hannah herself wanted when she reached the goal of motherhood. The two women spent their days together, doing wash and hanging it on the line outside; smoking cigarettes, drinking coffee and talking at the kitchen table; making bread and mowing the lawn with the lawn tractor. Grace kept her in a calm, predictable routine and Hannah realized that the routine made her feel sane for the first time in her life. She had always resisted normalcy, but she quickly realized that it made her feel more grounded in the earth and safe.

April.29, 2000
Dear Diary:

It has been almost a year since I quit work and school. It has been a quick year…lots of ups and downs. Grace and William saved my life and I do not know where I would be without them. Also, Jory, Lilly, Lou Lou and all the kids- they've all kept me <u>alive</u>. I was out in the field today and sat peacefully on the antique wagon, the dogs by my side. I just meditated as I watched the wild horses roam around the field, so strong and graceful. I walked slowly towards the majestic creatures and as I approached a sleek black horse made eye contact with me and began his silent gait towards me. A wash of calm overcame me. He held his head over the fence and nudged my shoulder tenderly; I hummed an organic melody as I stroked his velvety nose. It amazes me how this animal has the ability to love a complete stranger unconditionally. I have so much to learn from this animal.

Dear God, please help me find out what I was put on this earth to do. I feel like there are heavy weights attached to my weary body and I am slowly being pulled into a pool of quicksand. Lead me in the right direction-show me my path-let me feel at ease-help me to feel complete again and loved by you and myself. I think I'll read "Celestine Prophecies" and "Conversations with God" again. I need to read more and absorb more goodness from things. I can be spiritual and happy, I know because I've been there before.

Love Hannah

Watch out Girlie, you are biting off more than you can chew!

Hannah was thrilled to see an ad in the classifieds reading "Youth Worker needed at The Family Centre." Years prior to this she had done volunteer work there. She had worked with teenage girls that had been sexually abused, providing counseling and friendship to the girls. The job was fulfilling most of the time as Hannah felt as though she was truly giving back, and that her own suffering finally had a higher purpose.

Trashed
Winter 1993

The volunteering had ended badly though as Hannah had put her trust in a client. A girl named Heather that she had worked with ten years ago on a volunteer basis became homeless. Not able to let it go, Hannah had given her the keys to her bachelor apartment downtown. Hannah had previously been living with Ken, in the basement suite, and they decided to take a break for a couple months. She told the girl that she could stay there until she got back on her feet as Hannah was staying with Ken most of the time. The apartment was in a government housing complex and was subsidized as Hannah herself couldn't afford a higher rate of rent. Two days after she had given the teenage girl her keys she had returned to go and pick up some of her clean clothes and belongings. When she pulled up to the complex she noticed a shadow slip by the front second storey window of her suite. *"Good she's there"* thought Hannah. She buzzed the buzzer several times but there was no response. Next she tried buzzing her landlady Suzanne. There was an answer after two consecutive buzzes, "Yup! Who is it?" replied Suzanne in a thick, croaky voice.

"*It's Hannah from apartment #203; I can't get into my apartment.*"
"Hang on dear, I'll be right down." She replied curtly.
Suzanne the wiry haired landlady flung open the door with a lit cigarette dangling out of her mouth and said, "We need to talk!" Her voice was breathy from the short walk down the hallway.
"*What's going on?*" Hannah stated, knowing something was wrong.
"Well, did you lend out your apartment to some teenagers?" She knocked the powdery ashes into her cupped hand.
"*Well, yes…no actually just one of my clients, she had nowhere else to go.*"
"Well, there's more than one girl in there and they have caused nothin' but trouble the past few days. The cops have been round a few times askin' questions and everything."
"*Are you serious? I told her she could stay here, not her friends. She's so sweet, what kind of trouble could she be getting into?*"

"Well, prostituting themselves out the window is one thing! They pulled the screen off the window frame and sat there on the ledge propositioning all the men that were walking by. I had to convince the cops not to press charges against you; they thought you was the leader of a prostitution ring. But I told 'em you weren't the type to have nothin' to do with that."

"Oh, My God, Thank You so much. I had no idea the other girls were there, or that Heather would get into any trouble like that. Can you get me into my apartment so I can talk to her? Can you just wait a sec though, I have to run out and tell my boyfriend what's going on."

"Sure, I'll meet ya here in a couple; I have to dig out the keys anyhow."

After running back to the car and explaining the whole sorted situation out to Ken, they agreed that he should go around to the back door in case the girls try to run for it. She returned to the front door where the Suzanne was waiting with her plastic smiley face key chain containing a large mass of imitation brass and silver keys with masking tape numbers stuck to their round faces.

Hannah held in her anger as she made the ascent up the graffiti adorned stairwell. With each stair an intense surge of anger rose up like flames in the back of her throat…*How the hell could she do this to me after all I've done for her?* They reached her apartment door and Hannah pushed past Suzanne, *"Allow me!"* As Suzanne passed the key to her Hannah grabbed it a little too aggressively and flinched as the pain shot through her hand. An indent of the smiley face would serve as a reminder of this crappy day for a few hours. As she flung the door open she almost passed out when a sour, foul stench assaulted her, emanating from the 300sq foot home in a box. The bathroom was directly to the right, and she peeked in there with hesitation, holding back the vomit, she turned her head away quickly as she noticed brownish red toilet water with used tampons and excrement overflowing from the toilet bowl, and running onto her brand new chenille, floral bathmat. The bathtub was filled with toilet paper, condoms, stagnant water and filth. Hannah felt betrayed and violated. This was the first place she had lived on her own and they had come in here and trashed it within days. Everything was destroyed including her bed which was covered in filth and garbage. It was as though the girls had intentionally mistreated the apartment. Hannah couldn't help but feel as though Heather had some sort of vendetta out for her; why else would she have done this?

After assessing the damage, Hannah and the landlady looked out the front window where her boyfriend was parked. He was no longer in the car, so the women hurried out the back entrance. As they flung open the heavy steel door they noticed him standing there holding Heather's arm, her face tear streaked and full of fear. The four congregated and Hannah asked Heather why she had betrayed her like this. All she had to say was, "My friends made me do it, I'm so sorry! Please don't tell anyone." A few weeks after cleaning out her place and moving back in with her boyfriend Ken, Hannah decided she would quit volunteering at the Family Centre. She always wondered how a girl that was seemingly so nice could have screwed her over in such a terrible way. Was it an act of desperation, a bad choice in friends, or just sheer disrespect?

Karmic Intervention
Spring 2001

After some contemplation over whether the Family Centre would remember what had gone a decade ago she decided she had nothing to lose. Even her Dad had said "This is the job you've been training for your whole life." She completed her resume and printed it out on pale blue paper with fluffy white clouds scattered around on it. She thought this touch of whimsy would enable her to stand out from the other applicants. Finally she felt strong enough to get back to her life. She had stayed with the Dalton's for a year and now had moved into her own place with her kindred spirit Sarina. The girls had painted the walls of the 1950's house in very beautiful, vibrant salmon's and purplish blues. Their home always smelled of incense and fresh flowers and there was never a time when soul music was not being played. This was the best Hannah had felt upon hearing the news that she had Bipolar Disorder. She was ready to start her life over again…

A week later Sarina passed the phone over to her excitedly, whispering under her breath that it was the call she had been waiting for, The Family Center. She sat out on the front porch and admired all their potted nasturtiums while she listened to the long awaited call. They loved her application and were very interested in interviewing her the next day. Excitement rose up in Hannah and after hanging up the phone she ran in through the colourful stained glass front door and yelled excitedly, "*Sarina! Where are you sister friend! I have great news!*" Sarina's strained her wispy voice so Hannah could hear her, "I'm in my room Han!" Hannah sprinted through the house and jumped on Sarina's bed, both Sarina and her chubby white cat bounced up as Hannah landed. She flung her arms around her dear friend and sang, "*I got an interview!*"

"Oh my God Hannah, that is so awesome!

"*The woman that does the hiring said that she had hundreds of applications spread out on her desk and mine jumped out at her, she said she knew it was meant to be. How karmic is that. I feel very excited, but I am also a little scared. I've been in a cocoon for so long now; my wounds have just barely scabbed over. Now it's time for me to set out to fly the expanse of the sky.*"

"You're a perfect angel and those kids are blessed to have you as their guide to carry them through their hard times."

March 15, 2001
Dear Diary:

Today was quite a good day. I went to my orientation at the Family Centre. I was a little overwhelmed by all of the information that I got, but I think that's normal. I got two cases today; one is a teen who is promiscuous and hangs around in gangs-she needs a positive role model, her mother is manic depressive and is on medication. I am to help her learn to deal with a parent with mental illness. God, she sounds just like me when I was her age, except for the gang thing. The other girl is living with a good family but just needs to learn some basic life skills.

I think can really make a difference in this job, by showing the girls what you can really make of your lives. That even though times seem tough it is possible to get through. I must remember not to take my work home with me. That has been the cause of my demise in the past. I will give it all I have while I am there, but leave it at the door. This is going to be a challenge, but one I feel ready for. I must not let the Family Centre or myself down. I may feel like quitting now (retreating into my safe, predictable bubble) but I won't quit again- I know I am meant for this job, and like my Dad said I have been training for this job since I was 8 years old. I have walked down the same paths many of these girls have walked down.

Love Hanna

Dear Diary
March 31, 2001

There are no coincidences in life; our journey is set out for us before we arrive. It is a journey set by us and the things we go through allow us to learn lessons that allow our souls to flourish and grow. When you see someone and you instantly have a gut feeling about them, you know if they are good for you or toxic right away. If someone is new in your life and it feels amazing to be around them, you kind of get addicted to being with them, almost like your falling in love with them, your thoughts are slightly obsessive about them and you plan each moment leading up to seeing them again. Did we know these people before we arrived on this earth? As hard as it is to admit, I know I chose all my experiences so that I could teach and help others in the same situation. I often wonder how it feels to be a dark force on earth? Like how did Ross, or Shane and his friends feel after they beat me down? Did they feel powerful or did they feel remorse. Maybe their origins are different than mine, maybe they come from a different place, or maybe they chose their path as well, to teach them something...

Hannah's stomach was in knots as she fumbled for the address of her first client. She found it sandwiched in between the console and the passenger's seat. While she dug for it she felt the remnants of florescent orange Cheetos crumbs and car dirt enter her freshly washed fingernails. That threw her off her game a little, as she did not like to get her hands dirty at all! In fact, she was totally obsessed with having clean hands. Once she stopped at the lights, she was able to pour some of the water from her water bottle onto her hands, drying them off on her jeans. *Ah! That's better!*

She was getting close to the address on the paper when she noticed that she was in the middle of an industrial area. There were no houses or even apartments anywhere in sight. *"Could the address be right?"* Getting very agitated, she drove around searching for any building that could resemble living quarters. Finally, on the corner of the street and the avenue that was scrawled on her paper, she saw a dilapidated concrete building with the address spray painted in black on the side of it. There was garbage scattered all over the make shift parking lot. In the lot, there was only one car, a maroon Buick smattered with rust that was eating gaping holes in the body. Hannah felt terrified to get out of her car although it was the middle of the afternoon. Hesitating, she gathered her mahogany, leather briefcase; (a graduation gift from her Dad and Karen) locked the car up tight and headed towards the building.

She covered her hand with her sleeve as she opened the filthy steel door baring no window. The commercial Berber carpet was soiled and stained on the stairs going up to the third floor where she needed to go. Her chest began to tighten and she felt her heart drop thinking about the girl who lived here. The walls surrounding her in the stairwell were shades of gray and off white from years of filth. She finally reached apartment 302 and with much hesitation and fear knocked on the door. *"What am I doing here?'* she thought to herself. *"I could just run away right now and no one would know I was ever here, I could just quit.*" She heard footsteps approaching and the faint sound of Bob Barker's voice echoing cannily from a television in the background "We'd like to have you bid on those in dollars..." It was too late to turn back now. The door opened and the stench of cigarette smoke and old garbage almost knocked her off her feet; standing before her was a middle aged man, he was average height, had a swollen belly protruding from his plaid flannel shirt and GWG jeans, his face was scruffy and he smelt of stale beer .

"What do you want?" he said gruffly.

"I'm here to pick up Beverly, I'm Hannah, her youth worker" she replied sheepishly.

"BEVERLY, GET YER ASS OUT HERE, YOU GOT COMPANY!" He then turned towards Hannah barely making eye contact, "Have a seat if you want." Hannah cringed at the thought of sitting on the filthy orange, velour sofa covered in stains of unknown origin. "Thanks" she muttered in a forced cheery tone as she perched herself on the edge of the misshapen sofa cushion. She tried to avert her eyes from the filth piled all over the apartment as her anxiety levels were reaching peak levels. She longed for Beverly to get her ass in gear. The man who let her in had not yet introduced himself and sat silently on a green vinyl fold-up chair watching the kitschy game show on the old eighties style television diagonal to her, perched on a makeshift kitchen/card table. "BEVERLY!" He bellowed. "SHUT UP FRANK! I'M PUTTING ON MY GOD DAMNED MAKE-UP!" she hollered from the narrow hallway. Frank turned out to be Mom's boyfriend (number 12 or thirteen) and according to Beverly, quite an asshole just like the rest of them.

The two strangers finally made their way to an old pizzeria snuggled amongst the commercial building sites of the city's North end. Beverly opened up to Hannah instantly and the connection was strong. Hannah felt like the visit went very well. It was amazing to Hannah how similar the two actually were in what they had been through in their lives. They talked as though they'd known one another for years, and the three hour session seemed to be a success. While they were talking Hannah felt it hard to keep in all her experiences and just listen and offer support for once. She wanted to jump in and tell Beverly about all the shit she had been through so that Bev wouldn't think she had led a charmed life and couldn't relate. In her job training though her boss made it clear that it was unprofessional to open up to clients about you, the focus was always to listen and to focus on them.

On the second and third session Hannah tried to go over to Beverly's apartment, but both times the parking lot and building were deserted and no one answered the door. As hard as she tried to keep an emotional distance from her clients, she never stopped wondering what had happened to Beverly.

She was working full-time and had about nine clients at a time. Her emotional investment with the kids was intense and she had a hard time shutting off after work hours. Many a night was spent fraught with worry over her clients. In her heart she felt such a large responsibility for their success. Not being one of those people who could keep their distance was proving to be a real curse and as a result of the stress she began to notice that her illness began creeping slowly back, regaining control over her brain. She had hoped that the new love she found would overpower the illness, but her racing thoughts and dark hallucinations were beginning to conquer her. When life was no longer simple her mind had too many areas to focus on and would begin to struggle at keeping all the pieces held in place. It was as though she was balancing flaming torches on each of her limbs, struggling to keep them from falling down and setting her on fire.

Mailbox
2000-2001

While she was still safely hibernating at the Dalton's acreage she had, with much hesitation and fear started using a telephone dating line. The monotonous messages she had been receiving for months had provided an unsettling sort of comfort...

My name is John Smith and I am six feet, one inch tall. I have blue eyes and short brown hair. I don't smoke and I was raised Catholic but I don't go to church anymore. I like adventure movies, dogs, long walks and working out at the gym. I would like to meet a girl with similar interests...Oh! And I am 30 years old...

As she listened to these formulaic messages she felt like she was doing something dirty, or naughty. Was there anything to be ashamed of if she never followed through? She told no one of her secret nightly rendezvous with the telephone receiver. Giddiness overcame her when she heard the automated British woman saying "you have four messages in your mailbox!" An incredible sense of loneliness, and a craving for some romantic contact in her life drove her to this underground society. Feeling imperfect and wondering if anyone would accept her in her permanently flawed state she hesitated for many months to respond to any of the rote responses in her 'Love Link' mailbox.

Feeling very courageous on a particularly rainy day in March she decided to change her personal mailbox message to a poem…

There's a sparkle in my eye,

And I'm looking for a guy,

That sweeps me off my feet,

Whose humor can't be beat,

His smile must melt my soul,

His heart be true and whole,

A traveler he must be,

Off to Greece or our fair B.C.,

His presence I want to ignite,

Let's walk hand in hand on a starry night.

Or giggle until wee hours as the sun rises,

Or go to parties in disguises.

A beautiful woman inside and out,

Waits to find out what you're all about.

After two weeks with several of the same old "full of crap" responses her slight obsession with the service started to whiffle-waffle …

Lana

At this time Hannah was spending a lot of her time with her friend Lana. They had met many years prior while attending the Sexual Assault Centre group; she was the woman in the quilted skirt. Lana was a veteran of the service (resulting in several dates over several years) and armed with the knowledge that Hannah hated clubbing, now that she was medicated, she felt it was time to share this piece of information with her very desperate, very lonely friend. Lana had very specific rules that she followed when meeting up with anyone from the service:

Rule #1: On the first date meet them at a coffee shop for a quick cup of coffee.

Rule #2: Have your cell phone charged and tell a friend (me or Sarina) where you are and when you'll be home. Be Specific. Upon arriving and having your suitor show up, escape to the bathroom and call said contact person.

Rule #3: If the date is going horribly wrong get your contact person to call and come up with an escape plan.

Rule #4: Never let the guy walk you to your car.

Rule #5: Absolutely do not give him your phone number. If he's sexy let him give you his.

These rules worked for Lana, but she had been using the system for over a year and had never found a steady relationship from it. She was also made of thicker skin.

A Night of Fun-Gus

Tonight Lana took me in her room, slid a tiny treasure chest out from under blanket in her closet...she opened the weathered old chest and pulled out a crumpled up plastic bag filled with tiny delicate brown pieces...magic mushrooms...I had heard of them but stayed away from mind altering substances...What the hell, I was with my best friend...I choked the odd tasting rubbery morsels down and then we went to go say goodnight to her daughter...As we sat in her daughters tiny room the walls started transforming into florescent elasticized rubber...All her little trinkets made us giggle...Lana tapped a glittery unicorn mobile above Shannon's bed and the unicorns danced...We buckled over with laughter and Shannon looked at us like a stern pre-teen school marm about to give us the strap...We tried to hold ourselves together long enough to tuck her in and then we ran out of the house in hysterics...we ran down to the forest creek by her house and giggled like school girls...

All of a sudden swirls of rainbow coloured light filled the sky and the trees became illuminated by an angelic radiance...someone was calling me...calling me from the trees...tiny, vibrant voices...beautiful fairies danced in circles around me as I tried to catch them and sing their cheery tune with them...It was a vibrant fantasy painting come to life...We danced around the darkening forest path in the heart of the Mill Creek Ravine slowly taking layers of clothing off that restricted and confined us...As my naked skin tangoed with the cool, fresh night air I felt alive and invigorated like I had just taken a trip to the stars and touched one of them...or took a slide down a luminescent rainbow...Monkeys were swinging in the tall trees and I was yelling for them to come and play with me...Lana and I laid on the forest floor crumpling up fresh leaves, amazed by their tenderness and sweet scent...Lana and I were in exactly the same place and the feeling was so intense yet so organic and natural...When we returned to her darkened town house we laid on her shag carpet under a comforter and the energy was intense... That night we laid beside one another in her bed naked, yet innocent, the moonlight catching her soft blond curls gave her a golden aura...I felt such an intense love for the woman facing me...We each held giant life sized stuffed dogs and giggled until sleep came close...The next day would change the direction of my journey with my new love; and Lana maintaining the strong, independent solitude she had held onto for years...

The next morning the women were awoken by the sound of Lana's teenage daughter, she had jumped on the bed, cheery and refreshed with sleep. Quickly they covered themselves to hide their nakedness. Suddenly the previous night's escapade started to materialize in Hannah's memory. They casually hinted to Lana's daughter that they needed her to start getting herself some breakfast, a cover so that they could put their clothes on. After her daughter left the room, they turned their backs to one another in silence and started to put the clothes that were strewn on the floor back on. Hannah tried to change the subject by focusing on her telephone dating mailbox, she chirped in a false tone, *"Can I use your phone to see if anyone responded to my poem?"* Lana responded in an equally casual, yet forced tone, *"Of course, go for it!"* In a way Hannah felt like she was betraying Lana by anticipating the call of a strange man after the intensely spiritual and mystical night they had just spent together. In the back of Hannah's mind she knew that she would never be able to live that life, she needed as much normalcy as she could get.

Blind Date
April 2001

I picked up Lana's deep grey cordless phone and found a quiet corner of her townhouse to listen intently to the responses to my mailbox salutation...My heart started to pound so loud I could actually hear it beating like a weathered, bongo drum...I took out my mini coiled notebook and turned the smooth pages until I reached the page containing all my secret codes to access my personal mailbox…I dialed as quickly as I could with anticipation…There were three messages in my mailbox…I began listening to the first one…"My name is Tom Hardly and I…BEEP…"Your Message has been erased successfully!"Chirped the automated female voice…I was not even going to listen to those crap messages…then I heard it:

"I don't know where you end and I begin,
The precious moments spent in your company will make the stars shine brighter and the world seem like a more livable place,
Romance fills my heart and soul,
Rose petals will be spread at your feet and poetry will fill your ears if you take my hand and walk with me,
Let's take this journey through life as one."

My body was tingling with excitement…I was bubbling over with joy as I sprinted down Lana's stairs…I slid on the aged linoleum floor as I sprinted into the kitchen…"This is the one…I know it…he left the most beautiful response poem…" Lana forced out the most realistic, full smile she could muster… I think she could tell by the look on my face that I was shifting my heart over to this new "mystery" guy…We couldn't stay mutually single forever? Her and her daughter sang in unison, "Well, are you gonna let us hear it or what?" I hit redial and was once more connected to this mystical stranger…hearing his echoed voice on the speaker phone for the second time solidified my belief that he was the man without a face…

His name was Liam and he had left his phone number on a second message in her mailbox. She had decided that she would wait until after work to call him, so she would not look too desperate. So that night after work, she sat in her vibrant yellow kitchen at her vintage table; she slowly dialed his number on her cream coloured, stationary, rotary phone, smattered with vibrant fuchsia nail polish daisies. The phone rang several times, Hannah felt like if her heart beat any faster she might have a coronary right there on her kitchen floor.

Finally contact, "Hello!" The soft yet manly voice answered.

"Hi! Is this Liam?" she responded sheepishly.

"Yes, this is Liam."

"Hi, it's me Hannah; you left a poem in my mailbox…"

"Oh! Hi! I wasn't sure what you'd think, I am really glad you called me though, I liked your greeting."

"Thanks, I really loved yours too."

Our conversation felt so pure and natural it was as though we had known each other before. He knew just the right words to use and he was so genuine.

We didn't reveal too much about ourselves, but we did love many of the same things, though we also had a lot of differences, but it was refreshing. There was a slight hesitation in his voice when we talked about our future desires when it came to relationships. Having just finalized his divorce there was a lot of pain still lingering...he wanted to take things slow...this was a good thing. At this point in time I too needed to take things slow as I was adjusting to my new life and limitations. Feeling like a virgin again, like this was my first time in this new skin, body, soul and mind...I felt like this may actually work out well, we were both starting over and we both needed to be treated with kid gloves...

They spoke for three hours every night for the next four nights, it got Hannah through the day just thinking and anticipating their next conversation. On the fifth day Hannah had gone to the Dalton's acreage to pick up a few things. Upon arriving back at her home in the city and settling in she anxiously searched for the little blue notebook, her sweet salvation. Becoming frantic; she was like a crack addict desperately searching for a hit. She trashed her room looking for it, but it was nowhere to be found. The rest of the apartment was turned upside down, Sarina had come home and she too was searching for the tiny, navy notepad. After three hours of intense scavenging she collapsed onto the weathered hardwood floor and started sobbing...

"He was the one...Now he's gone forever...I never gave him my phone number or any information about me...I didn't even tell him my last name... Damn Lana's fucking rules to hell! I don't know what to do...I don't want to lose him..." Sarina held her as they rocked slowly back and forth intertwined... Suddenly Sarina whispered hoarsely "If it is meant to be you'll find one another, don't worry my soul sister, don't you worry..."

For the next month Hannah's thoughts were completely consumed with Liam. She relived each one of their conversations over and over in her mind. Work was a slight distraction, but she knew she wasn't putting her entire self into it any more. She felt so desperate and lonely but refused to move on, not wanting to give up the fantasy of him. Six weeks after their last conversation she received a phone call from Grace.

"I found something by the front door of our trailer when the snow melted. It is a small, navy notebook filled with numbers and names and stuff."

"OH! MY GOD! ARE YOU SERIOUS?" Hannah whooped with hysterical laughter at the very thought of it. Her little blue book survived the test of time. Buried under then snow for six weeks, only to be found when the snow melted by the heat of the warm spring sunshine. "I am coming there

right now to pick it up; I'll be there in 45 minutes!" She was so excited she was about to hang up the phone and run directly out the door, then she remembered, "*THANK YOU SO MUCH GRACE, YOU SAVED MY LIFE!*" She was too shy to tell Grace or anyone else where she had met Liam. All she told her was that there was important information in there. Her anticipation on the ride home was totally overwhelming, she had longed to hear Liam's sweet, gentle voice for so many weeks, for some reason she had never given up hope that they would somehow be reunited. Every time the phone had rang she picked it up quickly with the pipe dream that maybe he had psychically tracked her down somehow. Now she had in her hands on the magic book that contained her future...

She skidded into the long narrow, gravel driveway of her salmon coloured house, with its flat roof and rustic appeal. As she walked up the winding path etched with different varieties of wildflowers, weeds and yellow and orange nasturtiums, she looked up towards the brilliant, blue sky and thanked Mother Earth or the Universe, or God or whoever was out there listening for revealing her tiny notebook to Grace. She had not yet opened the book to see if its contents were even legible, avoiding the knowledge of it until she was ready, situated by the phone. There was so much water damage from being buried under the melting snow and slush that the possibilities of anything being legible were slim to none; known for her extremely optimistic attitude and she was not ready to admit defeat. As she entered the warm, cozy house she was welcomed with the familiar, herbal scent; *I love you sweet, sweet house, please God let me find him again! Please God please!* She kicked her shoes off and semi-sprinted to the wobbly table in the kitchen that housed the phone. She stared down at her notebook and continued her humble chant, *"Please, God if you are out there, let my notes be OK! Just give me a sign that he is the one for me."* She opened the book and noticed that the first page was just a large blue water smudge that had dried and shrunk down the size of the already tiny lined page. Frantically she searched for Liam's phone number or his mailbox information. As she flipped through the pages vigorously she felt her hope starting to dwindle; until she reached the middle of the notebook. There almost leaping off the page was Liam's mailbox number. His phone number had been up near the top of the page and had perished with the rest of the numeric flood victims. All of a sudden she remembered that having his information wasn't enough, she also needed to access her own information to get into the system. Flipping and re-flipping, scouring and searching, she came out empty handed; most of the pages were just large silhouettes of blue watercolour smudginess.

Her memory would have to withstand the test of time. She was one of those people that usually had an outstanding visual memory for words and numbers, uncannily in the same league as someone who had a photographic memory. As she picked up the phone she slid the spiral cord off of her blotchy page. First she called Lana to get the number for the system. Then she dialed it with a slight amount of hesitation…

"Welcome to "Love Link", Edmonton's leading telepersonal dating service, please choose one of the following options…" 1,5,6,9,…"Sorry, this is an invalid mailbox number…"2,5,7,9,"Sorry, this is an invalid mailbox number…"8,9,3,4" Sorry, this is an invalid mailbox number…" Who am I kidding, I have no friggin' clue what it is…What the hell am I going to do, I have to talk to him…I am dying inside…Oh! Oh! MY GOD! I know I can leave him a message in his mailbox without my information…O.K…leave a message…2,5,1,7,…"Hello, this is the mailbox of Liam Knight"…"Hi, this is Hannah, I know it's been a month and a half since we talked but I really felt we had a connection, I just lost your phone number and all my information for the system…I can't believe I'm breaking the number one rule by doing this but I don't have a choice and I really don't want to lose you, so here is my phone number, 486-3459…I hope you still remember me…I look forward to your call…

The hours on that rainy spring night felt like they dragged into days. Her anticipation was so intense she felt like she was losing her mind. She knew if he did not call by the end of that night she would surely be a basket case and be sent directly back into the Looney Bin. Luckily the phone had one of those extension cords that is about 15 meters long because that phone went wherever she went…out on the porch for multiple drags of Du Maurier Light King Size cigarettes; on her bed while she folded her second load of laundry; beside the bathtub while she had a long, hot, bath infused with lavender and patouli oils; in the kitchen while she made a batch of homemade cookies…R-R-R-R-ING!…R-R-R-R-ING! She held her breath, set the pan on the olive green stove, wiped the grease on the sides of her faded jeans and picked up the phone…*"Hello!"*

"Hi, is this Hannah?"
"Yes, it is. Is this Liam?" She tried to contain her excitement but it was about to burst out of her like Canada Day fireworks. His voice made her feel like she was home, were she belonged.

"Oh My God! I thought we would never find each other again. I haven't stopped thinking about you since the last time we spoke."

"I thought I would never hear from you again, so I quit using the system a few weeks ago. I had lost hope that I'd ever find you again. Today though, for some reason I felt like I should check my mailbox, just in case..."

"Oh My God!"

"When I heard your voice I was so relieved. I thought I had offended you or something, or that you just weren't interested."

"Oh! I am still very interested. I am so sorry!"

(She proceeded to tell him the whole story of what had occurred)

"I don't want to lose you again, can we meet tomorrow?"

"YES! I mean yes, sure I can, and I feel the same, where and when?"

"Do you like Italian food?"

"I do!"

"How about Sorrentino's on Whyte Avenue at 8:30pm?"

"Sounds perfect, I will be wearing red and I'll sit at the bar so you know who I am."

"OK! I'll see you there. Have a great rest of the night Hannah."

"You too Liam! I am so glad we found each other. Thanks for waiting. See you tomorrow night...Oh! Wait, what do you look like?"

"I'm like 5'7, 170lbs, with short salt and pepper hair, and I am a bit more than an occasional smoker!"

She laughed hysterically at his sarcastic humor, the way he mimicked the majority of the ads on the system.

"That's a relief, I lied, I am a smoker too, but I'm still in the closet after ten years."
Laughing with Liam felt so natural and easy...he was so unintimidating and so 'REAL'...He is going to be different than all the others, I just know it...I finally found a man...Oh! SHIT! What the hell am I going to wear tomorrow? I don't want to look too whorish, but I want to have an understated sexiness... look intelligent, but beautiful...

For the next several hours she tore clothes out of her closet and tried them on. Then she would run into the kitchen and perform a little runway show for Sarina. Some pieces were from Sarina's collection and others were from hers. Her manic energy and fervor was infectious, she had Sarina in hysterics. All the pieces had to be red though, so her choices were limited. Red brought out her rosy complexion and coordinated perfectly with her long, bouncy, strawberry blonde curls. Though she had gained some weight on the medication she looked more curvy and vivacious. She actually had adequate breasts instead of her tiny mounds from pre-bipolar days. The remainder of the night was spent primping and pruning for the next day. She shaved her legs, even though she had no intention of having them stroked, but she left her couchie wild and bushy. This would ensure that she would not sleep with him on the first date. It was about 3 in the morning by the time she finally drifted off to sleep. Her thoughts that night and the next day were consumed with him.

All those years of waiting were finally over. She knew in every intuitive cell in her body that he was the one that she had imagined all the years of her life; the one that she had waited for. He was her soul mate and she actually knew it this time. All of the other relationships were just there to pass the time or to teach her something. He was the man she saw for the past 25 years in her visions, when times had been dark; it was his presence that she felt. There was no denying that this was him, and she was finally going to be united with him.

During her client visits the next day she was distracted by fantasies of what that night would be like. Her clients could see that she was not really present. Knowing it was inappropriate to disclose information about her life she tried to withhold the excitement that was close to bubbling over. She was successful at keeping it in until the very last client. Her name was Penelope and her problems really weren't too tragic, so Hannah thought it OK just to expose this little harmless piece of information to her teenage patron. Once she let the headline slip her client lit up as though she felt like she had finally tore down the Berlin wall and saw what life was like on the other side; "The Secrets of the Mysterious Youth Worker Revealed!" Her client shared in her excitement and told her if she had to go early to get ready that was totally OK. At that moment Hannah and Penelope became friends.

Sometimes it is not only OK but necessary to open doors that are not meant to be open by society's standards. Roles are meant to be challenged, as we are all here to teach one another something, and if that wall does not get broken down, you will never know what the other person was meant to teach you.

Which red shirt should I wear???The v-neck with three quarter inch sleeves adorned with Chinese silk fabric? That one is sexy but understated... Or should I wear Sarina's red fitted jersey dress???I don't want to reveal too much the first time we meet...I like to leave something for the imagination... OK, I'll try this red dress on...Humph...It is tricky getting it on with all these Velcro rollers attached to my hair...Ouch! That frickin' hurts...Oooops! Crap there goes another roller...How much time is there? OK it's 7:30, I still have like twenty minutes give or take...No...I don't think I like the dress...it is too form fitting...it looks like I painted the friggin' thing on...totally not me...OK, well the only other red thing is that blouse with the Chinese fabric...That one is nice...I'll try it with my 'nice' jeans...That and my silver hoop earrings... that'll look fabulous...OK...I am not gonna get this bloody thing over my head with these rollers in...OK that should be enough hairspray...Ouch...damn it that hurts...OK last one...OH MY GOD! My hair looks like a beehive!!! Damn it...I knew I shouldn't have left them in that long...OK...I'll wear my red velour bra and panties...I have no intention of having sex with him on the first date...but it is good to be prepared in case of emergencies right??? OK, now for the shirt...Ooooo! I love it. PERFECT! OK...jeans and I'll wear my flat brown leather sandals...I have to be myself...no bullshit! If he doesn't like me for who I am then screw him! Now for this hairdo...OK I can press it down a bit flatter with the brush...now it's starting to look more natural... there! Got it! 7:40...I still have lots of time...Screw it I'll go early and have a drink at the bar before he gets there...

She arrived promptly at 7:50pm. More than half an hour sooner than she had told him she'd be there. When she walked in she quickly scanned the smoky, dimly lit lounge. One man looked directly at her as she was doing her scan. She stopped briefly to return the stare, just in case it was him. *He said he has salt and pepper hair...Is that him? I can't make out his hair colour in this light...He isn't walking over this way...I guess it's not him... Oh my god I am going to spew...I guess he's not here yet...I'll just wait at the bar for him...I am a lot earlier than I had said...He's probably not here...*

She boosted herself up onto the tall barstool, and removed her jacket slowly revealing the back of her red blouse to the lounge patrons. This way it was up to him to find her, now she just had to wait. The cold steel on the back of the barstool kept her from overheating with anticipation and the soft leather of the cozy seat cushion cradled her buttocks gently as she waited. Her urge to turn around and do another scan of the room was almost unbearable, but she did not submit to her urges. Now the ball was in his court. Forty-five minutes, three DuMaurier lights and two Crantini's later she started to tell the bartender her story...

I think he may have stood me up! After all this time and what we went through to find each other again, I can't believe he stood me up! Maybe he walked in, saw me and walked right back out...

All of a sudden while she was in mid-sentence she felt a gentle tap on her left shoulder and a quiet masculine voice "Are you Hannah?" She spun around slowly on her barstool to meet face to face with "him". She looked directly into his friendly blue eyes and felt like she knew him already. There had never been a time when she had felt so instantly connected to a man. *"Yes! I am Hannah. Are you Liam?"*

"I am. Sorry it took so long for me to come over here. I saw you come in, but I didn't think it was you. I didn't know you would be this beautiful." *Shit, I want to kiss this man hard on the lips right now! O.K. girl, pace yourself...*

He grabbed her drink and the freshly lit cigarette that lay idle in the silver ashtray and she grabbed her coat; then he led her over to an empty booth over by the frosted window. The warm glow that filtered through the creamy glass gave Liam the appearance of an angelic, almost surreal man. The bartender watched their blissful communion with a hint of jealousy. He had a silent yearning for the girl that had been at the bar. He thought maybe there would be a chance that he could be her knight if this blind date guy didn't show. But, being a veteran bartender he knew a 'love at first site' connection when he saw it. The moment that guy tapped her shoulder; he once again became the invisible face behind the bar. The guy all the women saw as a comrade, someone to tell their secrets to, not someone to share their lives with.

Time stands still as I sit here mesmerized by this incredible man...He makes me feel like I am perfect in my entirety...Our hands fit perfectly within one another...Our contagious laughter rings out into the tiny lounge...We have intelligent discussion...stimulating conversation that keeps me interested...I hang on his every word...He says with such confidence "I want to kiss you right now!" I say "Please!" We lean slowly toward one another over the table covered in wet napkins...my purse...an empty martini glass...one full and one empty red wine glass and a square, black, glossy dessert plate with a vanilla bean ice cream puddle nestled in the bottom of it...This most intense, gentle, passionate kiss begins across the table and ends with the two of us intertwined sharing one long booth seat...Never in my life have I experienced a kiss like this one...Time stands still and every cell in my body is like a piece of popping candy...as each cell is touched by the excitement running through my body they explode into a chorus of energy...Is this what true love really feels like... Have I just been going through the motions up until this point??? I know this is him. I am looking right into his face...his beautiful face...I have waited my whole life to meet him...His presence is so familiar...I know he is the one who carried me through all the darkness...I waited a lifetime to see his face...My time is now...My life starts right here...Right now...with this kiss!!! There has never been a more perfect kiss...He is so gentle...his mouth so familiar...so respectful of my traumatized mouth...I can tell by the gentle way that he kisses

that he will be respectful in a relationship...with my soul...in the bedroom...
he is the one...

    As the florescent lights came on and the vacuum started to whir, we realized
that we had shut the place down...the staff had become invisible to us...we
realized the night was ending and it hurt both of us deeply...We gathered our
belongings up in silence and we held hands as we started to leave...We thanked
the staff for extending their welcome so we could discover one another for the
first time...As the cold spring air hit us and the buzz of traffic resounded beside
us, we walked on the hard concrete towards the parking lot, we were silenced by
a mix of sadness and excitement...reality told me that I had to go home alone
and take it slow with him...so we planned a date a few nights away...Liam
would find a play for us to go to on Saturday night...That was three whole
nights away...it would feel like a lifetime now that I had found him...As we
started to walk up the hill into the parkade, the twilight air was filled with
the delicious fruity scents of LUSH handmade soap shop, we were silent...just
reveling in one another's company...It was hard to leave him that night, but
I could see my future when I looked in his eyes...

Darkness Overcomes Her

Late Fall 2001

Six months had passed and Hannah was still successfully employed as a Youth Worker for the Family Centre. Her focus was assisting troubled youth in straightening out their lives. Though her own life had followed a chaotic, unpredictable, destructive path she had an amazing gift. Her ability to read people and remain non-judgmental when people unloaded their secrets and fears to her, made her a rare commodity. All those months of attending, listening and putting rehabilitative plans into action began taking a toll on the freshly diagnosed Hannah. Slowly she started to stay up more and more at night, grappling with the racing thoughts in her head. Quietly she would rearrange cupboards and scrawl down notes in her journal to keep the dark thoughts at bay. As long as she was not left alone with her thoughts she was able to quell them. If left in silence or during times of silent introspection dark thoughts would corrupt her mind; demonic faces snarling at her, fading in and out, fire igniting and spreading out across her mind space, burning any positive, images that she tried to conjure up to replace the evil ones. The nights she spent away from her new love she dozed off by dawn to the flickering of her portable black and white television.

After months of racing thoughts, stretching herself too thin, dark images and lack of sleep, she began to start having images of her death. At first they were fuzzy and difficult to decipher, but the more she tried to deny the fact that they were there; the more they poisoned her mind. It got to a point where she was visualizing herself dying over and over in different, gruesome ways and she could no longer control the thoughts.

They were dominating her mind and she was scared and alone again. Her desire to hide this fact from Liam and her friends and family was stupid but she desperately needed to appear independent again. Taking two steps back was not an option. Jory, Lilly, Lou Lou, Phil and Grace had already done so much for her; she thought that if she didn't admit that she was sick again, maybe she would magically heal without anyone ever noticing. She couldn't understand why this was happening, she took her medication religiously.

Her life was better than it had been in a very long time; she loved her place with Sarina, she had fallen madly in love with Liam and she was great at her job and she loved it. Maybe it was too much too soon. The year prior to this she had slept 23 hours a day and hibernated out in the country, far from any of the stimulation that city life had to offer. She didn't want this new life; these new changes to end; the last thing she wanted was to end up in the hospital for months again. Her fear of losing it all outweighed her good sense to check herself into the hospital to get her symptoms straightened out again. She went to visit her daunting, authoritative psychiatrist; a serious, mid-fifties, mainstream man, who talked down to her like she was a child with no brain. Psychiatrists and Pharmacy people always made her feel vulnerable and crazy; they gave her looks of pity and unpredictability, as though they were ready in case she "lost it". Looks saying "I know you have a mental illness Ha!" When she took her spot across from him she felt like she was shrinking...

After a few weeks the thoughts that lay scattered throughout the day, completely invaded her mind space. She could not run from them anymore. The chase ended and they had her on the ground, smothering her so she felt like she was choking. This is what it must feel like to be in purgatory; demons dancing around zooming in and out and feeding on her vulnerable soul. It was as though another dimension had seeped into her view and she was coexisting with the evil forces that existed there.

Today when I went to see Dr. Gender at the hospital I took a ride in the glass fronted elevator...I was early and I needed to pass the time...I knew if I sat in the waiting room with the drooling, hunched over patients with white sludge gathering at the sides of their mouth I would feel too much like them, like I was turning into them...I had to stay away till just minutes before my appointment. I went up to the very top floor...As we ascended I felt consumed and claustrophobic...all of a sudden I was choking on my breath...People kept getting on and their incessant talking made me feel like I was spinning... Too many voices...I pressed down hard on the words that wanted to come leaping out...”SHUT UP!!!!!” We descended quickly and I had my face pressed up against the window, trying to avoid contact with any of the strangers surrounding me, trying to enter my invisible personal space...I stared at the ground and a flash of myself smashing through the glass, shards flying outward in slow motion catching rays of sunlight on their plunge, my body, like a rag doll crashing to the cement ground, exploding with blood and innards...I winced trying to push the horrific image out of my poisoned mind...I reached the bottom floor and ran to the waiting room in the Psychiatry unit...There was only one patient there...The patient looked just like a character on this skit I used to watch on Saturday Night Live...A woman/man named Pat...He/ she was cheery with her/his big, soiled baggy t-shirt, mousy brown crew cut, chubby oval face with female features and pubescent male facial hair popping out of her facial moles like tiny ‘jack-in-the-boxes”...I tried to retreat into a small ball as I hugged my scrawny legs into me on the light brown office chair covered in anonymous stains...I avoided eye contact...Her/his androgynous voice rang out “What are you here for?”, “I have paranoid schizophrenia and I pull chunks of hair out of my head when I'm sad...” I remained silent and uncomfortable...Her/his voice was loud and annoying...He/she was one of those people that wore her craziness like a designer jacket, announcing it to the world with pride...I knew I would never be that person...She maybe saw it as something unique about herself, a gift...For me it was the dirty secret that I wanted to keep buried...I didn't want people to look at me and whisper, “Oh! She's crazy! You can just tell.”

“Hannah, the doctor is ready for you!”

“Oh! OK, thanks, bye!” Now I figured it was safe to talk to ‘Pat’, it would probably make her day and the likelihood that I would run into her again was slim to none...I sat directly across from the doctor and spread on a winning smile in order to fool him into thinking that I was ‘fabulous!’ I was so petrified of ending up in the hospital, losing everything that I fibbed and told my doctor that everything was great! Fabulous! Perfect!...I should have received an Academy Award for the performance I put on for him...To be honest he intimidated me, he was an egotistical ass like many of my previous male bosses, he got off on overpowering his ‘weak’ and ‘fragile’ patients...I couldn't let him see my vulnerabilities, I needed him to stay far away...He spent his typical five minute interval with me (if you set an egg timer, guaranteed it would ring on cue!) and then shushed me out the door...I felt cheated and wished I would've said something about what was really going on...As I walked home I shook my body, thinking that by shaking it I would be able to escape the demons...I

felt like I must have done something very wrong, and karmicly it was passing over into this lifetime...

A month passed and the darkness overtook every aspect of my mind...My body was in a constant state of tension and my limbs shook uncontrollably...The thoughts could not be kept at bay anymore, they invaded during every waking hour and held me from getting the sleep I so ached for...Less sleep created more severe symptoms...I was drowning and felt like I could no longer gasp for air, my body was being yanked under water and I was starting to feel limp and helpless...It was getting harder to keep my mask on when I was around clients, friends and family so I began to retreat...

Three sleepless days of twenty four hour hallucinations of my death brought me to a moment in time where I was left alone...I laid on my bed in the fetal position and rocked back and forth rhythmically...I lost touch with reality as the darkness seeped into the sky, turning it black...My lover and my soul mate took turns holding me, speaking to me in mumbled tones I could not make out...I forced a response but all that came out of my mouth were archaic moans...They tried to hold me still and stop me from rocking but I was unresponsive so they let me continue...Reality slipped out of my grasp and eventually so did my lover and my friend, when they thought sleep had finally come to carry me away for awhile...The sun shone through the bright, green, gauzy curtains that hung from my window adhered with golden tacks... Something came over me and for a few hours I snapped back into reality, I felt like a Rubik's cube that had been jumbled and was now completely lined up and intact, all coloured squares matching up on each side...In the morning I felt like I was back on solid ground, but once I arrived at my first clients house I started to lose my grip...her voice sounded like mumbling and as I stared at her face mimicking an attentive therapist I had to try and remember when to blink on cue so I wouldn't scream at the top of my lungs as the demons began their dance in my head...

I called in sick for the rest of the day...I came home to an empty house and made sure I had nothing planned for that night...My only plan was to end these thoughts now...I went into the deep lavender bathroom and turned on the tap...I took my clothes off and walked into the kitchen, pulled out the cutlery drawer and pulled out the largest, most serrated knife I could find... As if possessed I laid the knife on the left side of the porcelain tub and climbed in...the water was hot so I felt an intense warmth come over me...as I slid into it I realized this would be the last time I would participate in the orgasmic feeling of sinking into almost too hot bathwater...I laid there and stared at the knife...Tears ran down my face as I realized this was the end for me...I *could not take one more moment of this haunting my mind was consumed with...It was taking me away from all the joy I finally had...I grabbed the knife and held out my slim ivory wrist...I ran the knife swiftly over my slight wrist painted with baby blue veins...as I slid the knife back and forth roughly over my skin I became aggravated that the dull knife was barely breaking the skin, so I switched sides...I punctured the skin and a light stream of blood began seeping into the clear water transforming it into a transparent pink pool...Suddenly I imagined my virginally troubled roommate coming home and finding me laying in a bathtub of bloody water lifeless and exposed...I couldn't do it too her so I got out of the tub and unplugged it...I stood there thinking of alternative ways to end the thoughts that invaded me as I watched the muggy, pink water swirl down the drain...*

I threw some clothes onto my flushed, damp, body...stuck Band-Aids hap hazardly onto my pathetic, fresh wounds and sat down on my bed trying to think of other ways to do it...ways that would be tidy and more respectful...I decided an overdose would be the cleanest way to do it...rummaging around in the medicine cabinet for anything I could take in large quantities... frustrated by the fact that I only got one week of medication at a time, specifically so that I wouldn't end it...Anyway, what would taking a zillion mood stabilizers do anyway? I found a full family size bottle of Sarina's pain killers...That would do it! I filled up the largest glass of water I could find and studied myself in the embossed mirror attached to my mahogany dresser...I knew if I didn't do it quickly I would never do it...I fired as many pills in my mouth as I could and swallowed them with the water...Trying not to vomit I gagged on every handful until the bottle was empty...I had just swallowed close to one hundred pain killers and just came to the realization that I had no fucking idea what that was going to do to me...If it didn't kill me, how would I be affected? What if Sarina came home before I was gone? What if she came after? Suddenly I started to feel weak and woozy, I fell like a ragdoll crashing to the oak floor in a hump...The chortle of the phone jolted me back into consciousness...It was within reach, I suddenly remembered that Lana and I were supposed to get together...I reached for the phone and my arm felt like Jell-O...I smacked the talk button and mumbled "Hello" in a desperate attempt to hide it from my friend...Lana knew instantly that something was wrong by the way I was slurring my words...She hung up the phone and minutes later I heard her swinging open the front door...She raced into my room and saw me slumped on the floor with the empty bottle still sitting innocently on my dresser...She grabbed my face in her hands and stared into my eyes..."HOW MANY DID YOU TAKE?", I mumbled, "all...", "Oh My GOD! Well how many were in

173

there?"..."it was full..."She picked me up and carried me to her car...in a few minutes she was screaming for someone to help her as her borrowed Jeep idled in the Emergency car bay...

Lana had trouble looking me straight in the eyes...I could tell she was petrified but also annoyed by what I had done...The nurses were cold and abrupt...It would have been easier if they had just screamed into my face, "WHAT THE FUCK WERE YOU THINKING YOU SELFISH ASS!" But no one knew about the torture my mind had endured over the past month...I felt as though I was in purgatory yet still on earth trying to mingle with the common folk...All I had wanted was to stop the images and the voices in my head, I really liked my life and I had no desire to end it...My desire to see what was next was being snatched by the chaos in my own mind...I just wanted it to stop...I just wanted my mind to be quiet...Shhhhhh...Shhhhh...

Two eight ounce glasses of charcoal (meant to coat the poison that invaded my twenty-five year old body)...Several 'pooh pooh, my shit don't stink!' looks from the nurses (who the fuck did they think they were anyway with their cartoon covered scrubs? I didn't find it funny!)...About twenty violent hurls of grey sludge mixed with speckles of pale blue regurgitated pain killer...Later I realized that the stereotypical rumors were probably running rampant around the Emergency room now..."She probably did it for attention!"..."She's got that Manic Depressive Illness, watch out for those ones!"..."Did she think taking pain killers would kill her?"...Those thoughts ran through my head briefly, but I quickly noticed that the dark thoughts were suddenly on hiatus... How interesting...It almost seemed like attempting to take my own life clued my mind in and magically the neurons were startled into firing appropriately for a brief moment in time...

A few hours after entering the Emergency ward my brother and his wife Lilly were filling the tiny holding cell with their uncomfortable, humorous banter, making a great effort to not be completely revolted every time I ralphed into the faded, blue, plastic kidney basin...Lana and Lilly took turns rubbing my back and sputtering out unique phrases of compassion, "There, there, just let it out!"..."Your doing great Hannah"...I wondered if this was what it was like to give birth, everyone cheering me on and trying to make me as comfortable as possible...Though instead of miraculously pushing a nine pound baby out of my swollen vagina, I was spewing creamy grey matter out of my mouth that was now so dry I felt like it was going to split apart...This was definitely not a heroic act...it was at the opposite end of the spectrum than having a baby... like night and day...yin and yang...

On hour five, a chubby nurse, with vibrant red hair and Betty Boop scrubs came into my vomit scented cubical of suicide and sang out cheerily, "Your boyfriend has been sitting out in the hallway for about four hours. He keeps asking about you and wants desperately to see you. Will you see him now?" I was touched, horrified and upset that no one had mentioned the fact that he had been there the whole time…Lana admitted that she had called him right after she found me and she felt it best that he not come in…I understood where she was coming from, we had only been dating a few months and I didn't really want him to see me like this…He knew last night that I was in trouble and he had faced it head on, with no judgments…While I was trying to figure out what to do, my thoughts were interrupted by my brothers concerned voice, "Who is this guy anyway? How long have you been with him? Did he cause this?" I convinced Jory that Liam had been nothing but supportive and a positive influence in my life…He respected me enough not to sleep with me… enough to take our time and get to know one another…we had reached another stage of intimacy…a stage I had never reached with any other man…I had let him into my soul…let him see my vulnerabilities and he had shown me his in return…He was the first man who looked into me, not at me…I pleaded with my brother to trust me and let Liam come in and be with me alone…He resisted, but finally realized that maybe the guy in the hallway was just the right man to take over the job of looking after his little, vulnerable sister…It was a hard role to let go of but he knew he could not keep saving me for the rest of my life…I needed to find my own way now…Jory held me and I felt my cotton, wrap around sack soak with his tears…tears of a new beginning… tears of relief…tears of letting go…My eyes welled up too and I returned his hug…no words were said, but if that hug could talk?… I had never loved my brother as much as I did that day…

Liam walked into the room and his eyes were bloodshot, tears were welling in his eyes and he was making a hopeless effort to quell them…He walked over to me with relief, held me tight and we cried in silence for a few moments… When we released one another he looked me straight in the eye and he said, "I waited my whole life to find you, I finally did. You are not allowed to leave me now!" I had still not explained to anyone why I did what I did…It was so cold and calculated…My mind was controlling the actions, not my soul or my heart…Finally I tried my best to explain briefly what I had been going through…He patted my leg, looked me straight in the eye and said, "You don't have to explain, I love you more now than I ever have and I know you're hurting. Please just do whatever it is you need to do to get help and know that I will be here, by your side every step of the way…"

EVOLUTION

"A butterfly emerges, still moist from the cocoon. This is how new life comes, softly, secretly among the green shoots."

-From the Rune Cards by Ralph Blum

The Man without a Face

Winter 2001

Liam had seen her at her worst and loved her through it all. After her overdose she had never expected to see him again. He was the most devoted friend she had during her third stay in a Psychiatric Unit. Jory also came every lunch hour with a slice of pizza, rescuing her from the puddles of industrial hospital mush. The day after the overdose a bouquet of the most beautiful flowers arrived from him. There were violet and fuchsia orchids; fresh, white lilies; sprigs of tiny, lavish ivy caressing the flowers; and a beautiful nylon butterfly hiding amidst the colourful medley. All of these stunning items sat comfortably in a shallow, round, blown glass dish swirling with pastel colours. Hannah felt undeserving of this bouquet. She hoped with all her heart that Liam knew that her attempt on her life had nothing to do with him. On first hearing his kind voice she had known that he was the man she was going to marry; a nice guy; a guy that would treat her well; a guy that had all the qualities she had on her list; a guy that would never hurt her or disrespect her; a man who had no desire to flaunt his ego; a man that seemed more evolved than anyone she had ever known; a man she strived to be like; a man whose calm demeanor could quell her racing thoughts just by his presence. When the pills had started to take effect his face has started to fade; now it was clearer than ever. Her recovery was speedy because of the support of Liam and her brother. They had taken her off of the Lithium and put her on Epival, an anti-convulsion medication that was working wonders for her as a mood stabilizer.

The more time I spent with him the stronger I sensed that he was the man, the visualization, who had carried me through the rough times...the man without a face…When we stared into one another's eyes we were carried into our private universe where stars lit our way and butterflies danced to celebrate our love…Anyone who has been in love knows that when you find the right person, that person who seems to get you more than you get yourself, you finally feel like you can stop looking…There is a major sense of relief…I knew that no one would ever hurt me again…I was safe now…He helped me see myself again…his love for me was so pure that I could not help but learn to love myself again too…His humble nature brought me to a place of trust that I had never reached with a man before…With others I always had an invisible protective shield up, with him I knew I could stand totally exposed and he would care for me and let me lead him into the protected parts of myself…

I had never met anyone so romantic before…If I went to his house it would be filled with glimmering candles and the smells of his cooking…he made the most fantastic lasagna I had ever eaten…we sat face to face in a sunlit nook in a tiny corner of his fifties style bungalow…His grey, scraggly dog Lennon with her loving eyes curled up on my feet…I swirled my melted mozzarella around my fork and wondered how many more meals we would share at this table… When we were doing the dishes I stared at the knife block and had the intense desire to pull one out and stab myself…Instead I turned to him and held him, inhaling his herbal scent…I realized that the pain was not over, but with this man by my side it was something I could get through…I hoped it was not too soon as the wounds of his divorce a year previous were still fresh…He took his chances and let down his walls even though he had been hurt terribly…she had used him…what a stupid woman, she had treated the most amazing man I knew like he was disposable and the likelihood of her ever finding someone like him again was highly unlikely…

The universe has a way of clearing your path when something new and necessary comes dancing into your life. Like a patchwork quilt the pieces all starting fitting nicely together. Once my medication got straightened out I felt what many consider to be called 'normal'. It was a feeling I was quite unfamiliar with, I was able to sit in one place and not have the uncontrollable urge to get up and do something, and my mind was quiet for the first time…

After I got out of the hospital we never spent a night apart unless I was visiting my sister in Calgary. If I tried to talk while we were falling asleep he would shush me with his tender kisses. His calm energy kinetically fused with my manic energy and the two did a tango of balanced choreography. Together we were more whole and functional. I took him out of his shell and he showed me the beauty of silence and quietude. After so many years falling asleep with the television on, lonely and scared it felt so right to fall asleep in his protective arms. Being exactly the same size made holding each other so perfect, it was as though we were created specifically for one another, like the snug pieces of a puzzle. He was never harsh or threatening in anyway. He took his time nurturing me intimately. He was the first man I could be with in complete darkness. Comfortable and secure I could doze off to la la land without having to keep the light on. He never woke me up demanding sexual contact. It was as though he could read me. How did this man, who led a fairly protected, 'normal' life, know what my boundaries were without me even having to tell him anything about my past? I really never thought it possible to sleep soundly next to a man without having to be on guard all night, ready to defend myself...

Liam had helped me evolve sexually, emotionally, physically, inside and out. He helped me erase the past, embrace the present and anticipate the future. For that I will always love and cherish him...

Liam also had the desire to escape the memories of his past so he sold his bungalow and bought a small condominium. The first time I went to see it I knocked on the door. He didn't answer but the door was open ajar, so I walked in. When I opened the door I dropped my bag and giggled with delight as I stared at the stairs leading up to the bedroom. On each stair there was a tiny glimmering candle summoning me tenderly to follow the path. There scattered on each stair were dozens of deep crimson, baby pink and white rose petals caressing my naked feet as I ascended them with a heart full of passion. Candles decorated the master bedroom and the bathroom, paths of silky petals leading into each room. Liam sat on the edge of the bed with his arms out. I ran into them and he held me like a child. I wept, but my tears were not of sadness, they were of a pure joy that had been foreign up until now, no one had ever loved me as much as this man holding me. He took every opportunity to show me in everything he said and did. On that night of my awakening, I bathed with him in water filled with rose petals; I made love to him for the first time in a bed of rose petals and slept in them intertwined with the man who now had a face...

Glacier National Park
August 4, 2002

Their wedding had been a glorious expression of who they were as a couple; one that none of the intimate participants would ever forget. They wrote their own vows and had an artist friend marry them. Members of their family made the trip to Glacier National Park and everyone set up camp for the August long weekend. The day before the wedding they drove down the narrow, winding, mountain "Going to the Sun Road" looking for the perfect spot to fuse their hearts and lives. On the side of the road there was a small sign reading "Sun Point", they had to skid to make it into the parking lot, camouflaged by foliage. There was a winding path through the trees that took them to a very narrow steep inclined path. Excitement rose within them; it was as though there was a magnetic field that was drawing them into its majestic energy.

They reached the top and stood in front of a pedestal describing the history of the location. They were at the top of a cliff with a bed of golden rocks that mimicked perfect seats. Surrounding the cliff was endless water, an artist's palette of blue hues. A gentle wind caressed her cheek, and she felt the familiarity of Liam's gentle arm scoop her into his warmth. Along the edge of the water were the most awe-inspiring silver mountains surrounding them in a complete circle. They said nothing to one another, the intensity of nature's artistry spoke to them; carried on the wind. This was the place.

The wedding day was unforgettable. Her six nieces adorned with fairy costumes, sparkly, nylon wings, magic wands and wreaths of flowers in their hair danced up the cliff towards their waiting parents to the song, "Kissing You," off the Moulin Rouge soundtrack. Hannah came up the mountain to "Wishlist" a Pearl Jam cover performed by the band they had formed after meeting (Hannah was the lead singer and Liam the drummer); her father was on one of her arms and her brother was on the other, he had a smile that was so intense, it spread like a wave onto each of the family and friends faces as they sat on the golden rocks, stunned by the beauty of their surroundings.

Liam had written her a beautiful poem to express his love for her, it was one that he'd written overlooking the river as the sunset and the inspiration shone out from his words:

On this day of beauty that defines our love; is there something I could tell you that hasn't already been said…A piece of me left to reveal; something yet unseen; or a gift left to give to you; something more…Maybe a thought you don't already know; or someplace in our hearts we haven't already been; some new high where our spirits could go;

We've given each other all of this!

The first time we locked eyes, entranced in loves stare; or when we leaned over the table for our first kiss; when I first learned of your immense capacity to care; or the first time I saw the world through your eyes; or our long talks, open with nothing to hide;

The first time we shared a good cry; or when I first knew what life could be with you by my side.

When without a word you made me realize who I could be.

Or the first time in the midst of a crowded room we were alone in our own world, just me and you.

When the first time the clouds lifted and the sun shone just because you smiled at me.

The first time I became aware that no matter how beautiful our love is, or how strong the bond that ties us, or when our love can't possibly fill us anymore. The next day, the next moment I looked at you, to my amazement, it only grew. This was the moment I knew I had to spend my life with you.

Hannah, I see the light of the world in you; You're my Angel; I Love You! Liam

Tears streamed down her face as she sang her vows in response, "*Thank you for Loving Me*", by Sinead O'Connor. They kissed several times before the "you may kiss the bride" part, sending chuckles across the participants.

After the wedding, they signed the papers and turned to one another and all of a sudden everyone became invisible. They were alone and consumed with the power of their love. Silence caressed them as they stared out at the mountains and glistening water below. They held one another and pressed themselves into one another. Gentle kisses and the power of what their eyes said to one another made them feel lost in the moment. The buzz of voices and the sound of cameras clicking were muted by their passionate connection. After a while they realized that all their friends and family were standing there watching them, also in silence, there was not a dry eye on that cliff. People remembered lost loves, new love, the search for love and they felt a universal connection to what Liam and Hannah shared that day after the vows were spoken.

Motherhood

November, 2002

The collapse of her own childhood past the age of three had her wondering whether she was fit to be a mother. A mother was someone that had to be dependable and self-assured so that her children would feel secure in her care. Now she could not turn back, the seed of life was already implanted in her womb. Hannah had exactly seven and a half months to get her shit together and become mother material. Getting married to Liam had helped set her feet on solid ground.

By the Light of the Harvest Moon

A decade prior Hannah had been told by several specialists that because of the abuse she had suffered she had too much scar tissue in her reproductive system to conceive a baby. Liam knew this so as soon as they got married they booked an appointment with a fertility specialist. He examined her one hot, muggy August afternoon and asked them to come back in a week for the results. They waited with a mixture of fear and anxiety for the call. The week seemed to drag on until the following Friday. The phone rang and to their relief it was the Doctor. He said they both needed to get on the phone. "Hannah and Liam, somehow over time your scar tissue has healed, you have the green light, congratulations, you can have a baby!"

I sobbed and released two decades of pain and resentment that I had been carrying towards the men that had hurt me and destroyed my body. I thought that because of them I would never be able to have kids and now it was as though someone had given me a precious gift. I needed to have my two children, the two I had imagined, my son and my daughter. I was giddy and delirious with love. It was possible to have and hold onto happiness, it seemed bad luck was no longer attracted to me. The condoms came off and the baby making process was on...

After finding out about my healed womb I relaxed and just enjoyed every sweet moment of married life. One evening we took a walk by the forest that lay parallel to the North Saskatchewan River. The sun was in the process of setting and all the other people had dissipated. We were embraced by solitude and surrounded by the whispers of the warm evening wind rustling the delicate leaves of the tall, lush trees. I felt as though I was backlit by a wondrous light. Liam turned me around and pointed to a luminescent, mandarin coloured moon that filled half the sky..."That's a Harvest Moon; they're called that because they are closer at this time in the autumn, when the farmer's collect their harvests. You look stunning in its glow. I'm so in love with you Hannah Knight." I answered with a kiss as we embraced and found a massive tree lying on its side.

By the light of the harvest moon we conceived our first child...

Holding On

When we found out I was pregnant we were transported to a fantasy life where all our dreams were finally coming true. Liam had always wanted children and I knew I was meant to have two; we never dreamed it would happen so fast...

After we celebrated we sat down and seriously discussed what we needed to do about my health during the pregnancy. The medication I was on was working but unfortunately it could possibly cause serious birth defects in the fetus of the baby. So with the green light from my new female doctor we agreed that I would try and go off the medication for the duration of the pregnancy. I had already quit smoking months prior to the news. It happened very quickly, but the thrill of having a life growing inside me made the withdrawal more bearable. My body shook, I was very irritable and my temperature shot up and down rapidly for the first week. I felt like a drug addict in recovery. Liam took some time off to help me get through the initial withdrawal phase. I had not slept without sleep medication in years so he would try and force himself to stay awake, rubbing my back and talking to me through the long stretches of insomnia. Liam was putting himself through everything with me, he never let me go through any of it alone. When he returned to work I became slightly manic and would drive around spending money on art supplies and second hand bargains. After clearing out the bank account a few checks in a row and watching the 400 square foot condo get cluttered, I begged Liam to take my car keys and my wallet. He was only to give them to me when I had a valid appointment or a specific trip I needed to take. I asked him for an allowance to control my spending. It killed him to be the enforcer of these things; he didn't want me to resent him for taking away my freedom. That made me love him even more. I made him act as my 'realistic, logical, practical' brain. Without my keys and wallet I felt slightly trapped, but it had to be done if we were going to get through this pregnancy with our finances and me intact. My mania worsened about halfway through my first trimester and I began hallucinating again. I tried to ignore the shadow people that milled around the apartment with me and the black insects that climbed the walls and black birds that filled the sky. Eventually I had to get a team of mental health nurses coming in everyday to check on me. I didn't always tell Liam because I didn't really want him to know how bad it really was. I was willing to sacrifice some things so that my child would be healthy...

Second Trimester

Feeling a flutter from within your own body, the flutter of your unborn child is the most majestic feeling. Your never alone, you and your child are connected in a profoundly intimate way; you are one heart, one soul for the pregnancy. I felt as though I was falling in love again, with the tiny person that floated in my womb. I fell in love with my body during the pregnancy and never imagined how beautiful I could be. I wore clothing that hugged my belly, and flowing dresses, cotton blouses with empire waists with tiny embroidered flowers adorning them. Every day I wrote in a journal, took pictures and documented all of the progress we were making...I kept myself busy by watching "Dharma and Greg", and TLC's "The Baby Story" every morning. I did prenatal yoga and took Lennon for walks in the forest by our condo. My body was blooming and I had been successful at keeping my illness at bay. I was not going to let my brain win or gain control. I did clear my schedule of anything that would cause me anxiety, which was basically every function where there were lots of people. I could meet one on one but I pretty much stuck around home. Certain people made me feel physically ill, like I was going to jump out of my skin; I avoided them...

I had to quit my full-time job at an Interior Design firm due to stress so I immersed myself in my art. I painted murals in all of the upstairs rooms. I rented a table on Saturdays at "The Paris Market" downtown and sold vintage lamps that I had hand painted. They each had a vibrant silk shade and whimsical beadwork. I never sold as much as my rent but it was quiet and the artisans there made me feel like part of a community. They were 'real' and humble people who truly appreciated the small, simple things in life.

Third Trimester

On a Friday I had borrowed the car to go to my Gynecologists office; she was famous for making you wait close to an hour for your appointment. On this particular day I was feeling very vulnerable. I was thirty five weeks pregnant and the weather was warm and muggy, making carrying this large belly quite the task. I had gained fifty pounds from eating almost a full container of Haagen Daaz, coffee flavored ice cream on a nightly basis (a worthy and better tasting replacement for cigarettes). Emotionally I was hanging on a very thin thread. As I sat on the uncomfortable chair in the office I felt the urge to break out in tears. I had come to most of my appointments (except ultrasounds) alone or with Liam, and I felt a horrible gap as I sat and looked at all the women whose mother's sat supportively by their sides. I had an incredible urge to slap them in the face. I wanted a mother to share this part of my life, someone to nurture me and the baby. Liam did what he could to get the time off work, but right now I just needed a woman's touch. Two young boys sat in the toy corner and started squealing and bickering. My nerves were like elastic bands being stretched so far that they were cracked and ever so close to snapping. A baby started to cry and I heard all the voices of every person in that waiting room but their voices were amplified and sounded like the screeching tires of a hot rod...I had to hold back my scream...I just held my head in my hands, covering my ears, trying to block it all out...The tears were uncontrollable, out they came with a vengeance...I couldn't hide, soon all eyes were on me and I heard a little voice to my left, it was a little girl about three years old with spiral curls and a pink fuzzy vest, "Why are you cwying lady?" I forced a smile at the little girl, picked up my stuff and flung open the heavy frosted glass door...I slid down the glass on the outside of the office and slumped over as far as my stretched body would allow, and then held my head in my hands...the skin on my belly was so taught it felt like it was going to burst but I welcomed the pain like an old friend...

The door swung open and one of the familiar nurses held her hand out to me...I started to sob as she put her arm around me and led me to a vacant room...she whispered, "next time you need to let me know and I will put you in a room until the doctor can see you." Her actions that day were heroic in my eyes...I just needed someone to carry me...

While I was sharing a bath with my favorite man, the life inside of me started to show signs that he was ready to arrive. My belly would harden completely and with that feeling came a pang of pressure that was uncomfortable yet oddly exhilarating. I knew that it was finally time to meet my little Ben. I wondered if he would look like Liam or me, what kind of personality he would have, how the labor and delivery would go. As Liam loaded the car I sat in his nursery and gazed at the birds and butterflies that danced on his ceiling backed by the flowy, sheer fabric and twinkling white lights that I had stapled up. I imagined him playing in his crib surrounded by the murals I had painted, one wall was a glorious sunrise with a large oak tree; another was the night sky with shimmery painted stars and quotes about motherhood and babies; the third a breathtaking sunset with a watercolour willow tree and the last a brilliant blue sky with white billowy clouds...

The intense pressure I felt to be 'the perfect mom' weighed on me when I realized that I was about to be the one in the responsible role. I had visited independence for a while, but my dependence on my friends and men had carried me along my journey. I would have to be strong for this little soul who chose to have me for his mom. During the pregnancy I had a reoccurring nightmare that I kept forgetting to feed Ben, it taunted me, like a carrot being dangled in front of a circus ponies face...

Twenty four hours later my son was placed on my naked chest as my husband held us, my sister silently wept, thankful she had made the three hour drive all the way from Calgary and arrived in time for the labor and delivery, and the doctors and nurses stood back and realized why they chose their occupation. He was perfect in every way. He didn't cry he just pressed his face against my warm, flushed skin and breathed quietly. Holding him and staring into his and my husband's eyes was the most magnificent moment of my life. My fears escaped and I was filled with the most confident emotions, I realized that I now had my very own family, with no dysfunction, no abuse, just a beautifully clean slate. The past dissipated and became buried so deep within me I felt like I was fresh and new. I defined what kind of mother I would be, not my past. I had no one to direct me but myself and my husband, and we would hold hands and learn the lessons of parenthood together...

After the commotion was over in the delivery room and we were brought to our stunning themed room; a room with a queen sized bed, a down comforter and Egyptian cotton sheets, a rocking horse in the corner, a mahogany dresser with a beveled mirror. Liam worked at the hospital so he made sure we had the best of everything and that all my needs were met, he never once left my side, this was something we were doing together, he didn't want to miss a beat...

As we lay together in our hotelesque hospital bed I placed Ben at my breast for the first time, his tiny eyes wandered as I moved my nipple trying to get him to latch on. He latched right away like a child who had been breastfeeding for months. He stayed there in between Liam and I as we all dozed off to sleep. The gentle sound of Ben nourishing himself at my breast was a meditative melody of life. Our first wondrous night as "The Knight Family"...

All of a sudden this intense feeling rushed over me. If I had to go through all those dark times to appreciate this quiet moment with my newborn son and my husband then all those years were worth it. My life changed drastically that night, I knew then and there that I would never be alone again. My grown man and my baby boy would transform my history ...

Leaky Breasts and Diapers

Until you have a child of your own you really have no clue what it is really like to have a baby. Your world completely changes and you see everything with a different set of eyes. Life is no longer about you and your needs; every moment is orchestrated by your new helpless baby. You are quickly transformed into the most generous, patient, nurturing soul, who lives and breathes for this life that just came into yours. You let your guard down and you release your ego completely; breasts are dangling, squirting and staining all your fat day shirts, but those full breasts are keeping that little boy alive and helping him thrive in his new life while still giving him an opportunity to have a physical connection to you, who carried him, talked to him, rubbed him and loved him while he was being carried...

Getting ready to go out as a family turns from a ten minute touch up to two explosive poops, three projectile vomits, two blouses and skirts, five diaper changes, a twenty minute feeding, packing and repacking the zillion baby items methodically. You go from being punctual to being lucky to get anywhere at all, but it's exhilarating! All of it! I loved every diaper change, every late night feeding, and every load of teeny, tiny pastel laundry. I felt like I was here to be Ben's mommy and the great love of Liam's life…

Focusing on him also helped me quell the bipolar symptoms that would creep up, tap me on the shoulder and remind me that I wasn't 'normal' or 'perfect'. The shadow people still tiptoed around the house, playing a dangerous game of 'hide and seek', taunting me and trying to reel me in. I just reminded myself that they weren't real; I just needed to get busy and shake them off. When I felt like I was drowning I would tread water as hard as I could and use all my strength to keep going. Liam was the most supportive man I could have ever asked for. He never demanded anything of me and was so thankful for the effort I made to have a beautiful, happy home. I think he felt as I did, that he was finally home…

A few days after we arrived home from the hospital my brother dropped my mom off for the day. She came offering a rainbow coloured blanket she had knit for Ben. As soon as she was in his presence I felt like I was suffocating. She kept taking pictures and acting like there was nothing in our history. The walls of my vibrant, raspberry coloured living room started closing in on me and I quickly picked up my swaddled son and stepped into the tiny backyard of our condo. I didn't know how to tell her she was not welcome to touch my son, that she hadn't earned the right! When I looked at her smiley, complacent face I wanted to slap it into reality. She represented all the horror of my past and I thought if she touched him my past would merge with my present. Several hours later and as many desperate attempts for my Mom to make excuses to hold my son I finally realized she would not give up until I let her hold him. I gave Liam a pleading look as if to say, "save me from this!" but I knew I couldn't escape the inevitable. I didn't want to get into all of the past right now, this was supposed to be the happiest time in my life and my Mom was here flaunting the past, waving it in my face as if to say, "Ne, ne, ne, ne, ne, I'm not going away, you can't run from me!" As I passed him to her the colour left my face and my body seized up. I felt like I was passing him to the dark side. She held him a total of two minutes, he squirmed and I said, "Oh, he's hungry, thanks, 'er, Mom". That was the last time I or my son ever saw my Mom…

Mother Earth Miracle

Hannah felt life growing within her for the second time. Liam had taken a second night job, several months prior, driving cabs to supplement their income Elated she called Liam on his pager to tell him; she typed in 911 which was the signal that she was pregnant and he was to call her as soon as he could. When Liam received the page, he was collecting his fare from a tall Asian man as he dropped him off at a seedy nightclub. The club had a colourful mural of a well-endowed woman with star shaped tassels on her naked breasts. He rushed the man out of his cab. Liam's stomach started flipping as he searched for the closest payphone. Three minutes later he finally found one in the parking lot of Humpty's Egg Place. He jumped out the door of the cab leaving it idling less than a foot from the cubicle and frantically dialed Hannah at home. She picked up before the first ring was even in progress…

"*We're having another baby!!!*"

"Are you sure?" Liam replied excitedly.

"*I did two tests, one right after the other and they were bright purple!*" Hannah shouted.

"I wish I could hold you right now baby!" Liam sighed.

"*Me too hon; I kinda wish I had waited till you were here, I just couldn't wait!*"

"It's O.K. I'm just thrilled babe. I love you and I'll see you in the morning."

"*O.K., I love you too, be safe!*"

"Bye Babe."

"*Bye.*"

191

After hanging up with Liam, she called everyone in her phonebook to tell them the news. This was not a time she wanted to be alone. Her closest family and friends stifled their fear and tried to sound purely elated for the couple. She had just gone back on her medication again after being off for two and a half years. She had stayed off for the year and a half that she breastfed Ben. Hannah tried to repress her fear for a while and just revel in the fact that there was a child growing inside her again.

As the evening progressed, she would periodically squeal with excitement. Sleep came slowly that night for Hannah. She wanted to feel Liam's arms around her and hear his breath gentle in her ear. The fears started to permeate her elevated state of mind. This was her first night off the medication that kept her sane and grounded. While pregnant with Ben she had fierce hallucinations while laying in the dark at night that bugs were covering her like a live blanket. She also had flashes of demons endlessly chasing and capturing her and her newborn son. Hannah hoped that she would be able to fight the hallucinations and run them out of her mind if they did come. For now, she wanted to try to remain as calm as possible and enjoy this new life force within her. Anxiety prevented her from drifting off to sleep; she tossed and battled the images and fears that were leaping in and out of her mind. Finally she heard the garage door open, the ignition turn off, the car door shut, the footsteps approach the front door, the key in the lock, the knob turning, the opening and closing of the door, the closet, the hanging of the coat, the banging of dishes in the kitchen, the footsteps to Ben's door, the opening and peeking in on Ben, the sound of the bathroom light flick on, the longest urination in history, the brushing of teeth, the opening of the master bedroom door, the clothes being removed and thrown on the floor, the sound of the mattress depressing under his body weight...

"*Liam*" Hannah whispered with anticipation and neediness.

"Your still awake my girl" Liam replied quiet and happy.

"*I couldn't sleep without you, I needed you.*"

"Can I spoon you and the baby?"

"*Of course, I love you, I'm glad your home.*"

"Me too, and I love you, go to sleep now Momma Love."

Liam drifted off to sleep first. Hannah's mind would not shut off but she hesitated waking Liam and telling him her fears although she really needed him now. She did not want him to worry or know that she was scared of what the next nine months would bring. During her pregnancy with Ben, she did not have the responsibility of caring for a seventeen-month-old child. How would she cope with being off all her medications for the entire pregnancy? As thoughts and fears raced through her troubled mind, she fought them off by placing her right hand on her womb and singing quietly to her tiny miracle.

The proceeding weeks flew by without incident, as there were many appointments to make and attend. Eventually the thrill and excitement began to dissipate as Hannah's manic symptoms began to creep back to life in her mind. One evening as she was watching the television with Liam she walked casually into the bathroom. She opened the toilet lid and the water in the bowl was deep, blood red in colour and was spinning rapidly. She blinked and shut the lid. Her need to urinate did not exceed her fear of what was in the bowl so she quickly walked out of the bathroom and back into the living room. Liam noticed right away that the colour had completely drained from Hannah's face.

"Are you O.K. Hannah?" Liam asked

"I'm fine, just nauseous." She responded making sure to avoid eye contact.

Liam was very intuitive and had always had a sixth sense, particularly when it came to reading Hannah. That and his gentle nature are why the two meshed very well as a couple, as lovers and as parents. He wanted to pry but knew that Hannah had to come to him first. Since finding out about the pregnancy, she had not discussed her fears with him. Silently, he wondered why. Did she not trust him? Was she afraid that he would think she was incompetent or unsafe around his child, himself or her and their unborn child? Yes! These were exactly the reasons Hannah was repressing her fears and not discussing them with anyone, not Liam or anyone else she had grown to trust. Mentally, Hannah was in turmoil, the old personality was taking over, the medication had worn off and the crazy, insecure, self-loathing, Hannah was being resurrected. She worked hard to hide this from the people she loved because she did not want to let them know she was this close to cracking. Hannah was a powder keg about to explode.

As Hannah was cooking dinner one evening, her blood began to boil. Liam had gone downstairs to play the drums and had left Ben with her. Ben was getting hungry and started pulling on her pant leg whining "Mommy, suppa!" repeatedly. Hannah felt the anxiety wrap tightly around her chest, the pain was unbearable…television blaring, Dr.Phil's annoying southern accent…the loud thundering of the drums emanating from below the linoleum…everything in the kitchen vibrating…the pressure of Ben's grip around her calf…Ben's whining "suppa, Mommy, suppa…" The stimulation was overbearing for Hannah and she felt her patience and reserve being stripped quickly from her. Bluntly she yelled down the stairs "*LIAM*", she noticed the rice water boiling over, water seeping through the space between the lid and the stainless steel pot, she ran to remove the lid and began stirring the drowning rice. "*Great the fucking rice is stuck to the bottom of the pot!*" She spat. Now all control was gone! "*LIAM!*" She screamed once more down the stairs. "*LIAM!*" She must have screamed five or six times and there was no reply from downstairs, just the sound of Liam's constant drum beat vibrating underneath her feet. Ben was frightened by her screaming as this was not something he was accustomed to hearing, his Mommy and Daddy had never fought before, they had not even argued in front of him. He covered his tiny ears with his hands and started to sob. Hannah scooped him up, flung the child safety gate open and bounded down the stairs, her temper flaring. Ben pulled his body away from hers in fear. She pushed the door open and looked at Liam, quickly he jolted up from his stool and ceased drumming, and he then took the headphones off. He looked at her stunned noticing the anger flaring in her eyes, "What's up?" "*I have been yelling your name for about five minutes, I needed your help and I didn't want to have to come down here with Ben. Are you coming up for supper or what?*" Hannah choked out violently. Without waiting for Liam's response she proceeded swiftly back upstairs to deal with the mess that was to be their supper. "Hannah!" he innocently yelled after her. She completely ignored him.

Angel's by Her Side

The buzzer gently vibrated in her ear as she woke up with a start, the clock read 6:30am. She was instantly alert and excited about reuniting with Lou Lou and her new baby girl. Hannah had been at the hospital in Calgary the previous day for the birth. The two sisters had been there for the birth of each other's children all along, this being Lou Lou's fourth child. She had gone back to Lou Lou's new home in Strathmore along with Jory and Lilly, Eddy and the kids and Eddy's mom after visiting hours had ended the night before. Strathmore was forty kilometers south of Calgary.

Hannah quietly dressed as not to wake Lou Lou's Mother-in-Law who lay sleeping peacefully in the bed beside her. She packed all her belongings, knowing that through her excitement she mustn't forget to eat for she had to nourish the life growing inside her. Quickly she grabbed a banana out of the oak bowl on the counter.

As she stepped out into the frigid dawn air, she found her first breath strenuous. She squinted to see her vehicle through the fog that lay thick in the dawn air. Letting the vehicle warm up she scraped a thin layer of ice that had made a delicate patterned film on all her windows in the night. She placed all her belongings in the trunk and sat in the car until it was warm enough to go. The small town was very silent as it was a Saturday and Valentine's Day, everyone was cozy in bed sleeping in with their families. Hannah had pangs of longing every time she thought of Liam and Ben. This had been her first trip away from both of them since her and Liam got married three years ago. Lou Lou had always been there for her and this was her time to be her older sister's strength.

She pulled into Tim Horton's and ordered a large herbal tea and a toasted blueberry bagel with strawberry cream cheese for her breakfast. As she pulled out of the Drive-Thru and onto the highway headed out of Strathmore towards Calgary her thoughts strayed momentarily from her sister and onto how dense the fog was and how sparse the vehicles on the highway were. As she turned onto the straight secondary highway her back wheels slid from side to side like a skater on a fresh, wet rink. In order to distract herself from the fear of not having much visualization she popped in the book on tape she had borrowed from the library to listen to for comfort. It was a murder mystery about a female bodyguard whose client was murdered while she was in the house.

Having always taken the small back highways from Edmonton to Strathmore to visit her sister she was not familiar with this highway. She had never taken the trek from Strathmore to Calgary before. She drove about 30 km's under the speed limit while the minority of confident drivers behind her kept passing hurriedly by. Her jaw became sore and tender from clenching it so violently. Just then she remembered in her excitement on leaving her sister's house that morning she had placed all her belongings in the trunk of the car, all she had in the car was the wallet that sat in her winter coat. She pondered whether she should pull over on the highway and take her purse out of the trunk as it held her in-laws clunky old cell phone. "*No*" she thought, "*I need to get to the hospital as fast as possible to be with Lou, she'll be waking up soon.*"

There was very little visibility on the highway and at times it seemed hers was the only vehicle on the highway for many miles. The companion lights of a leading vehicle would have been comforting to her right now.

Hannah's back began to ach from tensing it up so much. Thoughts of Lou Lou and her tiny new little girl made her journey more bearable, she could hardly wait to see them this morning. Along their rocky journey they had held hands and survived together, always being there for one another. There was nothing in the world that the two sisters could not say to one another. Lou Lou was the only one that knew both the deepest darkest parts of Hannah and the strong fabulous brilliant sides too. Hannah wanted so badly to care for her sister the way Lou Lou had done for her when she lay comatose in the psych ward five years prior. After the c-section yesterday Hannah had bathed Lou Lou lovingly and massaged all the built up fluid retention from the pregnancy out of her arms and legs. As she massaged her she did it with the greatest feeling of pure love. Lou Lou had spent her life taking on the role of Mother to Hannah. Hannah had attempted to reciprocate throughout their lives but Lou Lou always maintained a strong stubborn defiance to Hannah looking after her in anyway. Lou Lou had grown accustomed to always being the strong one that held everyone in the family together. In the recent years Lou Lou was more open to accepting Hannah's nurturing and had cried on her shoulder many times once the wall was broken down. That being why the journey was so essential to Hannah this morning, she really had waited her whole life for Lou Lou to let her reverse the roles and now was her time to give back…All of a sudden a sharp curve came out of nowhere on this perfectly straight highway… she veered away from the path of the oncoming traffic and tried to feel out the curve but she had hit a patch of black ice…she felt herself losing control of the car, a feeling that was foreign to her as she had never had a car accident before…the car spun clockwise a full 180 degrees…Hannah did not know if her and the child she was carrying were going to live…she placed one hand on her swollen belly and the other on the steering wheel… as the front end struck the edge of the ditch…

Oh my God! Please No! I love you Lela! I'm not ready to go now! Please God help us! Hannah screamed …the car flew up into the air and landed on its roof…then up into the air again and onto its wheels… the impact causing the metal to buckle in around them and the glass to shatter…the car continued the same sequence five times…the silence of the vehicle as it sailed through the air was deafening and terrifying…Hannah believed they would not make it…**No! I don't want to leave now…I love my life I want to keep going please don't take me now!**…she wondered if the vehicle would ever stop flipping…suddenly the vehicle made its permanent landing on a farmers barbed wire fence…luckily the vehicle landed on its wheels...by this point Hannah was sobbing uncontrollably unaware that she was covered in shards of glass...she looked around her and noticed the windshield was completely bashed in and all the windows were smashed except hers...she hyperventilated as she held her belly hoping that Lela had made it through this, she was only fifteen weeks and had not yet felt the baby move noticeably so she wasn't able to tell if the child was OK...shivering...*Where did my gloves go? Oh God! What should I do?...*her car was at least 50 meters from the side of the highway...invisible from the highway...pain like fire through her body...*Should I move?* Still in shock she pries open her door noticing that for some reason the glass and the metal of her door are completely untouched as if there were an invisible barrier guarding them during the crash...*Where's the cell? Oh my God!* She shook ferociously and as she pulled herself out of the car a searing pain shot up her spine...she searched the trunk for her mother-in-laws cell phone realizing that if she had left all her belongings in the car they could have flung around while the car rolled, knocking her unconscious...she climbed back into what was left of the vehicle and turned on the phone...the melting snow that filled her running shoes sent a painful shiver through her entire body...staring at the green screen of the phone she found it impossible to remember her sister's phone number, she had called her sister once or twice a day for years but her mind was completely blank, with each second she grew more frantic...*What the hell is the number? Please help me God what am I gonna do?* After a few moments each number appeared...as if someone had strategically placed them for her mind's eye to see...the air was so thick it was silent...each number she depressed was almost deafening...ring...ring...ring...*Oh God! They're all still asleep... what am I gonna do?* Ring...ring..."Hello! We can't come to the phone right now leave a message, chow for now, Bye!" Beep...*"Help me please! Someone please pick up the phone...I had a really bad accident and I don't know what to do! Help! Please pick up the phone!"*..."Hello!" Jory's wife Lilly answered groggily. "Hannah, what happened?"

"I hit a patch of black ice and my car rolled five times." She responded as she tried to speak through her sobs.

"Oh my God! JORY! EDDY! Hannah just wait there, don't move, Eddy is calling 911. Eddy and Jory are coming down there, where are you?"

"I don't really know. This curve came out of nowhere on the highway...I think the last sign I saw said Chestermere? I'm worried about my baby. Lilly I'm so scared I don't know what to do. I just

wanted to go see Lou Lou. Please tell them not to let her know. This is her special time I don't want to ruin it for her."

"How far off the road are you?"

"I'm really far, like 50 meters, I'm in a farmer's field and the car is facing the oncoming traffic."

"Are you hurt? Can you move?"

"I got out of the car to get the cell phone out of the trunk, my body really hurts though. Lilly I don't know what to do?"

"You're gonna be OK Han and so is Lela, we're getting help for you right now."

Hannah could not control her shivering, from shock, freezing; the dry, frigid air was blowing right in at her. The shards of glass that had showered her now felt like thousands of tiny pin pricks agitating her cold, aching, swollen body. She tried to focus on Lilly's soothing voice on the other end of the phone as she waited helplessly for her brother and Eddy to come help her.

Through the dense fog Hannah spotted a car slowing down on the highway beside her. The driver exited the vehicle and started a slow ascent towards her vehicle. The snow drifts in the ditch and beyond were at least a foot and a half deep. Vulnerability and paranoia cloaked her and made her chest tight...she felt like she was suffocating ...*"Oh my God Lilly, there is a man walking towards the car, what should I do, what should I do?..."* Han, just stay on the phone with me, don't hang up whatever you do." A scrawny, unshaven man with sparse brown hair and a faded leather Calgary Flames jacket materialized as he gradually trudged through the deep snow...he reached her car window and asked her if she was OK then offered her a hand getting out of the vehicle..

"I'm in pain; I need to stay on the phone with my sister-in-law."

"OK, but why don't you come and stay warm in my car? Can you move?"

"I got the phone out of the trunk so I should be OK, can you wait a sec. Lilly should I go wait in this man's car?"

"Yes." Lilly replied. "Stay on the phone with me though until Jory and Eddy get there OK? The ambulance should be there soon Eddy called before they left and they were heading there."

In silence the two strangers struggled through the packed snow, Hannah tried to hide the pain surging through her body. The heavy, wet snow saturated her runners and socks and began its ascent up her stretchy denim pant legs. Finally they reached his beat up old Honda civic. His car was only a few degrees warmer than outside but at least it was a barrier to the crisp morning wind chill. Hannah stayed on the phone with Lilly never speaking a word to the kind man, this she later regretted as he was the only one who stopped for her that hellish morning. She never even asked him what his name was.

Five hours later she was cradling Lou Lou's newborn baby Mady in her arms. While in Emergency they had promised to do an ultrasound to check on the baby, but after doing an array of x-rays and a Doppler test they opted not to. When Hannah tearfully asked why, the nurse retorted in a snotty tone "at this early stage in your pregnancy if there is anything wrong we won't be able to do anything about it anyway." Those words kept taunting Hannah as she held Mady in her arms; it took all her strength not to cry.

My Miracle

There were many ultrasounds done after the accident, but Hannah was not entirely sure if her unborn child would be O.K. Trying to care for Ben and deal with the pain from the accident proved to be very challenging. Her body ached for her to lie and rest, but her two year old taunted for her to be his playmate and the vibrant mother that he was used to. At this point in her life her desperate need for help was undeniable, but it was fiercely overshadowed by her need to be the 'ideal' parent for her son. A fear lingered within her, a fear that people would see her as an incompetent mother due to her illness slid her into a small corner, making it impossible for her to admit defeat. Her refusal to seek help for fear that her children may be 'ruined' crippled her at this point in time and many more times in the future…

Hold On
August 2004

She sunk slowly into the near scalding water, the pain from the heat searing yet soothing, exhausted her. All she could hear were the Jacuzzi jets humming loudly, the water spinning in competition with her mind, pounding against her stretched post-pregnancy flesh. She started to second guess herself for the first time since she gave birth to her wondrous little girl. She recalled her last appointment with Dr.Gender (her first psychiatrist) saying "I don't think it's a good idea for you to have children with your history Hannah." For the first time she wondered if he was right. It was different when she was alone; there was no one to bring along with her on this crazy journey called life. As she slid further into the water covering her head she felt like she was losing control again. In the past when it had gotten this bad she was unable to escape it for weeks. This time things were different though, her small family depended on her, she HAD to keep it together for them. As the jets beat water into the sides of her arms and legs she imagined the forceful water hammering the shit out of the stressful overwhelming feelings that lay invisible in her body. Upon climbing out of the searing water a sense of inner peace washed over her and brought her to a place that was lovely and manageable. The aftermath of giving birth was just so overwhelming that it had masked the beauty of the point she had reached in her life. Through her darkest times she had imagined what it would be like when she had her own family. She had visualized all three of their souls but they had always been faceless. Now they had all found her and she needed to hold on to that.

Dear Lela,

My precious angel you are now three months old. The sleep deprivation is tough on my nerves, so is having a rambunctious two year old, but when you smile you bring me back down to earth. Yesterday your Daddy took Ben to Tofield so we had the afternoon together. We listened to a compellation of my favorite music and my favorite Sarah McLachlan song came on. You were gently nursing as you drifted off to sleep at my breast, as the warm milk flowed from my body into yours I felt the most intense love for you. I could hear this beautiful music as I stared at your chubby, rose coloured cheeks, and your slight hand gently resting on my skin. I ran my hand over your tiny head; it felt like a fuzzy, warm peach. You finished your afternoon snack and leaned way back against my arm, your face had a sleepy expression of pure satisfaction as you giggled in your sleep. Your perfect tiny lips were dabbed with milk droplets, pursed in the sweetest expression of love. I cherished this moment as the warm tears began to flow. I laid you down in the room I had created for you, the pinkish glow warming your skin.

Love Mommy

Hannah looked forward to every moment spent with her precious daughter. When she was away from her it was like part of her soul was missing. The tenderness they felt for one another was a miraculous bond that only a mother and daughter can have for one another and no one can understand unless they have experienced it. Lela was very petite and had the most perfectly symmetrical features which made her amazingly adorable. Once she learned to smile there was hardly a moment were her tiny heart shaped face was not wearing one. When her mother smiled at her the world would stop moving and only the two of them existed in it. Hannah had an overwhelming sense that Lela was the daughter she had lost so many years ago. Lela was an old soul, Hannah could tell by the way she observed and listened to her surroundings. After waiting her whole life, she and her daughter were united at last.

Discovering My Spirit

Before medication, my meditations were filled with intense hallucinatory experiences. I was always unsure whether these hallucinations were real or a product of my unstable, meandering mind. I had not meditated since I witnessed my soul leave my body ten years prior. The experience was magical, but I feared losing control; and to me the experience was unexplainable. I was fearful of the power of meditation even though I knew it could be a peaceful way for me to really calm my manic tendencies. I strived hard to run from my racing thoughts and for a decade, every time I meditated I would sit face to face with these thoughts in a bloodthirsty wrestling match of consciousness.

Once medicated and stable I felt like even though I had everything I had always desired, the perfect nuclear family, the nice house, a vehicle that worked, friends I loved; there was still a gaping void in my life, a void calling out for meaning and depth, something that connected me with the universe; mother earth; the spirit world.

Organized religion left me with a sour taste in my mouth. Just the mention of a church or Jesus sent me directly into panic attack mode. All those churches and denominations my mom had exposed me to; the image of her speaking in tongues; the face of my 'religious' stepfather who infiltrated youth groups and bible camps for years targeting on the innocent, young holy children he was supposed to be mentoring.

The whole charade of brainwashing made me squirm and stifle my screams. The few times I had to be in a church for a wedding, baptism or funeral made me feel claustrophobic and unsafe. Just sitting on those hard, cold wooden *pews, looking at those hymn song page number organizers and Jesus fish wall hangings incited feelings of dread.*

Although I avoided organized religion I still felt a yearning to have some connection to something larger than myself.

If I was willing to commit to just one monogamous relationship with a solitary religion I would never feel the joy of experiencing all that the other world's religions had to offer. I could relate most with the Buddhist philosophies, but I was never willing to become strictly Buddhist.

When Lou Lou and I began studying different 'spiritual' philosophies and practices that hole started repairing itself. Reading Louise Hay's "You Can Heal Your Life", made me realize that I was very harsh on myself. Although I had been mistreated throughout my life, Me, Myself and I were the ones to blame for my self-loathing and negative self talk. On my way to work and home I would listen to Louise's CD program, "I Can Do It!" Lou Lou had sent it to me in the mail and that was her strict prescription. Louise became a surrogate mother, speaking to me about how to care for myself and change my negative thoughts into positive ones. Once I knew what I was doing I was able to dissect the reasons why I beat myself up so callously. I felt damaged and discarded most of the time; my mother had left me for men over and over again; my dad needed to escape from my mom; my siblings had families to care for; and friends flitted in and out of my life, growing tired of the constant drama, self-torture and passivity that just came with the package.

I had to start over once I was diagnosed with this socially unacceptable disease. I was not the same person on medication that I was before and people needed time to get used to the new me.

I worked as a librarian for a couple of years which gave me easy access to all the freshest, new age literature and I swallowed it up like a ferocious vulture. Through my spiritual readings I came to realizations about how to live the 'ideal' life, being happy and kind to all. I tried so hard to exist in this ideal state of perfection that when bad thoughts seeped into my mind I would beat myself up and feel like a failure. The words that were eloquently placed to heal me and change my life actually made me feel like I couldn't live up to those ideals. I had to stop reading them for a while. In a way I felt as though the authors were being a tad self righteous saying that they were living their teachings all the time. After all we are all human. I think it is more courageous for someone to admit their imperfections than flaunt how put together they are. My most cherished friends have patchwork pasts made up of colourful, chaotic experiences, and they wear those experiences on their sleeves like badges of honor. I believe the negative experiences are just as integral as the positive ones;

shaping us and teaching us lessons that we may not have otherwise learned. "Everything does happen for a reason" and "I wouldn't take nothing for my journey now" (Maya Angelou) are my philosophies on life; they have helped me make sense of the darkness of my past.

Psychic or Psychotic?
Winter 2008

Sometimes the lines between psychic and psychotic got crossed in my confused mind. When Liam worked nights I began to sleep less and my anti-psychotics were becoming less and less affective. They gave me a condition called Tardive Dyskenisia, where you start to have physical spasms, sometimes joined with horrid vocalizations. We would be quietly playing with the kids in the living room and my whole body would go into spasm, I would blurt out an animalistic yelp and retreat into myself from embarrassment. Eventually they began to happen so frequently I was beginning to get very uncomfortable physically and emotionally. They started to become painful and impossible to control.

Medication switches can be the kiss of death for someone with bipolar disorder and having Liam on nights made it a very inconvenient time for me to attempt it. The withdrawal symptoms of the medications I was on were similar to coming off of hardcore street drugs. I researched a new medication that didn't present the side effect as badly. Slowly my doctor and I weeded the old medication out and replaced it with the new one.

It felt like I was a crack addict coming off my drug, the side effects were so heinous; dry mouth, feverish, shakes, the intense desire to lay down and never wake up again, feeling uncomfortable in my own skin, like I was wading through a deep pool of quicksand. I was barely able to perform my duties as 'mother' and 'wife'. Liam stayed up most of the time and helped me as much as possible but when he was at work I struggled to keep my sanity. It had been such four years since my grasp on reality had slipped to such acute levels. I knew that I should be placed in the hospital, but we decided that we needed to handle it quietly on our own.

In the evenings I passed the time watching 'chick flicks', a way to escape the chaotic atmosphere of my mindscape. One evening I picked a romantic comedy called "The Waitress". The case looked cheery and upbeat: the waitress wearing a yellow uniform and a frilly, white smock; a classic Americana smile spread across her face; a tall, handsome man holding her and a creamy cherry pie in her hands. Reviews like, "delicious fun" and "a sweetheart of a comedy" scrawled deceptively across the case.

As I watched the film I felt haunted and disturbed. There was a comedic character with blonde hair and glasses who worked alongside the protagonist at the diner, she haunted me throughout the movie. I had never felt such fear and intensity during a movie before. My instinct told me to turn it off, but like a roadside accident I couldn't keep my eyes off the bubblegum coloured film. The main character was pregnant with an abusive mans child and she was fooling around with her gynecologist. She spent most of the movie trying to get away from the abuser and in the end she finally came out on top. At the end there was a scene where the protagonists' child walked down a wooded path in a frilly dress, hand in hand with her mom. After the movie I felt riddled with terror. I raced through the bonus material trying to figure out what negativity could be attached to the movie. The writer, director, producer was also the other waitress in the movie that haunted me. Apparently she died before the movie was released and the movie was dedicated to her. Not once did they mention the way she died. I couldn't let it go, I ran downstairs to my PC and researched her name. She was violently murdered; found hung on her shower rod. I wondered how much of the story in the movie was truth, and if there was a connection.

I slowly began to unravel, like a kitten's ball of yarn. The transition from 'normal' to 'psychotic' was as drastic and blinding as a brilliant camera flash. I was in a trance, I heard her voice taunting me and I believed that she was trying to speak to me. All the reflective surfaces in my house became conduits for her face, voice and presence. I ran frantically through the house taking mirrors and glass pictures off the walls, turning them backwards to ward off the voices. I piled all the sheets, towels and blankets from my linen closet over my right arm and began covering all the bathroom mirrors, frantic. I was conscious of what I was doing but was helpless to stop myself. I covered the shower rod with towels and squinted to avoid looking at it. Memories of my first psychotic episode flashed before me and I realized that I was in the next dimension, mingling with unknown forces. Were they creations designed by my unhealthy mind or were they intuitive insights into the human condition that I had picked up on during the movie. I'll never understand what happened psychologically to me that night, but for three weeks I was barely functioning in my roles, playing the part with what was left of my listless mind. The windows, mirrors and pictures remained covered for weeks. The kids asked questions, but in their quiet understanding, made it a fun game and never asked me to make things the way they used to be. I've told them that mommy has a disease in her brain and sometimes she has a hard time with it. They knew that I was not well and it seemed as though they compensated by helping out and being on their best behavior. My children showed me compassion in their innocent knowing that they too had to support me throughout this difficult period in our lives. Although I never wanted my illness to interfere in my present life, maybe it was good for my kids to 'see' that I too could be vulnerable and that they sometimes needed to be on the giving side.

As a parent who has suffered the life altering mistakes that my parents made, I have a tendency to try to be the 'ideal' parent. In an attempt to give my children the 'Brady Bunch' life, I start to burn out and when I make inevitable mistakes and then I beat myself up and berate myself to the point of self abuse. I realize now that if I can be 'stable and supportive' at least eighty percent of the time I'm doing OK. My kids need to see my imperfections; it makes us both more humble and compassionate people.

Hiding My Spirit

After conducting my own crash course in spirituality, I was in a nice, innocent place; a place of quiet surrender. In a way I was enticed by organized religion; I had no solid support system and many nights I sniffled around feeling sorry for myself. Church fellows could provide me with a surrogate family; bring me casseroles when I'm not well; have potlucks and sing songs around a bonfire. It was the sense of community that made me even consider it at times. The thought of being inundated with one set of ideals, of being 'on' and trying to 'fit' just to get some community spirit, made me squirm though. I realized that my true friends and family, the ones that looked at me with my mask off, soul exposed, loved me anyway, and they were all I needed.

The dynamics in my nuclear family are full of deep love, but are eternally branded with the dysfunction and violations of the past. I wear my spirituality in my heart, never to be exposed unless it is safe to do so. When I am too spiritual I feel disconnected from the rest of the world, so I save it for myself to cherish and for those few special individuals in my life that are free to express it. My most spiritual times mingle with hallucinatory, psychotic type experiences; there is a part of me that is stronger than I realize. I mostly keep it hidden; it makes me feel out of control. I think I need to stay on solid ground even though the deep spiritual connections make me feel more fabulous that I could ever imagine. It works better for me to keep those moments to myself and silently appreciate and cherish them. My spirituality is one thing I am in complete control of, something I can call on in times of need, something I can be open to when I need to seek understanding.

I feel most connected to my spirit when I am in the forest surrounded by tall, lush trees. It is as though I am connected to their energy. When I was in darkness I would sit outside on the grass and stare at the trees swaying, the leaves dancing and the wind whispering a love song in my ear. Nature is my synagogue and connecting with others is my form of worship. Now I appreciate silence and time alone. I am no longer frightened of myself and what lies deep inside my consciousness. My past helped me see others in a very real and compassionate way; I feel a connection with so many people because of all the experiences I have had. I realized that this was the journey that I needed to take in this lifetime; these were the lessons I wanted to learn. The support of my family and friends has taught me that I am worth loving and I have finally come to the place where I can truly say I love myself: scabs, bruises and all. I can look at my face in the mirror and it radiates a pure love that is finally tangible. My spirit is strong and loving and I feel that I could not ask for more than that.

Women Gathering

September 2007

Standing in line at the Earth's General Store she noticed a colourful brochure for "The Women's Gathering Event". She picked it up instinctively…

Vibrant jewel toned fabrics adorned with intricate multi-coloured swirls, florals and exotic birds of paradise…Warmth spreading itself over every visible space…Sunlight colourful and warm as it enters the room through thin layers of iridescent fabric draped on every window… An atmosphere of unconditional love, non-judgment and a deep seeded sisterhood…Guards were let down, 'real selves' were given permission to emerge and relish the spotlight and offerings to one another… Compliments and encouragements spread throughout the space.

A woman wearing a floral shirt, same as mine, her heart's desire to reconnect with her brother Jory, she in her 50's, I in my 30's…we had parallel experiences, there are no accidents or coincidences…fate is at play in this moment…Creativity and a collective consciousness of openness, awareness and a lucid grounding to the earth and our inner goddess…Moved to tears on numerous occasions.

Vibrant, colourful, flowing Gypsy garments…Restricting, conservative layers stripped off as the weekend progressed to reveal beautiful, flowing patterns, colours and our unique patch-worked individuality…No fear to wear garments that reflected exactly who we were.

A woman named Magda sat at the dinner table and it was as though she was a premonition of my mother, revealing her story about her lost lesbian daughter…"I too am a lost mother and my daughter's name is Maya."…we exchanged pain and sorrow, a sense of loss of our relationships, but for that frozen moment of beautiful time we looked into one another's eyes and saw the spirit of our lost loved ones... She was given the gift of seeing her daughters anguish through my eyes and I saw my mother's anguish in her eyes...It was as though a spiritual director was initiating every experience on the mapped out itinerary of events that weekend...

Not one moment existed outside of the spiritual realm...

A young Inuit woman with hair the shade of dark chocolate stands on the stage, comfortable in her own skin, her chubby, doll-like baby swaddled on her wide hip... Animal-like intonations emanating from the depths of her throat married with the most beautiful melodic notes... Bouncing gentle to the music, the baby mesmerized and soothed by the sound of his mother's sweet angelic voice...his hand on her heart...She is so young to be so evolved spiritually, proud of her culture, passing it on fearlessly to future generations with honorable grace....

Fresh whole foods to nourish our bodies as we are nourishing our souls... Lillian, adorned with a loose black t-shirt, a tie-dye peace sign over her centre, a long flowing, weathered jean dress, covered in rainbow coloured patchwork pieces...Her loose brown curls still damp from the early morning shower... I wonder with awe how amazing her day must be... I picture her bent over tending her organic vegetable garden, wide brimmed straw hat, hemp sandals, as her cat rubs gently up against her legs intertwining its body with her unshaven calves...Inside my soul this is who I am...A woman that is married to nature and ever far away from the technological revolution that today's society has endured...She has organized this intricately spiritual experience for many years to nourish every woman here, many of which are strangers... A hero in my eyes, someone who I hope to mirror one day in the future...Yet realize I am closer to that goal than I have ever been...

Returning to the essence of what was fabulous about my childhood, yet having the experiences on their own, not intertwined with the horrors that were latent almost thirty years ago...

All judgments', competition, ego vanishes before entering this sacred space...A room full of women that have suffered throughout their lives and are connected not by their suffering this time but by their healing...Many have never been mainstream and have tried to survive in the outside world wearing masks or attempting to conform. Feeling such a sense of ease that here in this space they are free to let their true inner selves shine forth...Peeling off the layers and exposing their soul they feel as though they have been set free... It is so beautiful to watch others go through this intense revolution while I am experiencing it...As I look at the face of the beautiful women I wonder what injustices they endured while in school...Were they picked on or scorned for their differences? Do they feel like I do?

In the evening the only light is the dim, flickering glow of dozens of colourful papier-mâché lanterns filled with beeswax candles...Swirls of patouli smoke dance around the room filling up our nostrils with the scent of herbs and earth...Straw baskets overflowing with brilliant silk scarves embellished with shiny beads, swirly embroidery and sequins...The tribal sound of the drums beating intertwined with the tender, childlike melodies of the flute...All of us dancing and chanting to the rhythm...Letting our guards slip slowly down our bodies and trampling on them with our spirited Celtic footwork... Though many of us have never played a percussion instrument it is as though our cells remember a time when we were mesmerized, and the spirit is moving within us making the movements and sounds flawless and organic...

Realizing that when this experience ends I will be permanently altered, the experiences leaving an indelible imprint on my heart...Not wanting to leave this community of nurturing mothers and daughters, trying to find their voice, or the right way down their spiritual path...I want to reach out and touch some of the women, or run up to them and profess my love wrapping my arms around them...These women are my mothers; my sisters; my friends; and I have been given the gift of spending the weekend in their presence...I too am a goddess and everyone there is helping me celebrate and honor my uniqueness...I belong...

Angel in the Water

September 2008

I saved my work and raced to the phone to dial my sisters' number. She had to be the first to hear that I finally completed the manuscript for my memoir. I was prepared for rejection, as it had been a couple months since we had last spoke. I was giving her the space I thought she needed to be at peace. Not wanting to force myself on her was my way of offering my understanding. The message was neutral and undemanding; "*Lou Lou, I have really great news, please call...I love you...I miss you...*"

Two weeks passed with no response from my sister. As I was sitting at my usual table at *Camilla's Coffeehouse*, listening to a live local band as I pissed around on Facebook, all of a sudden I was startled when my laptop was slammed shut. My heart leaped into my throat and I looked up at the wide eyes of my brother; "YOU HAVE TO COME WITH ME RIGHT NOW!" A lump of terror formed in my throat as I quickly packed up my belongings and followed him into the dark parking lot. As we exited the coffeehouse Jory looked at me sternly and said, "Lou Lou is missing, they found her canoe and lifejacket at the reservoir by her farm!"

"*WHAT! Oh my God, Oh my God!*"

"Grace and William are coming to look after your kids and you're coming with me to Lou Lou's farm. I'll meet you at your house. Pack up your shit fast!"

"*OK!*" We climbed into our vehicles and as I drove the shock set in and I began to shake uncontrollably. I was driving like a madwoman and the blood curdling screams that escaped my lips were unrecognizable.

"*Oh SHIT! Oh my God, Oh Lou Lou, NO, NO, NO, NO...*"

When I pulled into my driveway Jory held me as I sobbed. He said, "I don't know very much, but we have to get there now, hurry, go get your stuff!"

None of us realized how large that reservoir was. Its scope was twenty miles radius in total. The search was long, tedious and treacherous. Many years before water had been dumped into this large valley, on top of barbed wire fenced, rubbish and trees. Nothing had been removed; it had all been left there. My sister went missing in the most treacherous piece of water imaginable. Each night during the two weeks she was missing I had intense nightmares.

She was in a canoe in the middle of the day, in the middle of the reservoir and as she sat contentedly gazing at the innocent sunlight shining down on her a force came from the sky and separated her spirit from her physical body, pulling her into the clouds above her...Longing to see her I clenched my eyes shut and begged that same sky that captured her to take me too...I was on the shoreline and I felt a violent energy trying to pull me upwards...Fear made me wake with a start...I could feel Liam's breath on my back and realized I was laying in my nephews single bed, up against the wall, and Lou Lou was still missing. Sobs filled me and began pouring out waking my love. He pulled me into him and said, "Let's go downstairs we'll go outside for a few minutes." This had always been his technique for snapping me out of the dark places I visited in the night...

Each night of the two weeks I had nightmares of what the possible fate of my sister could be. I always wondered if they were premonitions or fears surfacing, but each one left me gasping for air. I felt like a twin, so deeply connected to my sister. I felt like I was living a nightmare; police officers driving up and down the deserted gravel road, the reservoir visible from the front of the house taunting and teasing. Going through the motions of social interaction was hard when inside I felt like I was crumbling apart. The exhaustion of helping with the household duties and waiting for an answer to the dreaded question of the loss of my sister made me crave the comfort of my home. I went home for just one night to recover from the intensity of the situation. I felt such guilt leaving my sister's four children but in order to survive this I needed to refresh myself somewhat. The afternoon after returning home I was alone at home with Lela. Liam had left for a few minutes to drive Ben back to school. The phone rang and I answered it;

"Is this Hannah Knight?"

My heart began pounding so hard the sound was echoing in my ears...

"Yes, it is..."

"This is Claire Severs from Vulcan Victim Services."

"Oh, Hi! How are you?"

"Well, I am so sorry but I have some news to relay to you."

"UH, Huh!"

"Your sisters' body washed up on shore this morning."

"Oh, OH OK, Thank You, I have to go now..."

"Hannah, Are you OK?"

"It is a relief to have closure, but hard to hear the result."

"Are you going to be coming back to Vulcan?"

"Yes, I'll leave right away. Claire I need to hang up now OK?"

As I hung up the phone I collapsed on the linoleum in my kitchen and violent sobs escaped my blue lips...she was gone and I was never going to see her again...never going to laugh with her...hug her...need her...talk with her...share my life with her...Oh my God, her kids and Eddy, how would they cope? What am I going to do now? I don't know what the fuck to do now... Lela came over to me, held my face in her hands and spoke maturely for her four years of age, "Mommy did your friend die? It is going to be OK." Her eyes filled with love and calm staring into mine as she held my face to hers. "Mommy, I'm sorry you're so sad about your sista." She stroked my hair and covered my face with her delicate kisses. I was astonished at how she knew just what to do, just what I needed at that, the single most tragic moment of my life...

It has been exactly two months since the death of my sister. After finding out about her death I had many more nightmares. I only had one, crystal clear dream. This disturbed me because we were so undeniable tied to one another for so much of this life, I just craved seeing her.

One night, I fell asleep and entered this dark abyss, large shadows where spinning around trying to devour me. I started screaming and tried to wake up, I dreamt I woke up and I was screaming but no sound was coming out, but I was hovering over my body, watching it scream silently. All of a sudden, in the dream, I was sitting on a couch, unfamiliar...in an unfamiliar house, but I could tell it was mine. I looked haggard and rough, with tousled hair, pimples, stained baggy sweats and a blue sweatshirt that was high around the neck, the kind I never wear because I feel like I am suffocating.

As I sat on the couch I noticed a figure passing in front of me, I looked up and it was Lou Lou just casually walking by, placing a gardening magazine on the table in front of me. She seemed like she had some job to do and was not even going to stop and say hi. I looked at her and she stared back at me with a serious tone. She looked healthy and proper, with a baby pink and mint green striped long sleeve shirt, with a wide neck and a bow on the left hand side and a pair of dark blue jeans. She glanced at me and I jumped up off the couch, she stayed calm and serious and I was so excited to finally see her. This was our conversation:

Hannah: How are you?

Lou Lou: I'm OK, How are you?

Hannah: OK I guess, when am I coming?

Lou Lou: Not for a while, there are things you need to do.

Hannah: (tears tumbling down her cheeks) I just miss you so much!

Lou Lou: (whispering) I miss you too (trying to hold in her tears as her face softens)

Hannah: (walking around the table and holding her sister to her, her sister is warm...) I love you so much Lou.

Lou Lou: I love you too (suddenly she walks away vanishing into the distance) I have to go, I'm sorry, I'm not supposed to talk to you right now.

After Lou Lou left I heard a knock on the front door. Liam and the kids were sitting with me all of a sudden. Liam said he would get it. He opened the door and there was a buzz of voices for short time, then he shut it again. He walked over to me and Lela and Ben were running towards me.

Lela: There are tons and tons of people waiting for you outside, they're sitting on lots of chairs.

Liam: Your Mom is here.

I walked slowly to the door, not knowing what to do.

Hannah: (to Liam) I look like shit.

Liam: Nobody cares what you look like Han. Just go.

I opened the door a crack and there were people of all different stage of my life sitting in a large circular shape all the way down the sides of my driveway. Mom ran to me and hugged me.

Mom: we just want you to know that we understand what you've been through and we are thinking about you.

It was comforting to see Mom and all those people but the fact that I saw Lou Lou just for a moment far overshadowed those acquaintances. There is no comparison for my sister's love. No one will ever be able to replace her. She was my mother, my father, my sister and my best friend.

I felt the bed depress as Liam climbed in to bed. I must have been returning from my astral travels as I was startled awake and fresh, hot tears were running down my cheeks. I cried because I wanted more than just a glimpse of my sister. I cried at the loss of my mother and the fact that she had not tried to reach out to me since my sister's death.

I have to stop now because I am crying in the corner of my favorite coffee shop and I fear someone may look at me or talk to me.

I have realized that when you just start to believe your life is right where you want it to be, it can come crashing down around you. The lessons keep getting fired at you and you continue to figure out what they are trying to teach you. This is the human condition and it is an endless cycle. You are on the bottom level at the beginning of your life and in order for your soul to evolve you need to learn the lessons of each of your personal tragedies. With each lesson learned you get to move up to the next level of spiritual consciousness. As soon as I could string intellectual thoughts together I felt this in my heart. At the age of four when my tragedies began I started making sense of this theory. It was what helped me go on. It became a challenge to face each situation and see what I could do to get past it and evolve spiritually. I knew these things before opening any 'spiritual books'. If you try and look at things at a distance and guess how they can be conquered it is easier to deal with what life throws your way.

Coming Full Circle:
A Love Story

October 2009

*Yoga in the living room illuminated with an orange glow...filtered light
from the setting of the sun through the triple sliding doors...The Pan flute and
a rushing waterfall soothes me as I slip into lotus position and lay my praised
palms on my outward spread knees...I begin to quietly whisper my mantra
"OM" and I hear a tiny voice mimicking me from the left...I peek over at the
couch and notice Lela getting herself comfortable in the same position I'm in;
teetering on the newly covered vintage footstool, her fuchsia pants adorned with
black and white spotted kitties and her golden curls tumbling down her bare
back... so free and absolutely glowing and beautiful...I felt such a surge of
pure love and realized this was one of those absolutely perfect moments, frozen
in time. I pretended not to see her, as capturing her unaware made the whole
experience seem more organic and true, she wasn't performing for me, she was
just enthralled by her practice.*

*Ben emerges and curls up with us under the velvety blanket in front of the
luminescent laptop screen and we watch a slide show of our most incredible trip
to Arizona appear on the screen as if perfectly choreographed to the pan flute
meditation music. Silent, with a mutual knowing that this moment would be
tainted if the silence was broken.*

*Moments of pure joy are scattered throughout my days as a stay at home
mom, wife and writer. I wonder if all mothers are given the gift of sharing
these discreet moments with their children. It hurts me deeply to see mothers*

looking at their children and not 'seeing' them. They skew their focus onto material desires and their children get lost in the plastic competition that is going on around them. I never want my children to feel invisible; I strive to make them feel 'seen' and 'valued'. The path of my life brought me here, to be their mother. Being their parent has been one of my biggest challenges and my biggest joy. With bits and pieces to draw from I feel lost and uncertain when difficult circumstances arise. My role models came and went, but I watched and gathered information. I stored it in my head for later use and filed it away for those days when I would come up empty and unsure.

I squint at all the men that passed in and out of my life, but I also appreciated each of them for what they taught me. They taught me that I could be loved and that I was beautiful inside. They played the role of father, partner, lover, protector and predator; each bringing me to a new realization about myself and my worth. They all contained bits and pieces of the man I sought for so many years, so I had tastes before he materialized. Mostly they filled a void that lay vacant, the presence of a man in my life, hopefully functional, but sometimes not. They kept me company on cold, lonely nights when I needed protection and unconditional love from someone; anyone.

An expression of love for the tapestry of incredible people, who entered my life and picked me up off the ground, tenderly brushed me off and made me see who I truly was. Gifts of friendship from amazing people that walked in and out of my life throughout my journey; all of them teaching me something valuable about life and myself; each acting as mother, sister, therapist and friend. Encouraging me to be a stronger woman, more confident and assured, willing to protect myself from harm, showing me to face myself head on and move steadily forward.

When I reunite with faces from the past, flashes of darkness seep back into my hermetically sealed world and I gasp for air...I realize it will always lay within me, latent but still flushed with danger...The new memories shift into those places in my brain, disposing of and replacing the old ones..

The enduring love of my brother and sister; a bond that was adhered with the bitterness of what life chucked at us; a relationship that strengthened as we aged and conquered challenges together; filling in the gaps that were left gaping open and exposed by our parents. Being together, a delicate dance of uncertainty and caution, fear and remembering, joyful yet always speckled with the pain of memories. Inevitably dulled with intoxication and harsh laughter to mask the intensity of what's hidden and trying to force it out. Having to distance ourselves from time to time in order to remain in the present, shielding ourselves from the past, pushing it to the darkest, furthest corner of our soul's closet.

I sit on the bench in front of my beautiful home as the magenta sun sets… Beautiful melodies ring out from my guitar and my nieces voices ring out intertwined with mine and their mothers…My brother, husband, father, stepmom and nephew watch with enchanted grins that spread tenderly across their faces…My stepmother captures the intensity of the moment through her camera lens so that none of us forget the magic of this moment…It was a long, hard journey for all of us to reach this pinnacle, but we are here and that is all that matters now…

A healed relationship with my father; at a time when I cherish his presence…No more secrets…I realize that he has felt the sorrow of losing me just as I have it felt for him…Unable to have me for so many years and losing me over and over again…My love for him intensifies when I see his face glow as he notices a beautiful moment etched in time with my children…I see how he looks at them and I know he is happy to be here, invited back into my life, unconditionally and safely…This heals me more than he'll ever know…It is a moment I have looked toward for my lifetime…

All of the songs that comforted me through the darkness lay in an overflowing binder… Each one strummed on my tangerine guitar, sung by my strong, raspy voice…filling the majestic night…my lover watches me with a tender smile as we witness the intensity of the setting sun in all its brilliance…As the night enters I am secure in the presence of my long awaited true love…laughter fills the warm wind that caresses us in the luscious backyard of our home…

The waves lap in; whispering musical notes of relaxation in my ears…The sun caresses my skin, giving me delicate kisses full of warmth…Writing has brought my pain to the surface in Technicolour detail…The words tumble out, carrying me back to the haunting windows of time, as if my memories are being projected on a battered, wall in my memory…Fleeting in and out and taking their final curtsey…Each memory stays and mingles only while welcome and then transforms into a mist, dissipating slowly into the universe and heavily out of my soul, for eternity…My motivation for completing this memoir being solidified by the fact that those dark memories were finally absent, remaining only in print for the rest of the world to see, relate to, and understand…

I look into my families eyes when I get lost in the past and they transport me back to the present…Through their dreams, smiles, eyes I see the future… It is a stunningly, majestic concerto of carefully composed notes… All of the soul searching and mistakes, all the relationships and failures, all the faces and experiences, all the sorrow and absolute joy shine their light, speaking to me, letting me know that all of this was my journey, my creation, leading me to my masterpiece...

The process of writing was long and treacherous at times; a seven year mission; a lifelong desire... The past haunting me, I wanted to push it away; put it off; but it lay, latent in the background, taunting, prodding, and bullying me... I'd stare at the blank page and images would flit across the page, nothing concrete until my eyes were ready to stay open...The time suddenly came and the words poured out like a rain onto dry thirsty grass...No stops, no doubts, just pure thought transformed into poetic prose...The motivation ached in me to reach the end of my story, close the book and move on...I have not one regret about my past. It all brought me to this place of quiet surrender...It has taught me to appreciate tiny nuances that unfortunately many people miss... It allows me to not only have compassion but a connection with so many souls that are waiting for a hand to reach out, lift them up and hold them close for a while...My healing allowed me to hear and relate...There is no greater gift in this life than connection with other souls...It is a lost art that needs to be resurrected, brushed off and polished for our future generations...

Many children dream of being ballerina's or firemen, I always had the same dream, to one day write my story and share it with the world...

The man came, then the boy, and finally the girl. My path to them was treacherous but they chose me, and I chose them...Our union is a celebration of pure love...

Thank you for sharing my journey...

I am Home...

P.S. As I watched the sun kissed faces of my children, watching the miraculous flight of hundreds of butterflies, one with brilliant black and blue silken etchings landed gracefully on my shoulder. People stared in silence as the butterfly stood motionless speaking to me with the powerful language of nature. The butterfly playing the role of gatekeeper for my future...

Epilogue

A Note to My Readers

After you've read this book I encourage you to start writing your own stories. If you're not comfortable writing, just try sharing them. As a society we need to stop holding back our true selves. The more we hide from the truth the more it takes a toll on our bodies, minds and spirits. Life gets too fast and we forget to slow down and notice the simple things in life. Try turning off, settling down and spending time in silence with yourself. Whether your journey has been rocky or smooth, your stories are important to share. Writing and telling them provide us with an emotional and spiritual release of all that lies subconsciously within us.

My bad memories were clouding all the positive aspects of my childhood; I refused to let them knock out all the good anymore. I had passions, loves and abilities that came from somewhere and I no longer wanted to let the traumatic experiences from the past ruin my life; past, present and future.

If you're a little strange or quirky remember we all are and don't be afraid to be who you really are. You will love yourself so much more. Maybe you'll feel like you don't fit in, but you will attract the right people for you, people that will make a positive impact on your future. Those of us, who walk around shielding ourselves with a false front, feel tortured, blocked and distant from ourselves, need to learn to let go.

You are your toughest critic. Mothers and Fathers, be careful with your children. Sisters and brothers remember you can be the strongest connection to your past so your bonds need to be nurtured and loved.

I wrote this book because it was the last part of my healing; if you gain anything positive from it I will have done my job.

The End
&
The Beginning